TEACHING THE MEDIA
International Perspectives

LEA'S COMMUNICATION SERIES
Jennings Bryant/Dolf Zillmann, General Editors

Select titles in Media Education (Robert Kubey and Renee Hobbs, Advisory Editors) include:

Christ • Media Education Assessment Handbook

Christ • Assessing Communication Education: A Handbook for Media, Speech, and Theater Education

Davies • Fake, Fact, and Fantasy: Children's Interpretation of Television Reality

Hart • Teaching the Media: International Perspectives

For a complete list of other titles in LEA's Communication Series, please contact Lawrence Erlbaum Associates, Publishers

TEACHING THE MEDIA
International Perspectives

Edited by
Andrew Hart
University of Southampton

LEA LAWRENCE ERLBAUM ASSOCIATES, PUBLISHERS
1998 Mahwah, New Jersey   London

Lawrence Erlbaum Associates, Inc., Publishers
10 Industrial Avenue
Mahwah, New Jersey 07430

Cover design by Kathryn Houghtaling

Library of Congress Cataloging-in-Publication Data

Teaching the media : international persepctives / edited by Andrew
Hart.
       p.   cm. — (LEA's communication series)
    Includes bibliographical references and indexes.
    ISBN 0-8058-2476-6 (cloth : acid-free paper) — ISBN 0-8058-
2477-4 (pbk. : acid-free paper).
      1. Mass media—Study and teaching. 2. Media literacy.
    I. Hart, Andrew.   II. Series.
P91.3.T445   1997
302.2'07—dc21   97-40263
                                                                CIP

Books published by Lawrence Erlbaum Associates are printed on
acid-free paper, and their bindings are chosen for strength and
durability.

Printed in the United States of America
10 9 8 7 6 5 4 3 2 1

Contents

Foreword

The Media Education Revolution

Len Masterman
University of Liverpool, England

Why should we bother to study or teach about the media? In the past, teachers have given three different answers to that question, and those answers (and the practices that followed from them) have formed the three great historical paradigms of Media Education.

The earliest answer to the question *"Why study the media?"* ran something like this. The mass media are really a kind of disease against which children need to be protected. What the media infect is the culture as a whole. Culture is contaminated by the media's commercial motivations, their manipulation and exploitation of their audiences, their corruption of language, and their offering of easy, low-level appeals and satisfactions. What makes the media such a problem according to this analysis is that they produce a counterfeit culture, which is a direct threat to genuine culture and to authentic cultural values. Crucially, this is, among other things, an audience problem. It is not simply that popular culture and high culture cannot somehow coexist. Clearly, at one level they can. The threat comes through the corruption of the audience. The very future of serious literature itself, for example, was held to be absolutely dependent on the existence of a serious literate readership to sustain it. Without the existence of that discriminating reading public, literature itself would wither away. As early as the 1930s, contemporary newspapers, magazines, and advertisements were seen as actively destroying that serious reading public. The media demanded and therefore produced, shorter attention spans and an appetite for the sensational, expressed in slick, smart, and superficial language. This constituted an attack on the very foundations of serious reading and indeed, serious engagement with any art form.

If the media were a definite kind of cultural disease, then Media Education was designed to provide protection *against* it. Media Education was an education against the media, and contrasted the manipulative nature of the media with the timeless values of real culture, as embodied supremely in literature. That earliest paradigm is now popularly known as the inoculative paradigm (Leavis & Thompson, 1933). Educators allowed a little media material into the classroom only in order to inoculate students more effectively against it. On the whole, media teachers today represent a powerful lobby against that way of thinking about the media. But it is still probably the way in which most other teachers view the media. And you will still see remnants of that old inoculative view within the most progressive Media Education practice. For example, teaching about advertising is still almost universally teaching *against* advertising, rather than an attempt to develop an understanding of how advertising works, of the role of advertising agencies, or of the function of advertising within contemporary media.

What effectively put an end to the dominance of the inoculative paradigm was the arrival in schools in the early 1960s of a generation of young teachers whose intellectual formation owed as much to the influence of popular culture, and particularly cinema, as it did to print-based culture. Such teachers were apt to argue that the films of directors such as Bergman, Renoir, Bunuel, Fellini and in particular the French New Wave directors actually possessed as much intellectual energy and moral seriousness as anything that was being produced within European or American literature. They produced a new answer to the question: *"Why study the media?"* It was to enable students to discriminate not against the media but within them—that is, to tell the difference between the good and the bad film, the authentic and the shoddy television program, and work within popular culture of some integrity and work that was merely commercial and exploitative. This was the 'popular arts' paradigm (Hall & Whannel, 1964) that emphasized the idea that popular culture was every bit as capable of producing authentic works of art as was high culture. It gave Media Education a new agenda and a renewed energy in the 1960s, but by the mid-1970s almost all of that energy had been dissipated.

There were three principal reasons why the 'popular arts' paradigm failed to produce an adequate foundation for effective media teaching. First, Media Education was still seen as essentially protectionist. It was a somewhat paternalistic exercise in improving students' tastes. It was still based on a very negative view of the media preferences of the vast majority of students, and was always likely to be resisted by them for this very reason. Second, it remained an evaluative paradigm, which was severely disabled by the fact that there were no widely agreed standards or criteria available for actually evaluating the media. Media teachers found themselves in very uncertain territory when they wanted to demonstrate precisely why this newspaper or television program or piece of popular music was superior to that one. There was also a dangerous tendency for good to be equated with middle-class tastes, and bad with working-class tastes. The kind of media material which teachers tended to like— European films shown in film societies, television documentaries, and serious newspapers—was self-evidently good. Hollywood movies, tabloid newspapers, and television game shows—the kind of material liked by students— were bad. Third, it was not simply a question of the practical difficulties of discriminating between the good and the bad in the media. There were major doubts, I think, about the very appropriateness of applying aesthetic criteria at all to a vast range of media output. Was there really any point in trying to discriminate, for example, between good and bad news bulletins, advertisements, sports programs, or weather forecasts? The 'popular arts' movement was, essentially, a way of legitimizing film studies. It privileged film, within the study of the media, as the one popular form with unchallengeable claims to having produced works of authentic merit. But it provided a distinctly limited way of illuminating the media as a whole. By the 1970s it was becoming clear that a Media Education that was to have any relevance at all for students had to give preeminence not so much to film, which in terms of cinema going was by now somewhat marginal to the experience of most students, but to television which was much more central to their experience.

During the late 1970s, a number of media teachers began to see and make connections between their own down-to-earth classroom concerns and the general drift of a number of structuralist ideas, particularly in the areas of semiotics and ideology. Semiotics firmly established the notion of the media as signifying systems that needed to be read critically, rather than windows in to a reality that had to be accepted. It established, that is, the first principle of Media Education as being that of *nontransparency*, and its dominant concept that of *representation*. No less important, semiotics undermined at a stroke all of those apparently immutable distinctions between the culturally valuable and the apparently trivial on which Media Studies (and Literary Studies before it) had been based. Semiotics' purpose was to reveal and decode, not to make aesthetic judgments. Because both were equally signifying systems, semiotics was able to make a scandalous equation between for example, *King Lear* and a Big Mac. The way in which theories of ideology moved during the 1970s curiously dovetailed with these developments. There was a marked movement away from that traditional notion of ideology as a body of dominant ideas and practices imposed from above on subordinate groups, which resulted in false consciousness. Rather, following the rediscovery of the work of Antonio Gramsci, ideology came to be equated with 'common sense', with what was most natural and 'taken for granted' about our ideas and practices. Dominance was achieved, that is, as much by consent as by imposition.

For Media teachers, these developments in semiotics and ideology pointed in precisely the same direction. They pointed to the fact that the ideological power of the media was very much tied up with the naturalness of the image, and with the tendency of the media to pass off encoded, constructed messages as natural ones. They demonstrated too, that questions of power were central to discussions about the production, circulation and consumption of images and representations. They raised questions about which groups had the power to define, and which groups were only ever defined. They established, in other words, the importance of a politics of representation, and thrust Media Studies into the heart of some of the most important political and social questions of our time.

What was being achieved throughout the 1980s was a widespread international movement of Media teachers out of traditional discriminatory aesthetic paradigms into more broadly political and representational ones. Teachers were also working out some of the more radical implications of this shift for classroom practice. For what soon became apparent was that we were talking about something more than a change in subject content. What was being proposed were radical changes in teaching objectives, in classroom methodology, in methods of evaluation, and indeed in teachers' and students' understanding of what constituted knowledge.

The answer that this third paradigm—the representational paradigm—gave to the question *"Why study the media?"* went something like this: "In contemporary societies the media are self-evidently important creators and mediators of social knowledge. An understanding of the ways in which the media represent reality, the techniques they employ, and the ideologies embedded within their representations ought to be an entitlement for all citizens and future citizens in a democratic society." In working through the implications of this paradigm, teachers found themselves working in new ways in the classroom. In fact, they were beginning to answer what is probably the most important question faced by educational systems in the late 20th Century and beyond: What constitutes an effective democratic education for majorities of future citizens?

As the research in this book so vividly shows, some of these models of Media Education continue to have life in today's classrooms. But these international studies also embody the struggle to move beyond the old paradigms to ensure that teaching strategies and school curricula develop in tandem with the pace of change within the media themselves. Let me end this Foreword by suggesting two major themes with which Media Education has to grapple now and in the immediate future.

First, it is not possible for anyone living in the current commercial media environment to be media literate today without understanding that the primary function of commercial media is the segmentation and packaging of audiences for sale to advertisers. Until now, Media Education has been based on a premise of the most astonishing naivety that the primary function of media has been the production of information or entertainment. What we have principally studied in Media Education have been texts: television programs, newspaper stories, and magazine articles, for example. But these are not the chief product of commercial media. They are what Canadian critic Smythe (1981) called the 'free lunch': the means by which the real product of the media, from which its profits are derived—the audience product—is brought into existence. A critical understanding of the basic techniques and tenets of marketing and of the nature of the audience product will need to be brought to bear on the study of all media texts and institutions and will, I believe, have as central a place in the analysis of future media as such concepts as authorship had within film studies in the 1960s, and representation and ideology had in the 1980s. Second, the growth of commercial media has been accompanied by the increasing impoverishment of public service and pluralistic media. The spaces in which we, as members of society, can communicate with one another without governmental or commercial interference are being closed down dramatically. As Media teachers, we need to develop an explicit commitment to the principles of open and universal access to information, and to preserving the independence from undue commercial influence or government interference of at least some producers of information. Teachers working within public educational systems already have a commitment to the maintenance and defence of public information systems, and they have to find ways of expressing this not in terms of an uncritical partisanship or on the basis of a narrow anticommercialism, but rather as an open and generous allegiance to democratic values. And that entails, as always, putting all of the arguments to our students but leaving them with the responsibility for making their own choices.

Very large issues are at stake in struggles over the future configuration of the media industries. Should information be regarded as just another commodity or does it have a social value? Is it preferable to produce information which meets general social needs or information which makes a profit? Is access to information a right or should it be restricted to those who can pay? Is the production and circulation of information an extension of property rights or does it lie in the public domain? It is scarcely an exaggeration to say that the future shape of all cultures and the future health of all democracies lie in the ways in which they answer these questions. But without the existence of an informed and media-literate public these issues may not ever be debated. It is our crucial role as Media teachers to ensure the continued evolution of that critical public. It is a task worthy of our energies well into the next century.

REFERENCES

Leavis, F. R., & Thompson, D. (1933) *Culture and Environment*. London: Chatto & Windus.
Hall, S., & Whannel, P. (1964). The Popular Arts. London: Hutchinson.
Smythe, D. (1981). *Dependency Road*. Norwood, NJ: Ablex: New Jersey.

Acknowledgments

Systematic research is expensive, especially if it has an international focus. This international project could not have taken place without the commitment and enthusiasm of a large number of collaborators. I thank Southern Arts, Television South, and own university's research fund for contributing toward the costs of the original *Models of Media Education* project in England. But, apart from a little local financial support in other countries, the project has depended entirely on the voluntary participation of all the collaborators and the facilities provided by their own universities to encourage their research. It has not been easy and it has not been quick, but it has been helped considerably by new technology in the form of e-mail and electronic document transfer. So I thank all the contributors for their patience in this process, and offer my apologies for anything that has been lost in transmission or translation.

We have depended, too, on the help of researchers, most of whom remain anonymous and unpaid. But John O'Kane and Tony Benson were both briefly funded as researchers in the United Kingdom and, as experienced English\Media teachers, made invaluable contributions to the project. We would all like to thank the many teachers and pupils who appear in the different studies and who generously gave of them to let us into their classrooms and their confidences as we explored their approaches to Media teaching. Except where it was impossible, their names have been changed throughout the book to preserve confidentiality.

Even so, without the advantage of meeting occasionally at international conferences to discuss our work in depth, the international project would never have been successfully completed. I therefore thank the organizers and participants in conferences in England, Northern Ireland, Canada, and Spain between 1992 and 1996, especially the Guelph conference in 1992 and those at La Coruna in 1995 and 1996. Finally, I hope these studies demonstrate the vital importance to our educational futures of devoting time, energy, and financial resources to classroom-based research with practitioners.

—*Andrew Hart*

1

Introduction: Media Education in the Global Village

Andrew Hart
University of Southampton

Despite faster and more efficient communication systems across much of the world, international comparative studies in education are currently suffering some neglect. In most countries, the dominant interest in educational processes and practices elsewhere seems to be focused on 'quick fixes' or finding cheaper options for their educational problems. As individual nations have receded into a narrow concern with the control of domestic educational expenditure, interest in the diversity of educational approaches as reflections of different social and cultural contexts or of different educational goals has suffered. In many cases, this has led to conservative and even retrogressive developments in education.[1]

Although media ownership, production, and distribution have become increasingly internationalized and even globalized, educational responses have not kept pace with these developments. The microinteractions of the classroom seem strangely detached from the macrodevelopments in technology and culture. Increased use of media in informal education does not necessarily mean an increased understanding of the processes by which this informal education occurs. Paradoxically, the correlation between media usage and media understanding may be an inverse one, as Marshall McLuhan hinted in his assertion that we "look at the present through a rear-view mirror. We march backwards into the future" (McLuhan & Fiore 1967, pp. 74–75). Like science fiction writers, we are chained forever to re-presenting the past, even when we wish to address the future.

---

[1]I thank members of the *Southern Media Education Research Network* for their continuing interest in this research. In particular, I am grateful to Andrew Goodwyn of Reading University and Graham Murdock of Loughborough University for their contributions to the development of some parts of this chapter.

There has been much rhetoric but little research on Media teaching. This study is the first international perspective in the English-speaking world that systematically examines empirical strategies for the teaching of Media. It is also the first to focus on Media teaching with 14- to 16-year-old students. By contrast, most accounts of Media teaching to date have been concerned with arguing a case (often polemically) for Media Education or providing resources and strategies for Media teachers. There is a dearth of basic research, if research is seen as a process of investigation that is public, systematic, controlled, and critical of its own methodological weaknesses (Cohen & Manion 1994, pp. 4–5, 40). Local research needs a global context and there is a need for comparative studies, so that the few local studies that have been attempted are not seen in isolation.

Research on classroom strategies for Media teaching is still in its infancy. Previous studies have focused on general discussion of theoretical approaches and have often looked at Media Education 'programs' without grounding such discussion in actual classroom teaching approaches. Such abstraction can be extremely misleading, especially when it relies on secondary sources of information. For example, Piette and Giroux's (1997) unusual account of the European Media Education movement 's origination in Finland treats published educational resources as if they were actual sequences of teaching, failing to distinguish between a publication for the classroom and what actual teachers have done with it. The geographical distance of such reports from their sources is very apparent and invariably diminishes both their validity and their value. In a similar way, Brown's (1991) work on 'critical (television) viewing skills' often relies on secondhand reports that ignored actual developments and focus on virtual ones. He provided useful detailed accounts of funded and voluntary programs in the United States, but nothing on actually observed lessons. There is very little reference in his work to actual classroom practice and only one reference to an actual research project in the United Kingdom, conducted by Butts (1986) in Scotland in the mid-1980s. Such work as Brown's is necessary and valuable, but it is geographically and methodologically limited. It is best described in his own words as providing "a pragmatic invitation … [for] … explorers and practitioners" (p. 330).

In the United Kingdom, there have been other studies of classroom practice, notably the British Film Institute's (BFI) most recent report (Learmonth & Sayer, 1996). But, as its title implies, this report is a study of 'good practice' that relies on reporting on the work of the strongest teachers in schools specially selected for the quality of their work in this field. The report, based on eight secondary schools in the United Kingdom, is helpful in drawing attention to some of the commonly found strengths and weaknesses of Media teaching, but its primary focus is on appropriate inspection criteria for the evaluation of teaching and learning. It is not explicitly concerned with the relationship between teacher perspectives and classroom practice. It reports on a very small number of Key Stage 4 (KS4; ages 14–16) lessons, providing detailed information about only one of these (Learmonth & Sayer, 1996,

p. 36) It cannot claim to be research in the standard Cohen and Manion sense because it neither declares its research approaches nor critically discusses its methodology. It is impossible, therefore, to assess its validity as research.

Some significant studies have focused more on learning theory than on teaching strategies. The work of Buckingham and colleagues in England offers a series of rich and detailed explorations of student–teacher and student–student interactions in Media classrooms that has been very productive of new questions about learning processes. It has also played a useful role in relating Media learning to language-learning theories. But it does not focus on teaching strategies or processes, nor does it reveal and reflect on its own methodological weaknesses. This makes it very difficult to use in any comparative way (Buckingham, 1990, 1993a, 1993b; Buckingham & Sefton-Green, 1994).

This book describes an international project based on research that began in England. It aims to initiate a more fruitful dialogue about specific educational approaches within some of the major English-speaking nations throughout the world. It does not seek to offer a comparative evaluation of different paradigms for Media Education or different teaching models in practice, but does seek to explore the diversity of educational concerns, goals, and classroom practices. This exploration will help to define existing models in different countries more precisely and to make them more visible and more accessible. The purpose of this research is not evaluative but illuminative. It will enable and encourage readers in different parts of the world to gain new perspectives on Media teaching, to examine teaching approaches that differ from their own and to reflect on their own, practices with a view toward understanding them more fully and enhancing their effectiveness in the classroom.

By providing detailed case studies of current work in different parts of the world, this book enables tentative comparative analysis of various Media teaching paradigms and practices in different cultures within the English-speaking world. The case studies do not claim to be representative of Media teaching in any of the contexts studied. Although they are firmly placed in their own historical, cultural, and curricular context, there is no claim that they provide any basis for generalization toward reliable surveys of Media work in different countries. The research is partial in three senses. First, it is limited in scope because it reports on a small part of a much larger picture, and focuses on a fairly narrow and localized range of work, mainly within the teaching of English. Second, it is highly selective because all the teachers in our samples were chosen to participate because of their known involvement in Media work. Third, it is partial because all the contributors to the book are acknowledged advocates of the potential value of Media Education within formal schooling.

According to one authority on language teaching, there is an "enormous lack of descriptive work in classrooms" (Brumfit & Mitchell, 1989, p. 6). This is especially true of Media Education classrooms and this study, therefore, provides valuable new information. Specifically, it addresses the following major issues:

1. How are teachers living in the new multimedia world, both in their personal lives and in their classroom practice? How do they see this world in relation to their personal philosophies of teaching?
2. How are schools responding as institutions? To what extent do school policies recognize the importance of young people's extracurricular culture?
3. What influences are exerted by national and local curricular authorities? Do current formal curricula encourage engagement with new media technologies?

The participants in the international project agreed to adopt a common research framework for the diverse social and cultural settings in which we knew that Media Education was happening. In the event, we were able to keep this framework constant in only four of our six settings. In the United States and Canada, we were unable to establish the necessary conditions for the research framework to operate formally and had to rely on adaptations of ongoing work with slightly different orientations. The Ontario research draws on particular concerns with personal biography and acquired critical discourses as potential determinants of teaching strategies, whereas the Massachusetts study is firmly located in a program of Professional Development for teachers. In the latter case, it is also clear that Media teaching is not confined to the teaching of English and is emerging in various ways within other curriculum areas, frequently under the title of 'Media Arts.' However, both North American studies provide some remarkable insights into the texture of work in their own contexts and some vital points of contact with the other studies.

These differences are reassuring because they emphasize that the residues of curricular colonialism are not universal. If the Northern Ireland, South African, and Australian studies clearly reveal discourses that echo debates about English teaching that began in England, then the North American studies show that varied vernacular strategies are developing.

There are many different notions, even within the English-speaking world, as to what is meant by Media Education. Even when we are clear that we are dealing with teaching and learning *about* the media rather than the *use* of media (educational technology) in the classroom, there is still much potential for confusion. (In North America, the term 'Media Literacy' is often used as well as Media Education and is discussed in more detail later in the relevant chapters.) As was noted in an earlier international collocation of Media work:

> Media Education in practice is now so varied and takes place in diverse contexts such as educational or community based institutions, religious organizations or popular movements; in some situations teachers alone organize programs, while in others professional media workers are involved. (Bazalgette, Bevort, & Savino, 1992, p. xii)

These differing approaches are related to, but not necessarily predicated on, a wide range of curricular frameworks, from statutory requirements in England,

Northern Ireland, and Australia, to much more informal arrangements in North America and South Africa. It was because of this range of context and practice that this study was deliberately limited to predetermined curriculum contexts and age groups, and for this reason we attempted to maintain a consistency of research methods across cultures.

In England, some clarity and continuity have been achieved through various attempts in recent years to define Media Education within the National Curriculum for English. The details of these developments are explained in the next chapter. For now, it may be helpful to note that in this book, the emergent term 'Media' is used for convenience as a simplified way of referring both to general 'Media Education' in English or across the curriculum, and to the more specialized subject 'Media Studies.' We may soon be able to speak as easily and confidently of 'Media' as we already can of 'English,' as is already happening in some schools. Even then, however, we shall need to recognize the wide diversity of practice encompassed under the term, for example, in the differing emphases which teachers and courses place on practical as compared to analytical work.

THE NEW MEDIA ENVIRONMENT

The development of new media technologies, new media forms, and new institutional structures is certainly a global phenomenon. The spread of the Internet has accelerated the more general process of 'mediatization'[2] of experience that Mattelart (1991) analyzed so incisively. It is a crucial aspect of the development of the 'global village.' This 'mediatization' is not only enlarging and altering our vocabulary, but has already begun to affect the actual form of everyday communication and interaction. As McLuhan (1964) put it, "we have leased our central nervous systems to various corporations" (p. 79). He correctly and provocatively diagnosed the "Age of Information and of Communication (in which) electric media instantly and constantly create a total field of interacting events in which all men [*sic*] participate" (p. 264).

McLuhan (1964) predicted that conventional educational processes would be fundamentally altered in the 'global village' in response to new electronic communication processes. He saw education as, ideally, a form of "civil defense against media fall-out" (p. 208). But he did not foresee that educational institutions and processes would fail to keep pace with technological and corporate development. For the educational response has been neither global nor radical. This dislocation between the accelerated pace of development in information and communication

---

[2]However ugly this term may seem to English speakers, it is preferred here to the even uglier form 'mediazation' used by Thompson (1990) in *Ideology and Modern Culture,* where he defined it as "the ways in which the symbolic forms in modern societies have become increasingly mediated by mechanisms and institutions of mass communication" (p. 75).

technology (which, it is currently estimated, doubles in power and halves in cost every 18 months) and the sluggish conservatism of educational systems is a major problem in the West. It is not one that will be solved simply by increased access to new information and communication technology. It requires a radical overhaul of educational curricula and methods.

We are entering an age of multimedia in the sense of a new, increasingly enveloping and involving media environment that is experienced as an interconnected whole. Media culture has massively expanded over the last few decades. There is a range of new media: cable and satellite TV, home computers, video recorders and camcorders, new 'online' interactive services, video discs, and other consumer-oriented interactive software. There is also a growing interpenetration of media as genres, themes, and contents flow from one to another with increasing ease as a result of the movement from analogue to digital coding and the consolidation of communications conglomerates.

Technological and statutory developments have led to significant changes in the ways in which young people interact with the media. Various forms of deregulation have led to the increasing availability of specialist and streamed services that no longer fit the traditional models of broadcasting. Technological developments have facilitated increasingly creative interactions with media artefacts. These practices include 'scratch' video, the use of 'dub' and mixing techniques in live and recorded music and the reworking of still images through digital manipulation. At the same time, computer technology has increased the opportunities for relatively sophisticated production in sound and in still and moving images. Increasingly, these are distributed through the Internet, thereby changing the relationships between young people and commercial media industries. Indeed, the development of broad-band networks that abolish the 'tyranny of distance' and allow a continual, interactive flow of cultural productions, information, experience, and expertise of all kinds is widely seen as the pivotal innovation in the emerging array of 'new media.'

Optimists see schools' ability to use these developments as a basic precondition for building a society able to take full advantage of the movement from an industrial to an information age. They point to the potential for creating a more open society, a more informed and participating citizenry, a more fluid and innovative culture, and a more flexible and appropriately skilled workforce. This view is shared by both major political parties in Britain. The U.K. government has placed particular emphasis on the need for schools to promote 'network literacy' and has funded a number of pilot projects linking schools to broad-band networks. It has also stressed the wide ranging educational potential of the 'information highway' and sees schools acting as computing and communications hubs for local communities. To facilitate this, it has secured an agreement that British Telecom will install links in every school in the country at zero cost, in return for permission to offer entertainment services over its networks.

As the experience of computing in schools has shown, however, simply intro-ducing new technologies does not ensure that they will be used either fully or flexibly. The ways computers have been received and used in schools reflect current social reality. A number of British commentators have pointed to economic and organizational realities, high running costs, and lack of appropriate training for teachers. But there is also a cultural reality that is shaping the ways new technolo-gies are used in schools and how pupils relate to them. The 'new media' are being introduced into a situation where there is a complex network of established connections and disconnections between schooling and the mass media environ-ment. These relations can create openings and opportunities for flexible innovation in teaching and learning around 'new media,' but they can also erect symbolic barriers. The rhetorics and pleasures of pupils' leisure-time involvements in media often sit somewhat uneasily alongside school-based initiatives (Murdock, Hart-mann, & Gray, 1992).

There is a need to conduct systematic research on these issues now. If we are to develop strategies and policies that maximize the potential cultural, social, and economic benefits of innovations in communications, we urgently need better and more comprehensive information on which groups of young people are currently moving into the multimedia future, on how they are using available possibilities, and on the dynamics that promote or inhibit their involvement. Understanding the changing role of schools, as 'gatekeepers' of young people's cultural experiences and competencies, is absolutely central to answering these questions.

Media, Culture, and Education

The issues discussed so far are embedded in a wider set of relations among culture, environment, and education. Culture is used here in the broad sense of the clusters of meaning through which people make sense of the world, together with the ways in which these understandings are expressed publicly through language, artefacts, and social practices. Command over culture requires access to the appropriate resources for interpretation and innovation. Passing on the stock of existing culture and the skills to reproduce, replenish, and adapt it has long been seen as central to a society's survival and growth. Children and young people are at the center of this process. They carry culture forward into the future.

Since the beginning of the industrial age, when commentary on the 'condition of culture' began to gather momentum, it has been obvious that complex modern societies produce a plurality of cultures. Amidst this diversity, three cultural spheres have emerged as particularly important:

1. The 'official' culture supported by the major public institutions: museums, libraries and, most important of all, the formal education system. Schools

define what forms of knowledge and expression are to be considered valuable and how they are to be approached and used.

2. The culture produced by the major commercially organized communications, information, and leisure industries.

3. The vernacular cultures grounded in the life of particular neighborhoods and/or social groupings (class, ethnic, and religious) that exist on the margins of official and commercial culture.

The demarcation lines between these three cultural spheres are, of course, fluid and permeable. There is continual traffic across borders. However, schools face a particular problem. They are the main institutional mechanism for passing on 'official' culture as inscribed in curricula. In Australia, in common with other excolonial nations, there has been a rejection of an earlier 'official' culture, and there is now some uncertainty and a continuing struggle to establish a canon which adequately reflects vernacular cultures. In England, schools are increasingly charged with handling an agreed canon that reflects previous national and colonial certainties. Their negotiations with commercial and vernacular culture are therefore fraught with difficulties.

These difficulties have intensified in the last two decades as a result of specific social and educational changes. First, the complex and heated debate over what should constitute 'official' culture has intensified. On the one side stands the project of installing a National Curriculum that specifies what is central and what peripheral, what constitutes the cultural core, when it should be taught, and how the outcomes should be measured. On the other side, we have an increasing awareness of cultural diversity and relativity fueled by a variety of changes, for example, the arrival of a postcolonial polity and the ensuing debate about multiculturalism, the vogue for postmodernism with its associated valorizations of difference and relativity.

As a result, teachers in the classroom (and particularly English and Media teachers) face a range of new pressures and dilemmas that are accentuated by changes in the cultural formations outside school. Second, as noted earlier, the media environment that surrounds schools and that engages pupils has become more complex, more pervasive, and more integrated. Finally, the new centrality of media culture to young people's experience is arguably strengthened by the erosion of the sites that previously sustained and passed on vernacular cultures through family and community networks, and by the decay of public space.

Many young people no longer experience media texts as complete entities. Rather, they seem capable of relating to and enjoying a series of fragments and of 'parallel processing' many media events simultaneously. Traditional 'effects' research has focused on audiences as passive objects, but more recent ethnographic approaches see audiences as informed subjects who respond actively to texts. Qualitative studies have shown how different media genres relate to diverse 'taste publics,' how the social dynamics of domestic contexts relate to media usage and how new communication technologies are being integrated into domestic settings (Moores, 1993; Silverstone, 1994). Studies of young people's usage of television and a range of other media (Buckingham, 1990, 1993a, 1993b; Buckingham & Sefton-Green, 1994) have begun to outline a developmental model of new forms of literacy in terms of narrative, discursive, and modal competencies. These competencies are more than skills. They are social practices that develop by means of 'spontaneous' acquisition and by 'scientific' or more systematic learning experiences. Seen together, these developments in cultural practices and in research perspectives make this an appropriate moment to take a systematic look at the way schools, pupils, and parents negotiate the formation of cultural futures.

THE *MODELS OF MEDIA EDUCATION* PROJECT IN ENGLAND

Previous Research

The only previous substantial work on Media teaching took place in the early 1970s when the Schools Council funded a pioneering investigation into how schools were responding to the burgeoning media culture around television and pop music, and the ways in which teenagers' involvements in this culture were affecting their commitment to school and their educational performance (Murdock & Phelps, 1973). This large-scale survey found that 80% of teachers in grammar schools and 42% in comprehensive schools sampled felt that the study of the mass media had little or no legitimate claim to classroom attention. The findings were widely used and debated both in Britain and elsewhere, but in the 20 years or so since then, there have been no further detailed large-scale studies.

Since then, the rise of qualitative methods in Media Studies has, however, provided much more detailed and nuanced accounts of children's and teenagers' media experiences and their relation to changing patterns of social division, family structures, everyday life, and personal identity. Within education there has been a vigorous debate about the use of media in schools and about the value of Media Education. More recently, these arguments have been given added impetus by the rise of increasingly interactive media. As the influential Cox Report in England noted, in this new context, Media Education must aim "to create more active and critical media users who will demand, and could contribute to, a greater range and diversity of media products" (DES, 1989, 9.6). Yet we currently lack an adequate evidential context for such debates because no recent study has returned to the full range of questions raised by the 1973 study and explored them systematically across an appropriate range of contrasted educational settings.

The original *Models of Media Education* research project in England (Hart & Benson, 1993) explored major questions about aims and methods for Media teaching among teachers of English. It uncovered several areas of uncertainty about Media teaching and identified a range of models that English teachers draw on in the classroom at KS4 (ages 14–16). The project produced detailed descriptions and analyses of a wide range of approaches to teaching about the media.

A survey carried out in the Hampshire area in 1988 revealed a very wide range of understandings of and attitudes toward Media Education, but offered little insight into the detail of classroom practices. When asked to describe their own practice by questionnaire, respondents often seemed to rely on indistinct memories of significant moments that they had not managed to connect into a coherent program of studies. The structured interviews that were conducted with teachers for the *Understanding the Media* project (Cooper & Hart, 1990; Hart, 1991) somewhat reduced the problem of subjective recall by enabling a greater depth of investigation.

Unlike Buckingham (1990, 1993a), whose early work on Media Education concentrated on problematizing many of the claims made for Media teaching in secondary schools and on providing a revisionist account of Media learning in the context of children's social development, we were only incidentally concerned with pupils' learning. His critical look at the claims made for group work in developing social skills, learning to work under pressure, understanding team structures, providing opportunities for self-reflection and exploring the idea that reading texts is a process of negotiation is helpful. He endorsed the view that if pupils share their pleasure in texts with their peers, their understanding is developed. Similarly, some of his most recent research (Buckingham, 1993b; Buckingham & Sefton-Green, 1994) is concerned with the growth of children's evolving understanding of television modes and processes, particularly in terms of how this operates in informal social settings. Although the questions of what and how children learn are also central to understanding how teachers teach, the focus of this project was explicitly on the latter.

Research Methodology

Classroom research has long been animated by major theoretical and methodological debates that can be sketched only briefly here (Hammersley, 1993). It may be helpful, however, to discuss the two methods used in our own research to collect two distinct sets of data, through structured interviews with teachers and through systematic observation of selected lessons.

In the 1960s, the dominant method for studying classroom phenomena was systematic observation. Large samples of teachers and students were observed at regular time intervals or for specific periods, and recurrent events and interactions were recorded according to a predetermined coding scheme. One of the best known of these is Flanders' Interaction Analysis Categories (FIAC), but there are now more than 100 others. Systematic observation has been frequently criticized as having some major flaws (Delamont & Hamilton, 1984; Walker & Adelman, 1975). For example, using predetermined categories may prevent insight into unpredicted complex behaviors. At the same time, arbitrary time sampling neglects and may distort'natural' classroom interaction patterns, and restriction to classroom settings ignores the contexts of teacher and student cultures, and the assumptions and intentions which envelop them.

Although this research method has been ably defended (McIntyre & Macleod, 1978), it is clear that FIAC and other coding systems are not equally suited to all classroom situations. FIAC is particularly appropriate for coding talk in a 'transmission'-type classroom but produces difficulties in coping with talk in small-group contexts where pupils talk to each other. The external systematic observer is also unlikely to understand, let alone to code adequately, many of the detailed connotative aspects of classroom talk. A great deal of talk in 'open' classrooms necessarily remains hidden.

During the 1970s and 1980s, an increased emphasis on "naturalistic study of everyday settings employing relatively unstructured, qualitative methods" (Hammersley, 1993, p. x) gained favor among classroom researchers. Through the influence of several different but interlocking approaches (in particular, ethnography, ethnomethodology, interactionism, and phenomenology) there has been a marked shift away from the study of large samples and the use of quantitative analysis and statistical explanations towards the production of 'thicker', more in-depth data based on ethnographic techniques. Amongst a range of interpretive and qualitative approaches, the case-study method has come to dominate classroom research.

Unlike full-scale ethnography, which necessarily involves extended periods of intensive participant observation, case studies have the distinct advantage of enabling research results and recommendations to be produced within a useable timeframe, because they reduce the amount of necessary researcher time spent in a given setting. At the same time, case studies offer the subjects who participate a greater measure of control over the research process through negotiated access to data and publication of findings. Both of these factors are especially significant in school settings, where teachers are both extremely busy and have a legitimate professional interest in classroom research that may enhance good practice.

The case-study approach using ethnographic techniques emphasizes description and analysis rather than theoretical perspectives. It does not involve the rigorous setting up and testing of hypotheses so much as the evolution of appropriate theoretical explanations for the data collected. Although our experience and previous research have suggested some potentially reliable hunches, our approach in this project was heuristic rather than demonstrative, illuminative rather than revelatory.

The main research question that the project began with was:

- **What are English teachers doing when they say they are doing Media Education at KS4 (ages 14–16) in secondary schools?**

In light of our earlier experiences in interviewing teachers informally (Cooper & Hart, 1990), we used structured interviews to investigate teachers' motivations, aims, and anxieties in greater depth. We also carried out systematic observation of lessons and included a debriefing process with the teachers interviewed. Eleven teachers were interviewed for about 1 hour each during a 6-month period in 1992. A Media lesson (also averaging about 1 hour) was later observed by the interviewer. Interviews were recorded on cassette and transcripts sent to the interviewees to check for accuracy. An essential conclusion to every interview was to ask for a brief description of the lesson we were to observe and a full account of the lesson's aims.

Our basic research question was made operational by focusing on two major subquestions:

- **What Media Education aims are apparent?**
- **What forms of Media Education are apparent?**

The setting for observation was the classroom, of course, and the focus was on the teachers' instructions, questions, responses and other actions. Coding of teachers' strategies was carried out according to a systematic observation schedule, but not according to a given timeframe. Because the judgment of an event's significance was entirely in the hands of the lesson observer, observations were necessarily high inference. But, as with all systematic observation processes, they have the distinct advantage of being made explicit. The main variables were as follow:

- Declared teacher aims
- Key concepts (implicit or explicit reference)
- Lesson introduction
- Content items
- Method (structure/organization/development)
- Teacher-defined tasks/pupil activities
- Resources
- Lesson conclusion

More detailed indicators of these variables included, for example, lesson follow-up, room, furniture, equipment, noise, interruptions, response, timing. The 'Key Concepts' identified were based on the BFI's 'Signpost Questions' shown in Fig. 1.1. These provided a robust but flexible framework for coding different conceptual focuses in both the lessons and the interviews.

Using this form of coding for observation meant that we were able to avoid some of the recurrent criticisms laid at the door of the ethnographic case-study approach. For example:

1. The observer's personal biases may distort the data.
2. Because ethnographic studies focus on what is observable, the narrower the focus of the study, the more likely that important variables may be omitted.

WHO is communicating with whom?	AGENCIES
WHAT type of text is it?	CATEGORIES
HOW is it produced?	TECHNOLOGIES
HOW do we know what it means?	LANGUAGES
WHO receives it and what sense do they make of it?	AUDIENCES
HOW does it present its subject?	REPRESENTATIONS

FIG. 1.1. 'Signpost Questions' for Media Education (after Bazalgette, 1989, p. 8).

3. There is a bias toward recording appearances rather than offering explanations.
4. Results may be merely descriptive (Hammersley, 1993, p. xvii).

We drew on a number of reflexive strategies to counteract these potential weaknesses. The most obvious of these was to make the research methodology explicit at each stage of the process, both in terms of its rationale and its operation. This meant critically examining each decision retrospectively and being aware of unpredicted variables that may have influenced the collection and analysis of data. It meant revealing the 'natural history' of decision making, and making it possible for readers of the formal project reports to form their own inferences and conclusions from the final account. Such reflexivity meant including the mistakes and misunderstandings, rather than trying to cover them up.

The biggest danger of our approach, however, was the potential 'demand effect' on teachers. The lessons were all observed in classrooms, had all been planned in advance, and were explained to the observer. So, although the settings were naturalistic, the lessons may not have been 'natural' ones. They may have been specially provided as 'showcase' lessons for the benefit of the observer, whose interests were always explicit. This seems unlikely to have happened in practice, however, because there seems to be so little consonance between the predetermined aims of lessons discussed with the observer and what actually went on in the lessons themselves. (Other explanations of this dissonance are possible, but they are not flattering toward teachers.) It may be argued that it is not at all natural for teachers to clarify aims before a lesson and stick to them. Yet lesson planning is a foundation element of Initial Teacher Education and provides the backbone of most Professional Development courses and resources, so this is hardly a valid objection.

There were also considerable advantages in having two sets of data, one from the structured interviews and one from the systematic observation of lessons. On the one hand, the empirically observable events of the classroom could be enriched and illuminated by the contextual data on teachers' assumptions, goals, and strategies revealed by the interviews. On the other hand, bearing in mind the weight of evidence showing that what teachers do in classrooms cannot be extrapolated from their own accounts of their intentions or retrospective recall, the classroom observations provided a wealth of empirical data which facilitated comparative analysis. There is a danger, of course, of merging the two sets of data irresponsibly so as to fill in gaps in either set of data. This danger was overcome, however, by carefully keeping them in separate analytical domains.

A list of questions was devised to provide the basis for the structured interviews with teachers before the classroom observation took place. These questions sought to differentiate classroom approaches to Media Education in terms of aims, content, and methods. In addition, the questions attempted a brief exploration of the teachers' previous experience and their perceptions of Media Education's status in their schools. This approach was adopted on the grounds that teaching does not take place in a cultural vacuum.

Sample Selection

Schools were chosen after enquiries to appropriate authorities about centers within a 50-mile radius of Southampton University known to have an interest in Media Education. The selection of schools was made by a study of addresses supplied by the Southern Examining Group of schools in Hampshire and Dorset known to be running General Certificate of Secondary Education (GCSE) Media Studies courses, the mailing list of *Southampton Media Education Group*, lists of secondary schools supplied by Hampshire's four Divisional Education Offices, lists held by Hampshire Schools Inspectorate of schools known to be teaching Media and, in particular, to have entered candidates for GCSE Media Studies in 1991; and personal contact with heads of English Departments. The Southern Examining Group's list provided 5 of the 11 schools visited. Three were chosen from s known to have sent teachers to Media Education courses at Southampton University and a further 3 were gained through personal contacts. Ten of the schools are in Hampshire and one is in Dorset. Area education offices were most helpful in sending addresses of all the centers in their areas.

Fourteen centers were contacted through heads of English Departments. Only 2 centers failed to reply, while a third showed interest but dates proved impracticable. Although the intention had been to interview and observe on separate days, six teachers expressed a definite preference for completing both sessions in a single visit. The choice of individual teachers to be interviewed and observed was largely in the hands of heads of Departments, although it was clear that we needed to meet teachers with a commitment to Media Education. The selected sample either volunteered or was asked at Department meetings because of their known interest in Media work.

Interviews

With the teachers' agreement, interviews were normally recorded on audiocassette, but notes were taken in order to make supplementary questions possible. The interviews generally lasted for about 1 hour and were based on a common set of structured questions (see Fig. 1.2).

Background

What is your main teaching subject?
In what areas of English teaching are you most interested?
For how long have you been a teacher?
For how long have you been teaching Media?
Can you describe the process by which you became interested in Media Education?

Support

What percentage of your current teaching time is given to Media work?
Does this include any Media work outside English?
What proportion of KS4 pupils have experience in Media Education?
What other Media work is done in the school?
Are you able to draw on the expertise of other staff or outside agencies?
Does the school have a policy for Media Education?

Aims

What are your aims for your pupils?
How do you think pupils respond to Media work and to your approaches to it?
Is your teaching influenced by your own views about the media or society?
What would you say are the key concepts in Media Education?
Are there any concepts with which you have difficulty?
How do you see Media Education developing over the next ten years?

Methods and Content

Can you describe in general terms your approach to Media work in the classroom?
With which areas of Media work do you feel most comfortable?
Are there any topics or concepts you tend to avoid?
Which resources do you find most useful?
How far do you find it necessary to produce your own resource material?
If you were advising a teacher new to Media Education about resources what would you say?
Has your work in Media Education influenced what you teach in, or how you teach, other subjects?
Has teaching Media Education given you any surprises?

Focus

Can you describe the lesson I am going to observe?
How does it connect with previous or anticipated lessons?
How does it fit in with the remainder of the English curriculum?
What are your aims for the lesson?
Why do you consider these aims worthwhile?

FIG. 1.2. Questions for structured interviews.

The main aims of the preliminary interview were to discover what the teachers intended to do in the lessons we observed. We also wanted to formulate a preliminary description of these lessons so that the we would be tuned in to significant elements and approaches. It might often be important to understand the personal and social constraints that influence the teacher's approach. A teacher might, for example, perceive the attitudes of the other members of the department to be skeptical of Media Education. In these circumstances, a perceived need to justify lessons in terms of the development of language skills or to set tasks that emphasize written composition might influence the mode of teaching. Similarly, a teacher might bring to Media Education a background of literary theory, semiology, or industrial experience, for example, that might strongly influence the selection of, and approach to, themes. For these reasons it was thought worthwhile to explore the backgrounds of the teachers involved in the research and their perceptions of the status of, and support for, Media Education within the department and school.

Although the original aim of the interviews was to establish the specific aims of the lesson to be observed, it was one of the rewards of the research that these interviews also proved to be extremely revealing of the continuities and differences in teachers' approaches and perceptions. It soon became clear that much longer interviews could be justified for the value of the data obtained. Teachers were very articulate and often expressed appreciation of the opportunity the interview had given them to explore and share their thoughts.

After analysis of the interview transcripts, profiles of the interviewees that focused on their preferred teaching styles were returned to the teachers for comment and addition. The main purpose of returning the profiles to the teachers was to provide a check on their validity, so that they might act as reliable frameworks for interpreting the lesson observations that were to follow. It was also, however, a courtesy to busy professionals who had given time and effort to assist with the research. Teachers often complain that they are asked to take part in research projects but rarely hear any accounts of the work done or see any benefits to education practice. Every effort was made to emphasize the expected value of the project in developing recommendations for the practice and resourcing of Media Education.

Lesson Observations

Observation of a lesson took place as soon as possible after each interview. The observer did not normally participate in the lesson. Note was taken of the balance of time for the parts of the lesson, the nature and style of questions, the degree and nature of pupil participation, the resources used, the tasks set, the concepts available to pupils, and the language used by teacher and pupils (see Fig. 1.3 for a copy of the observation form). An account of each lesson was written and sent to the teacher concerned for comment. Audiocassette recording and photographing was used with the consent of the teacher.

Figure 1.3. LESSON OBSERVATION FORM

School_____   Date _____199_
Teacher_____   Year _____
Duration of Lesson_____   Nos. Girls ____ Boys_____

Aims

_____

Concepts

_____

Resources

_____

Introduction

_____

Content

_____

Method

_____

Pupil Tasks

_____

Conclusion

_____

Other Observations
e.g. follow-up, room, furniture, equipment, noise, interruptions, response, timing.

FIG. 1.3. Lesson observation form.

All teachers gave permission for their lessons to be tape-recorded and for photographs to be taken. Observation was normally from the rear of the classroom so as to be inconspicuous, although teachers always introduced the observer to the class and had usually told pupils in advance of the visit. Where group work was a major part of the lesson, the observer was usually invited to sit in on or talk to groups.

There were problems in observing lessons. The presence of an observer is inhibiting for most teachers, who might consequently be tempted to play it safe with lessons that were unlikely to prove challenging. Teachers in fact displayed great integrity in continuing with established programs of work rather than offering one-off favorite lessons, but this usually meant that the lessons observed were part of a sequence, often of three or more weeks' work. The project's constraints of time meant that teachers' favorite lessons could rarely be seen—a project of at least four terms' duration would be needed to ensure that this difficulty could be overcome. Instead, teachers were given the chance during the interview to describe favorite lessons.

The research methods and instruments adopted were relatively simple and transparent. We laid no traps, attempted no trick questions and kept the participants as fully informed as possible throughout. We invited them to a follow-up conference when the research was in draft form to meet external consultants on the project, and to another conference to discuss a Professional Development book (Hart & Hackman, 1995) that we prepared as one of the means of disseminating the research.

Outcomes

The lessons we studied and the teachers we interviewed revealed the teachers' limited experience of media processes and agencies. This meant a restriction of range to relatively familiar areas. Like media texts they studied with pupils, the teachers were strongly constrained by their own institutional and 'production' contexts. Agency, Industry, Institutions and Production, which are arguably most central to teaching about the media, were rarely addressed by the teachers. At the same time, although there is as yet little research to substantiate it, these are probably the areas in which pupils have the least expertise (see final chapter for a more complete discussion of this issue).

It was noted earlier that our method of identifying teachers' purposes before the lessons were taught may have been responsible for an element of artificiality in what we observed. In reality, however, having both structured interviews and lesson observations supplied us with a set of case studies that illuminated one of the most interesting areas of the problem we were examining: the relationships among the experience of the teachers, the scope of their lessons, and the Media expertise they were able to draw on with confidence.

THE INTERNATIONAL *MODELS OF MEDIA EDUCATION* PROJECT

As a result of the success of the *Models of Media Education* project in England and contacts with other researchers, a collaborative project was established to develop the research internationally. The 1989 Lausanne symposium organized by Jean-Pierre Golay, the 1990 *New Directions* colloquy in Toulouse, and the 1990 conference in Natal, South Africa, were all crucial opportunities for Media educators to meet and discuss their own work and developments in their local contexts. The 1992 *Constructing Culture* conference in Guelph, Ontario, run by the Association for Media Literacy, went a step further by enabling leading Media Education researchers to meet and discuss potential collaboration in this project. Participants in the international project agreed to use the same methods and instruments that were developed for the original English project, with similar cohorts of students and teachers, in order to provide a relatively fixed lens through which classroom approaches in different educational and cultural contexts could be observed.

Three years later, in June 1995, many of the participants in the study met again during the fourth *Pedagoxia da Imaxe* at La Coruna, Spain, for the first 'World Meeting' of researchers on Media Education, where the successful completion of nearly all of the studies initiated in 1992 was confirmed. Most of the contributors met again in June 1996 at La Coruna for the fifth *Pedagoxia da Imaxe* conference to finalize their work. This book is the final result.

The international project focused on:

- Conceptions of Media Education within English teaching .
- Perceived problems and rewards of teaching and learning about the media.
- Teachers' attitudes to Media Education both as a theoretical discipline and as a classroom subject.
- Teachers' aims for their students.
- Teachers' prior experience of media institutions.
- Key concepts with which teachers feel most confident, and the sources from which their understanding of these concepts derive.
- Favored resources and the ways in which these are used.
- Teachers' expectations for the future of Media Education.

Debates between conflicting views about the media of the future have strongly influenced current thinking about appropriate forms of education. Our research has identified a range of teaching models that will help conceptualize a wide range of practices among teachers of English. It shows how classroom strategies and practices in different countries are responding to the new technological developments and ideological debates. By providing two distinct but related sets of data on Media teachers' rationales for their work (from in-depth interviews with small samples of teachers) and Media teachers' classroom methods (from systematic observation), the study has created a new basis that enables us to begin to:

- Document the different understandings, purposes, and practices of Media teachers in a range of international locations.
- Make a comparative analysis of different approaches to Media teaching both within different national and between different international locations.
- Encourage discussion of appropriate models for different locations and purposes.

- Facilitate discussion of appropriate methodologies for classroom research in Media Education.
- Provide a basis for the continuing development of Media Education as a discipline and for further research in Media Education.

Although they may sometimes appear to, teachers do not function independently of larger controls. What we are able to explore through the lens of comparative analysis is the extent to which national, regional, and district cultures and policies impact on local practices. There is a necessary (and desirable) tension between the allocative controls of statutory educational frameworks and the operational controls of individual teachers in their classrooms. The spaces, resources, temporal frames, and class sizes they operate within strongly influence, but do not completely determine, their aims and methods. So too with their personal biographies and goals. Our interviews and observations gave us insights into some of the complex interactions between cultures, teachers, students, resources, methods, and curricular contexts in educational settings. We have experienced a series of adventures into the minds and classrooms of teachers who are attempting to relate their curricula and methods to developments in information and communication technology and the cultures of young people.

There are some general similarities of approach and some sharp differences that demonstrate how important it is to resist the temptation of 'exporting' models of good practice to inappropriate contexts, and to reject some of the colonialist assumptions that have deeply affected English teaching around the world during this century. Our findings show, above all, that we need to think globally but to work locally if we are to develop approaches to Media Education that systematically address increasingly powerful 'mediatization' and globalization processes and at the same time create classroom strategies that genuinely reflect the vernacular demands of different cultural contexts.

REFERENCES

Bazalgette, C. (Ed.). (1989). *Primary media education: A curriculum statement.* London: British Film Institute.

Bazalgette, C., Bevort, E., & Savino, J. (Eds.). (1992). *New directions: Media education worldwide.* London: British Film Institute.

Brown, J. (1991). *Television 'critical viewing skills' education.* Hillsdale, NJ: Lawrence Erlbaum Associates.

Brumfit, C. J., & Mitchell, R. F. (1989) The language classroom as a focus for research. In C. J. Brumfit & R. F. Mitchell (Eds.), *Research in the language classroom* (pp. 3–15) Basingstoke: Macmillan.

Buckingham, D. (1990). *Watching media learning.* London: Falmer.

Buckingham, D. (1993a). *Children talking television: The making of television literacy.* London: Taylor & Francis.

Buckingham, D. (Ed.). (1993b). *Reading audiences: Young people and the media.* Manchester: Manchester University Press.

Buckingham, D., & Sefton-Green, J. (1994). *Cultural studies goes to school: Reading and teaching popular media.* London: Taylor & Francis.

Butts, D. (1986). *Media education in Scottish secondary schools: A research study 1983–1986.* Stirling: University of Stirling.

Cohen, L., & Manion, L. (1994). *Research methods in education* (4th ed.). London: Routledge.

Cooper, G., & Hart, A. (1990). *Understanding the media: Interview transcripts.* Southampton: Southampton Media Education Group.

Delamont, S., & Hamilton, D. (1984). Revisiting classroom research: A continuing cautionary tale. In S. Delamont & D. Hamilton (Eds.). *Readings on interaction in the classroom* (pp. 3–24). London: Methuen.

Department of Education and Science. (The Cox Report). (1989). *English for ages 5–16.* London: Her Majesty's Stationery Office.

Hammersley, M. (Ed.). (1993). *Controversies in classroom research* (2nd ed.). Buckingham: Open University.

Hart, A. (1991). *Understanding the media.* London: Routledge.

Hart, A., & Benson, A. (1993). *Media in the classroom.* Southampton: Southampton Media Education Group.

Hart, A., & Hackman, S. (1995). *Developing Media in English.* London: Hodder.

Kubey, R. (Ed.). (1997) *Media literacy in the information age.* New Brunswick: Transaction.

Learmonth, J., & Sayer, M. (1996). *A review of good practice in media education.* London: British Film Institute.

Mattelart, A. (1991). *Advertising international.* London: Routledge.

McIntyre, D., & Macleod, G. (1978). The characteristics and uses of systematic classroom observation. In R. McAleese & D. Hamilton (Eds.), *Understanding classroom life.* Slough: National Foundation for Education Research.

McLuhan, M. (1964). *Understanding media.* London: Abacus.

McLuhan, M., & Fiore, Q. (1967). *The medium is the message.* Harmondsworth: Penguin.

Moores, S. (1993). *Interpreting audiences: The ethnography of media consumption.* London: Sage.

Murdock, G., Hartmann, P., & Gray, P. (1992). Contextualizing home computing: Resources and practices. In R. Silverstone & E. Hirsch (Eds.), *Consuming technologies: Media and information in domestic spaces* (pp. 146–160). London: Routledge.

Murdock, G., & Phelps, G. (1973). *Mass media and the secondary school.* Basingstoke: Macmillan.

Piette, J., & Giroux, L. (1997). The theoretical foundations of media education. In R. Kubey (Ed.), *Media literacy in the information age* (pp. 89–134). New Brunswick: Transaction.

Silverstone, R. (1994). *Television and everyday life.* London: Routledge.

Thompson, J. B. (1990). *Ideology and modern culture.* Cambridge: Polity Press.

Walker, R., & Adelman, C. (1975). Interaction analysis in informal classrooms: A critical comment on the Flanders system. *British Journal of Educational Psychology, 45,* 73–76.

2

Models of Media Education in England and the Secondary Curriculum for English

Andrew Hart
University of Southampton

A recent issue of the British Film Institute's newsletter *Media Education News Update* (MENU; 1993, p. 1) suggested that:

> There is still much confusion over whether Media Education just means that the media are a convenient way of bolstering traditional English teaching, or that it entails specifically studying the media themselves. We think it must mean the latter because the former takes no account of existing knowledge and how it ought to be developed during schooling. To develop this effectively, teachers must receive adequate guidance; the production of such guidance must, in the long term, be based on the knowledge, skills and understanding that Media Education should be building.

One of the main reasons for this confusion is not specific to Media Education, but shared by most other disciplines. There is undoubtedly a dearth of classroom-focused studies of teaching strategies. That is why the Models of Media Education project was originally established in England, as explained in the Introduction to this book. This chapter explains the curriculum context and presents the main findings of the English study, including detailed case studies of two teachers and their lessons.

RECENT DEVELOPMENTS IN THE MEDIA CURRICULUM

The role of Media teaching within English is widely seen as one of helping pupils enjoy a wide range of media and develop an awareness of how they work. It involves accepting the validity of the specific meanings that young readers create through their reading of many different kinds of texts. Media Education was defined in this way in the report of the influential Cox Committee:

> Media Education ... seeks to increase children's critical understanding of the media....[It] aims to develop systematically children's critical and creative powers through analysis and production of media artefacts....Media Education aims to create more active and critical media users who will demand, and could contribute to, a greater range and diversity of media products. (DES, 1989, 9.6)

Ultimately, pupils should be able to speak independently and with confidence about the characteristic forms and pleasures of a whole range of various texts. This process necessarily involves them in becoming more active media readers and audiences. As they become increasingly able to create a critical distance between themselves and the media texts they value, they are moving toward a kind of autonomy that helps them articulate their own 'voice'.

According to this approach, the essential task for teachers is not to make qualitative distinctions between literary and media texts nor to place them on some form of hierarchical scale. Rather, it is to help pupils learn how to evaluate for themselves any kind of text according to content, form, and context. Knowing about the contexts of production and consumption is a necessary basis for understanding how to read texts. The realization that texts are constructed rather than discovered is central to the development of higher level reading skills.

The question of curriculum location is almost as fundamental as those of purpose and content. If Media is to be taught at all, decisions must be made about where, when and by whom. Should it be a subject in its own right, an integral part of English, or a cross-curricular concern? The term 'Media Education' has been widely used in England during the 1980s to refer to secondary school (ages 11–16) work on the media within English and across the curriculum in, for example, the 'Cross-curricular Themes' work prescribed by the National Curriculum. It is also a term that makes particular sense in a Primary or Middle School context. Its weakness is that it may be rather bland in reality. Its virtues include its generality and its innocuousness.

The strategy advocated in the British Film Institute's (BFI) document *Secondary Media Education: A Curriculum Statement* (Bowker, 1991) was to argue primarily for a cross-curricular approach under the title Media Education rather than for the more specialized term of 'Media Studies'. This cross-curricular framework was developed originally in the *Primary Curriculum Statement* (Bazalgette, 1989). 'Media Studies', on the other hand, is largely reserved for specialist General Certificate of Educational Studies (GCSE; examinations at 16+ years of age), Advanced Level (examinations at 18+ years of age) and undergraduate University courses. It has been seen by some as a political risk, because it suggests distant echoes of the 1970s' work of the Glasgow University Media Group and stereotypical accusations of 'left-wing bias'. Yet specialist understanding of Media Studies is highly desirable if strong forms of Media Education are to develop, rather than some of the weaker forms that currently appear in many schools.

Study of the mass media has been growing in popularity in English schools at least since the 1960s. The main impetus for this growth came from teachers of English, many of whom saw themselves as protectors of children from the 'false consciousness' that the media were believed to inculcate. It was this invasion of consciousness that Marshall McLuhan perceived in the 1960s. The media invasion was a subliminal one, operating beneath the threshold of consciousness. In a famous phrase, he warned that the content of the media was "like the juicy piece of meat carried by the burglar to distract the watchdog of the mind." (McLuhan, 1973, p. 26). This fear of the seduction of the innocent was to dominate the early years of studying the media.

In the 1970s and 1980s, Media Education in the United Kingdom grew rapidly, with the creation of new Secondary level courses in Film Studies and later with new courses in Media Studies and national examinations at age 16 and 18, as documented in the Schools Council survey (Murdock & Phelps, 1973). The availability of the videocassette recorder (VCR) gave an enormous boost to Media work and made the study of television the dominant focus. However, there was a tension over what kinds of texts were legitimate objects of study: those valued by teachers or those valued by pupils? This tension led many teachers to examine their own attitudes in more personal, less theoretical ways, and some recognized the hypocrisy in routine condemnations of what were major sources of information and pleasure for themselves as much as for their pupils, especially when they formed an important part of pupils' cultural identities.

During the 1980s, both Media Education, mainly in secondary schools, and Media Studies, mainly in higher education, were fast growing areas. After a long period of antipathy toward the mass media, especially from English teachers in secondary schools, there was a noticeable change of attitude. During that time, for example, the National Association for the Teaching of English had its own working party on Media Education. Actual provision in the education system was patchy, however, and mainly existed where enthusiastic individuals or groups were developing their own ideas.

In 1988, a National Curriculum was proposed for England and Wales. Many individuals and groups (such as The BFI) lobbied for the inclusion of Media Education. Media Education was included first in the Cox Report's proposals for National Curriculum English and then in the Statutory Orders themselves (DES, 1989, 1990). In reviewing dominant curriculum models for English teaching, Cox (DES, 1989) featured five main approaches.

1. A *"personal growth"* view focuses on the child: It emphasises the relationship between language and learning in the individual child, and the role of literature in developing children's imaginative and aesthetic lives.

2. A *"cross-curricular"* view focuses on the school: It emphasizes that all teachers (of English and of other subjects) have a responsibility to help children with the language demands of different subjects on the school curriculum: otherwise areas of the curriculum may be closed to them. In England, English is different from other school subjects, in that it is both a subject and a medium of instruction for other subjects.

3. An *"adult needs"* view focuses on communication outside the school: It emphasises the responsibility of English teachers to prepare children for the language demands of adult life, including the workplace, in a fast-changing world. Children need to learn to deal with the day-to-day demands of spoken language and of print; they also need to be able to write clearly, appropriately, and effectively.

4. A *"cultural heritage"* view emphasises the responsibility of schools to lead children to an appreciation of those works of literature that have been widely regarded as amongst the finest in the language.

5. A *"cultural analysis"* view emphasizes the role of English in helping children towards a critical understanding of the world and cultural environment in which they live. Children should know about the processes by which meanings are conveyed, and about the ways in which print and other media carry values. (2.21–2.25)

Media Education established a firm foothold, notably within the 'cultural analysis' approach, in schools and in post-6 education (where curricula allow for more flexibility and specialization). The Cox-based English Order recognized explicitly the value of nonliterary and media texts and required that they be given some attention. Media Education was seen by Cox as part of "the exploration of contemporary culture" (9.4). Cox recognized that Media Education approaches should be part of every English teacher's practice, that "the kinds of question that are routinely applied in Media Education can be fruitfully applied to literature" (7.23); and that "Media Education has often developed in a very explicit way concepts which are of general importance in English" (9.9). These questions and concepts are listed by Cox as "selection (of information, viewpoint, etc.) editing, author, audience, medium, genre, stereotype, etc." (9.9). The questions resolve themselves into "who is communicating with whom and why; how has the text been produced and transmitted; and how does it convey its meaning?" (7.23).

This was the first official recognition of the subject. As a result, all English departments in secondary schools and all teachers in primary schools were required to incorporate Media Education into their English and language work. This initiative produced a flurry of supporting materials and books aimed at helping teachers to achieve this end. There was also an expectation that Media would be taught in other parts of the secondary curriculum and even across the curriculum, as in primary schools.

Many teachers, however, remained either lukewarm about Media Education or, in a minority of cases, even hostile to it. Nevertheless, the trend was toward an acceptance of Media Education within English, and a receptiveness in schools for Media Studies. Some secondary teachers and whole departments welcomed it wholeheartedly. A report on English by the national Inspectorate (HMI) during 1990 to 1991 observed that at Key Stage (KS) 3 (age 11–14), most English departments had incorporated information technology (IT) and some elements of Media Education into their work. The BFI continued to lobby for Media Education to be included in a much broader sense in, for example, Art and Geography, or in a broader sense as a cross-curricular element throughout the school.

This period (1990–1995) has been characterized by enormous changes in schooling in every dimension. One feature of this was a concerted attempt to revise the National Curriculum toward a much more traditional (and so-called) skills-oriented approach. The thrust was to get rid of the 'cultural analysis' model, and to insist on the preeminence of a 'cultural heritage' model. Teachers resisted these changes, but most of their energies went into fighting attempts to introduce simplistic national tests for 14-year-olds in English.

Media Education was mainly sidelined in these battles. There was a flourishing of classroom materials and of groundbreaking small-scale research, but there is little evidence to suggest that Media Education has now entered the mainstream. However, Media Studies at General Certificate of Secondary Education (GCSE) (for 16-year-olds), at 'A' level (for 18-year-olds), and at degree level has continued to grow year by year. An estimated 30,000 candidates took public examinations in Media or Communication Studies in 1995.

In Scotland, where Media Education has established itself firmly, two very detailed surveys within 5 years show strong developments, supported by the Scottish Film Council (SFC) and by local and national education authorities, in both primary and secondary schools (Brown & Visocchi, 1991; Butts, 1986). In England, the BFI, in conjunction with The National Foundation for Educational Research (NFER) undertook a survey of schools in late 1993 (Dickson, 1994). The sample was small (482 schools and colleges), and the response rate was moderate, providing only 189 replies. There was no opportunity to cross-check these responses with the actual practices in the institutions themselves. In spite of these reservations, the survey showed that: Most institutions claimed that they were teaching some Media Education within English, and in 67% of these it was also taught somewhere else in the curriculum; almost three fourths of respondents considered that they devoted between 10% and 25% of curriculum time to Media Education; 69% of respondents thought Media Education was "very important."

The National Curriculum for Art, after going through many similar changes to the English curriculum, also envisages space for Media teaching, especially in relation to image analysis and construction, still photography, and video work.

The Current Context

Despite these developments, Media Education has not achieved a high status or become a major focus within statutory education. Many teachers see the 'new' (post-1995) National Curriculum as further downgrading the position of Media Education within the 5 through 16 curriculum. However, the statutory document can be read either literally or 'between the lines'. The frequent references to media texts do suggest a serious intention to address basic media issues. Yet they still neglect such important aspects of Media as Representations, Audiences, Agencies, and Institutions. Committed Media teachers will look for and find many openings, whereas those who are less convinced or enthusiastic may well ignore the opportunities for Media work that it envisages. Those who wish to include Media will need to integrate it with linguistic and literary study more comprehensively than before. The most direct reference states that:

> Pupils should be introduced to a wide range of media, *e.g., magazines, newspapers, radio, television, film.* They should be given opportunities to analyze and evaluate such material, which should be of high quality and represent a range of forms and purposes, and different structural and presentational devices (ref) (DES, 1993, 20).

This provides a sufficient toe-hold for the committed and the existing specialists, but it offers little scope or pressure for others to develop or change.

Yet the 1994 draft Order for English inspired more responses than any other and seems to have produced significant changes in the final Order. More than 6,500 educationalists responded to it, of whom over one third complained that there was too little reference to Media. What emerged as the post-1995 curriculum is a more balanced, if still flawed, framework for English teaching. 'Texts' are no longer exclusively literary. Media work features in all three Attainment Targets: *Speaking and Listening, Reading; and Writing.* There is an appreciation of the importance of the visual, and a recognition of the importance of practical work. The dominant 'cultural heritage' perspective has been tempered by a concern for 'cultural analysis'.

There are also new developments such as the General National Vocational Qualification in Media Studies. The Business and Technical Education Council syllabus continues to include study of the media. However, these latter qualifications are likely to have more impact on colleges than on schools.

Currently then, Media Education is surviving in schools, and Media Studies is growing rapidly. It is likely that Media Education will now also grow. This growth will come through a combination of changing technology (especially computer technology), and through the next generation of teachers that is growing up in a media- and technology-oriented world.

Whatever growth in Media Education and Media Studies there has been in schools and colleges, there has not been a corresponding expansion of training and development opportunities for teachers. The result is that many work in isolation with little more than examination syllabuses to guide them. In-service support for

Media Education has been severely reduced over the last 2 years as a result of funding changes and a National Curriculum focus on the core curriculum areas. Some teachers have simply inherited responsibility for Media courses from enthusiastic teachers who have moved on. Although some of these 'substitutes' often become enthusiasts themselves, they can too easily find themselves overwhelmed by the scope of the subject and by the unlimited material from which to choose.

Because few teachers have been formally trained in Media Education or Media Studies, there is inevitably a wide variation in theoretical understanding and classroom practice. Notions of Media Education may vary from showing a video recording of a Shakespeare play to the critical study of media institutions and audiences. Some teachers have rejected analytical approaches in favor of creative or technical ones. Others justify the subject for its implicit methods alone, arguing for example, that its emphasis on group work and projects develops social skills. However, apart from Buckingham's (1990d, 1993; Buckingham & Sefton-Green, 1994) work, little is known empirically about teachers' actual classroom practices.

The BFI *Secondary Statement* (Bowker, 1991) offers some excellent examples of Media work reported by English teachers themselves. Some of them show clearly the special expertise that English teachers can bring to the study of media in the classroom. Although such accounts may be useful in the context of action-research projects designed to enhance teachers' roles as reflective practitioners, they are not the products of systematic research.

There is a great deal of work being carried out in English classrooms that draws on media materials and processes. The BFI\NFER questionnaire referred to earlier (Dickson, 1994) showed that nearly 90% of English teachers in 189 schools and colleges surveyed used television for showing 'film-of-the-book' adaptations of literary texts. The focus of learning in such contexts is often what is learned *through* Media work that is central to the aims of English. But some work is also concerned with learning *about* the media. It is important to distinguish between them, not because one approach is any more effective or worthwhile than others, but because they are actually different and therefore lead in different directions. The goals pursued by each approach can, therefore, be best reached if we have a fuller understanding of the strategies, methods, and forms of organization that are appropriate in each case.

A Leeds University study (Brown, 1990) was carried out in conjunction with the Training Services Agency as part of an evaluation of initiatives in English teaching. It began with a broad concern with 'English for participation', and suggested a wide range of appropriate models for the development of such work in English. The report argues that "English has emphasized inward states, private forms of knowing and expressions of the uniqueness of experience (and has neglected) the social dimensions of experience." But if pupils are to develop as speakers and writers, they need to "participate as well as reflect" (Brown, 1990, p. 181).

The classroom approaches studied in Developing English for the Training and Vocational Education Initiative Project (DEFT) were selected therefore, for their specific emphasis on: *language*, which goes beyond the personal and literary into the more public domain of working in teams, decision making, persuading people, transactional processes, organizing, informing, and helping people; and *content*, which includes experience as contributors to technological and economic processes or other aspects of work experience. (Brown, et. al. 1990, pp. 6–7). In summarizing their evaluation of these projects, the researchers explained that the best writing they found was when: "the writers were looking outwards, engaged in informative not introspective acts, seeking as much to change the world (or their part of it) as to understand it, or themselves, better" (Brown, et al., 1990, p. 182).

Common to most of the projects evaluated was an engagement with *non-literary texts*. These were often of a quite conventional kind, such as formal reports. But what was new about this approach was that the reports were based on pupils' experience of work situations, rather than simulations. As a result, when more than one individual reports on an experience in the same context, detailed comparisons become possible and a critical sharpness is added. The transfer of this kind of alertness to the production and analysis of media texts may also, become more likely and more natural.

For example, unlike the well-established routine of devising mock advertisements for nonexistent products, producing real promotional materials for clients demands that pupils address relationships between audiences and styles with great care (Brown, 1990, p. 174). Andrews, the DEFT Project's independent evaluator, concluded that these approaches produced not only greater personal involvement and more accomplished writing from pupils, but also major advances in oral competence. He attributes their increased confidence in interviewing, decision making, and other forms of oral work to a greater range of communication tasks associated with "real audiences and outcomes." He also claimed that the DEFT Project developed imaginative involvement in practical contexts that link easily with conventional literature-based approaches, and that 'Knowledge About Language' was also developed through interaction with speakers and writers in quite new social contexts (Brown, 1990, p. 144).

There are certainly some problems, as Buckingham (1990b, 1990c) has pointed out, in incorporating work on the media within English. Redefining 'texts' to include nonliterary ones was difficult enough for Cox and the National Curriculum Council (NCC), and may also be difficult for some English teachers. The post-Dearing revisions maintain this more comprehensive notion of 'text' as including nonfiction and nonliterary forms. But they do not offer a coherent framework that will help teachers approach such texts systematically and analytically.

However, if there really are problems in leaving the teaching of Media to English teachers, there are even more problems in expecting teachers of other subjects to handle it. It is relatively easy to quantify and show the presence of 'media' in many different subject areas. But what is meant by 'media' in these different contexts? What kind of teaching is going on? What kind of learning is happening? Without detailed research, these questions are impossible to answer. As a result, many accounts of whole school involvement in Media Education may have more to do with public relations profiles than with a genuine curriculum. As the external pressures on schools increase, there is a danger of creating a 'virtual curriculum' that bears little relation to classroom realities.

THE *MODELS OF MEDIA EDUCATION* PROJECT

Most of the teachers in the original English study accepted the mandate of the Cox-based curriculum for English, that Media Education should be a part of pupils' education throughout their secondary education, or even earlier. There was very little anxiety about the subject proliferating into other disciplines and most felt secure about their own contributions to any cross-curricular initiatives. On the other hand, none of the schools concerned had yet developed a school policy for Media Education, and in some cases the teachers interviewed proved to be unaware of Media work being done in other departments. Some expressed anxiety about attitudes of colleagues in their own departments, and feared some disapproval of what was sometimes seen as the study of ephemera (Hart & Benson, 1993).

At this stage in the development of Media Education (i.e., during the lifetime of the Cox-based curriculum before the post-Dearing revisions noted earlier), we expected to find that the approach of English teachers emphasized skills of analysis and comprehension. We felt that there was likely to be an inclination to work on the familiar territory of advertising and newspaper language. Teachers, we supposed, would seek to justify their work in terms of language development with a recognition that the media provide a stimulus to the practice of oral skills. Literature and Media work might well be linked, with considerable use of televised adaptations of novels and plays. From this might come some study of audiences, representation, and narrative forms.

The Cox-based curriculum in place during 1992 confined its attention to the Reading Attainment Target, with particular emphasis on KS 3 and 4 pupils (ages 11–16). According to the National Curriculum English Attainment Target 2 (DES, 1990, 3–11; Reading, Levels 5–10), pupils should be able to:

Show in discussion that they can recognise whether subject matter in non-literary and media texts is presented as fact or opinion ... [5c];

Show in discussion and in writing that they can recognise whether subject-matter in non-literary and media texts is presented as fact or opinion, identifying some of the ways in which the distinction can be made ... [6c];

Show in discussion that they can recognise features of presentation which are used to inform, to regulate, to reassure or to persuade, in non-literary and media texts ... [7c];

Show in discussion and in writing an ability to form a considered opinion about features of presentation which are used to inform, reassure or persuade in non-literary and media texts ... [8c];

Show in discussion and in writing an ability to recognise techniques and conventions of presentation in non-literary and media texts, and judge the effectiveness of their use ... [9c];

Show in discussion and in writing an ability to evaluate techniques and conventions of presentation in non-literary and media texts, and judge the effectiveness of their use ... [10c];

Select, retrieve, evaluate and combine information independently and with discrimination, from a comprehensive range of reference materials, making effective and sustained use of the information. [10d].

Aims and Assessment

One of the benefits of the recently created GCSE examinations in the United Kingdom has been that syllabuses have had to provide clearly expressed aims and objectives. English teachers had in many cases become so used to basing their teaching on past examination papers and taking many of their aims for granted that this approach had considerable novelty. The introduction of explicit aims and, in particular, learning objectives enabled teachers to reexamine their work, and to remind themselves of a discourse that had perhaps become underused. With the new emphasis on coursework, teachers found that each assignment needed to be justified in terms of objectives, but that in the case of Media work the concepts were sometimes unfamiliar.

Although our teachers listed between them 29 aims for the 11 lessons, it was clear that some were uncomfortable with identifying specific Media concepts and saw the lessons in terms of textual approaches familiar from literature work. The aims of each of the 11 lessons we observed were stated as shown in Table 2.1.

Our analysis suggested that of the 11 lessons planned, 3 declared no Media aims at all, 5 aimed at a balance between Media and English (mostly Literature), and only 3 conceived of the lessons purely in Media terms.

In terms of the 'Key Concepts' criterion, the range was relatively narrow, with more than 50% of all emphases falling within the three most frequently addressed areas as shown in Table 2.2. In fact, the last four were mentioned specifically by only one teacher, a probationer who had recently completed a Media course and whose lesson did address her aims. It was also, at 1 hour 40 minutes, the longest lesson we observed.

There is scope for some difference in how these aims are classified, for example, is 'design pictorial representations' image analysis or representation? Clearly it is

TABLE 2.1

Aims of 11 Lessons Observed

1	**Promoting a Pop Group**
1.1	To understand how the pop music business operates, and to be aware of the limitations on the artists in controlling their product.
2	***Jane Eyre* as a TV text**
2.1	To raise awareness of the importance of producing evidence for opinions.
2.2	To bring into sharper focus some important aspects of the literary text.
3	**Analysing Advertisements**
3.1	To develop skills of analysis and deduction relevant to other texts, especially poems and novels, and to life skills.
4	**Promoting a Pop Group from a Novel**
4.1	To reinforce understanding of the characters and themes of the novel.
4.2	To learn to work as groups and to negotiate tasks.
4.3	To work to a deadline.
4.4	Tp practise writing in a style appropriate to pop magazines.
4.5	To consider the requirements of a teenage audience.
4.6	To design pictorial representations of ideas.
5	**Analysing Comics**
5.1	To look at the ways texts function beyond the literal meanings of language, specifically through symbols, cultural icons and implicit values.
5.2	To understand the concepts of Audience, Narrative, Institution, Genre, and Expectation.
5.3	To examine the varied responses readers might make to a text.
5.4	To make comparisons between narratives and representations in comics and in *Lord of the Flies.*
5.5	To study a mass medium in terms of who is communicating what to whom and with what effect.
6	**Visual Treatment of Poems**
6.1	To gain understanding of the nature of television audiences and their appropriate language registers.
6.2	To improve understanding of the poems.
6.3	To make an assessment for GCSE Oral Communication.
7	**Lifestyles**
7.1	To see media representations as constructs mediated by bias.
7.2	To test the understanding of previous work on lifestyles.

(continued)

TABLE 2.1 (continued)

8	**Sunday Supplements**
8.1	To examine the ways magazines cater for particular audiences.
8.2	To understand the language registers appropriate to specific audiences.
9	**News Broadcast based on Biblical Episode**
9.1	To encourage pupils to look more carefully at television news broadcasts and at the ways in which news is presented.
9.2	To discover how far pupils' perceptions of the news is affected by news values, especially in the presentation of violence.
10	**Reading a Pop Video**
10.1	To gain experience in reading visual messages that are part of pupils' lives.
10.2	To understand the idea of imagery in the study of literary texts.
10.3	To encourage the habit of close reading of apparently simple texts.
11	**Perceptions and Representations of Careers**
11.1	To look at, enjoy, and reflect on a television play related to pupils' own recent experience.
11.2	To relate pupils' actual work experience to their fantasies about their futures

TABLE 2.2

Frequency of 'Key Concepts' in Lessons Observed

'Key Concepts' Central to Lessons	Frequency
Audiences	5
Language	3
Image Analysis	3
Institutions	2
Mediation	2
Representation	1
Narrative	1
Genre	1
Categories	1

TABLE 2.3

Literature-Related Aims in Lessons Observed

Aims Related to Literature	Frequency
Textual Analysis	5
Thematic Work	2
Narrative	1
Character	1
Imagery	1

both, but here we have to trust our coding category during the observation of the lesson. If we look at the aims which relate more specifically to Literature study, we find the balance as shown in Table 2.3.

Teachers' aims that referred directly to Audiences and Language made up nearly half of the specifically Media aims. Awareness of Audience as a concept is probably the borrowing from Media Education that English teachers in general have most enthusiastically embraced. Its relevance to literary study, to imaginative writing, and to oral work has been a valuable extension to English studies, and it has linked closely with recent emphasis on language registers. On the other hand, it can be argued that teachers may have been interested in the concept of Audiences as a direct response to these uncertainties and anxieties. What was happening, perhaps, was that English teachers were seizing on this area as a more accessible way into areas of Media Studies where they felt less secure.

Some of the teachers had trouble bridging the gap between their own experience of the media and the varied experiences of their pupils. Some found that there was scarcely any, or even no, overlap. With the world, attempts to draw from pupils observations on their tastes in programs, music, newspapers, and so on, with which the teachers were largely unfamiliar, proved intimidating. By focusing on Audiences, the teachers seemed to find a way of gaining acceptance for their own tastes while helping pupils to value their own experiences.

Work on images seemed to mark a movement away from a language-directed approach to specifically Media concerns. What was striking about these lessons, however, was that the work was almost entirely 'uncritical' in that the emphasis was on seeing the images studied as models of good practice on which to base pupils' own work. Indeed, comparisons with poetic imagery were often made without irony. This approach extended into the next category, Institutions, where pupils were presented with accounts of media institutions as having their own imperatives that were apparently perceived as inevitable or even to be copied. The idea that institutional ethics might be in any way problematic did not emerge. In one case the approach seemed to be linked to the school's own attempt to promote itself in the local community, each being used to justify the other.

This model of institutional acquiescence seemed to be general except in the two schools that dealt with the next concept on our list, Mediation. In both cases, Mediation was interpreted as bias and pupils were warned of its effects. The similarity to work on literary texts is obvious, though both teachers were imaginative in their approaches: one showing that a Bible story would inevitably be distorted by media presentation, and the other encouraging pupils to compare their real-life experiences with the fantasy representations of their age group in color magazines.

SELECTED CASE STUDIES

The first case study to be described was of Jane, who was teaching in a rural comprehensive school. In the lesson observed, she and her class studied a Pop video. The class consisted of 23 boys and girls in Year 10. The lesson observation took place on June 5, 1992 from 1:20 p.m. to 2:10 p.m.

The Interview[1]

Jane was in her first year at her present school but had been teaching for 9 years. She earned her degree from Nottingham University where she met Len Masterman. Her first teaching post was at a secondary school in Nottinghamshire, where there was a flourishing Media Department, and she taught Media as an option for pupils not wishing to study Literature. It was not an examination subject, however, and indeed she has not yet had the opportunity to teach the subject for any form of external assessment. The school was a base for development work with the University, which helped to develop and strengthen her interest in Media work.

She moved to Hampshire after 3 years and was surprised to find little evidence of Media activity in schools. She was offered an allowance to develop Media Education in the English Department. Discovering the existence of the *Southampton Media Education Group*, she attended meetings in an effort to build up resources, and began to learn of other agencies. When the Head of Department went on maternity leave, Jane assumed the post and was unable to continue her Media initiative. Moving to another school, she found that Media was not considered important; indeed, the Head seemed hostile to the idea. At the same time, changes in GCSE combined with anxieties about the National Curriculum were making school officials nervous of new initiatives. Only when she moved to her present post did she find a Department Head who was enthusiastic about Media work, and a supportive English team. Her enthusiasm restored, she found that she was increasingly integrating Media ideas into her English lessons.

---

[1]Throughout this section, G = girl, B = boy, T = teacher.

Methods

Jane's methods can perhaps be best described through an understanding of her other English interests. If forced to choose one area of English in which to specialize, she would opt for teaching short literary and nonliterary texts. In reading these with classes she draws on reader-response theory introduced to her at Nottingham University and supported by her Department Head for whom it is "the main idea." She enjoys allowing pupils to offer their personal responses to stories without her intervention. Close reading of texts then becomes easier and more acceptable to classes, and coursework becomes more interesting because pupils see that their ideas are valued and worth exploring. "It's starting from a different end, that's all. Once you have elicited their response you start teaching very hard—just a different emphasis from the old-style GCE."

This approach makes the introduction of various kinds of text into the classroom more acceptable to pupils. Jane is particularly concerned that pupils should be alerted to the constructed nature of television programs. She demonstrates that messages are created and ought not to be taken at face value. "I remember a pupil saying to me after we'd done something on *East-Enders,* 'Oh, Miss, I couldn't watch it properly after we'd done that lesson ... ' I felt good about that because she was watching it properly ..."

She believes that schools should teach the ways advertisements often try to manipulate consumers, and that children should be helped to think about the construction of what are presented as facts, especially in news and documentary programs. But she feels that the presentational features of the media must also be recognized, and that techniques for studying literature are relevant in looking below the surface at other levels of meaning.

> We try to look at television and film appreciatively, especially by looking at extracts. The pupils chose the pop video we are going to be looking at next. We would not have chosen that particular one, but looking at it in advance to prepare the lesson, we realized that it is incredibly complex.

Frequent use of 'we' indicates how closely the members of this department work together, sometimes team-teaching but more often sharing teaching plans and working on material at the same time in order to compare notes immediately afterward.

Personal Approach

Jane believes that pupils are not made explicitly aware of her own political or social views, although on issues like race or gender it is sometimes not easy to appear objective.

We were looking at news items when the Los Angeles riots happened. This led to a discussion about Ku Klux Klan attitudes and we asked how they would feel if they were black. Then John played them Billie Holliday's *Strange Fruit*. It's difficult then, I suppose, to hide how you feel.

You can be a fascist in the classroom, I think, by the way you put the desks out or the way you expect the children to answer the questions you ask them.... I'm probably what the government would think of as a trendy teacher, I suppose, because I don't put them in rows and they're allowed to talk without putting their hands up. Rather than in the material I choose, I think they would know my views from the way I treated them and the way I expected to be treated by them.

Resources

The department prepares much of its own material and, having recently completed the Royal Society of Arts Information Technology Certificate course, Jane enjoys preparing worksheets for her classes. In addition, they all contribute to their newspaper cuttings library. Useful books have been *Eyeopeners* (Bethell, 1981) and *The Language of the Media* (Davies, 1987, 1988).

Pupil Response

Jane believes that the department's approach gives pupils confidence. They are willing to say what they think, and in this way teachers gain insights into their thought processes that other methods tend to hide. As this is a major justification for 'response approaches,' Jane has found few surprises in teaching Media, but she recalls that while teaching in Nottingham she was surprised by what she discovered in studying film extracts in detail and slow motion. "I didn't pick up but I was equally surprised at what I didn't pick up to begin with." This sense of being on a voyage of discovery with her pupils was implicit in much of what Jane had to say.

Key Concepts

The BFI 'Signpost Questions' (see Fig. 1.1) are not central for Jane or the department generally. They are developing an ad hoc approach based on sharing best ideas but, when pressed, Jane admitted to a reluctance to engage with issues of ownership and control, which she believes pupils find "deadly boring.... I am happy with what we are doing but I can see that there is more to it."

The Future

Jane believes that Media Education is in danger of becoming marginalized.

Six or seven years ago it probably took off as an area in its own right, and I think it *is* an area in its own right but I think the National Curriculum hasn't helped Media purists to let it become a separate subject. It seems only at some further education institutions and at higher education level that it exists as an entity. For schools going straight down the National Curriculum line I don't think Media is a high priority … you could get away with doing very little.

Her experience is that other departments have selected areas which suit them. "So the Humanities Department do comparative journalism.… Drama and Art look at their own aspects and that is probably how I see it developing with different subjects taking it under their umbrella."

Overview of Lesson Observed

Jane led the class through a close reading of a pop video they chose themselves. She adopted a relaxed, 'Friday afternoon,' approach, inviting the class to share her pleasure in the pop video they had chosen. By admitting her own surprise at its complexity, she disarmed those pupils who were inclined to resist the idea that it might be worth studying. The lesson was divided into very short units that enabled the class to move steadily into a deeper analysis of the video's content. The fact that she had previously studied the video with her colleagues meant that she was able to share in the pupils' sense of discovery while retaining the confidence to accept fresh observations from some extremely observant pupils. The focus was on Language, Audience, Mediation, and Representation.

Lesson Aims

The aims of this lesson were:

1. To gain experience in reading visual messages that are part of pupils' everyday life.
2. To understand the idea of imagery in the study of literary texts.
3. To encourage the habit of close reading of apparently simple texts.

The lesson was part of a one-session-a-week (Friday afternoon) unit on popular music developed by three members of the English Department, including the department head, to encourage 'wider reading' around the work being done on poetry and imagery. Popular music is seen by the team as embracing more than is commonly understood by 'pop', and here includes folk songs and jazz. The sequence of lessons had been:

1. Small groups wrote down the names of all pop groups and titles of songs which they felt had a message or deeper meaning. Groups allocated one of the songs to each member to find a recording and write out lyrics.
2. Groups were re-formed according to themes of chosen songs, for example, war, religion, politics, education, or drugs. Each group prepared a tape and presentation of the songs.
3. One group wished to make a video presentation. The teacher provided a pop video of *We Don't Need No Education!* by Pink Floyd, which was watched and discussed by all groups.

4. Groups produced and presented their audiotaped programs of thematically based songs. The video group showed their unedited video based on Billy Bragg's *Sexuality*. They had the assistance of an ex-pupil currently studying media at a further education college.

5. Classes worked in poetry writing sessions, producing their own 'poetry of protest.' Film of the Los Angeles riots, pictures of lynchings of black people in the 1930s, and the imagery in Billie Holliday's *Strange Fruit* were used as stimuli.

6. The teaching team identified themes worth pursuing on the basis of interest shown by pupils. These included: the Pop Industry, Image Creation, Poetry of Protest, Media Promotion of groups, and lyrics through video. Coursework assignments were prepared to cover these themes.

7. A selection of pop videos was shown to the groups, and one of these was voted most suitable for detailed study.

Resources

Resources included the following:

1. Pop video of *Stand* by *REM*.
2. TV and video player.
3. Enlarged print photocopy of lyrics.
4. Photocopy of adapted shooting script.

Lesson Introduction (15 minutes)

Jane reminded the class of their choice of pop video the previous week, and explained that the purpose of the lesson was to look at ways of presenting music visually. Their choice was *Stand* by *REM*, a video some of the pupils had thought too simple to be worth studying.

Pupils watched the video closely and then spent 5 minutes, without discussion, writing down their thoughts about what they had seen. They were advised to write in sentences or notes but not to attempt a scatter diagram.

Lesson Development (20 minutes)

After the viewing and writing, Jane invited pupils to read out their observations. Three pupils commented favorably on the dancing and the reinforcement of the lyric's message through images; they noticed that pictures on a screen behind a team of dancers changed more frequently and in subtler ways than they had realized during casual viewing. It was on this point that she intended to build the lesson, and she commented on her own surprise in previewing the video.

A boy known to Jane for his robust expression of his ideas was then asked to read his comments:

B: I don't like this song. It's got a rhythm on the video involving chickens. The song's pointless.... There's no meaning in the song and there are so many scene changes you can't follow the video, so you don't know what's happening.

His contribution created the expected reaction and she asked the class to vote on whether they disagreed. He was happy not to have attracted much support, and the class monitored his reactions from that point. Interestingly, he was prepared to modify his views as the lesson progressed. He began to interpret the many changes of image for himself and showed considerable perception in the face of some good-humored teasing about his antipathy to chickens.

Jane then asked the class to watch the video again without sound.

B: Karaoke!
T: (laughing) No, it's not karaoke. I'm not going to play the sound because I want you to focus on the visual image ... and I want you to write a list of four different strands in the video.
T: You see that theme several times. You see four people dancing on the compass points. Those are strands—images which appear again and again. The words are repetitive and so are the images.

After watching the silent video, pupils wrote their four points and discussed them with partners. Jane asked pupils to read out their lists and then invited them to say what they had noticed that they had missed on previous viewings.

This provoked an interesting discussion about the location and meaning of the images. Some, for example, seemed unfamiliar with the idea of a weather vane, whereas one boy was able to identify the one shown as from Lord's Cricket Ground.

Lesson Conclusion (15 minutes)

Jane then moved into what she described as the third stage of the lesson. She had prepared an adapted script on which the pupils were to log the first 17 seconds of the video. In this brief section there were 10 shots. The pupils described them in about 10 words each in one column against the accompanying part of the lyric. They collaborated on the first two shots to make sure all pupils understood the task.

The first two shots lasted barely a second each. Five shots were logged before the bell ended the lesson, with some shots needing to be repeated when a few pupils failed to notice changes that the more observant had commented on.

Lesson Analysis

It was obvious that the experience of watching in this way had been a revelation to some of the pupils. An apparently simple pop video proved to be both complex and subtle, illustrating the lyrics in ways which went beyond their originally perceived meaning. In the early stages of the exercise, some pupils argued that it was pointless way as these videos are not meant to be studied in depth. What emerged, however, was that each pupil had observed differently, and some had taken a great deal even from a first viewing. Further, pupils saw that paying attention to the video improved their understanding of the song's message. By the end of the lesson, even the skeptics had become enthused and one, on leaving the room, actually thanked her for the lesson.

The second case study was of Kevin, who was teaching in an urban comprehensive school. In the lesson observed, he and the class discussed perceptions and representations of careers. The class consisted of 11 boys and girls in Year 10. The lesson observation tool place on June 17, 1992 from 1:20 to 2:30 p.m.

The Interview

Kevin has been teaching for 15 years, 9 of them as Head of English at his present school. His chief interest is in "pupils' experiences with the way they respond to text, the way they can empathize with texts in all genres from poetry to documentary." He sees it as part of his duty to encourage pupils to be prepared to examine all texts that have affected them from whatever source, and to bring them into the classroom environment for analysis and debate. His own choice of class texts is in no way circumscribed by this approach; *Macbeth* with its themes of ambition, deceit and determination can, if pupils' response is respected, be seen as at least as relevant to their experience as any modern text.

Interest in Media

Kevin claims that he has always thought of Media work as part of English studies, and his interest in film, stage, and music have made the idea of exploring and communicating feelings, relationships, and ideology through the media integral to his teaching approach.

> I came from a very musical background and that's part and parcel of my approach. I like the whole idea of performance, whether it's doing it myself or sharing or being part of a performance, and I see that very much at the heart of the sharing approach to enjoying a text.

As a Winchester Cathedral chorister, he was accustomed to TV cameras, microphones, and the disciplines of the media from the age of 9. Kevin trained at King Alfred's College, and Winchester provided him opportunities to familiarize himself with media technology. His teaching, particularly at his present school, has maintained his media awareness. The school has worked with broadcasters on a documentary on vandalism; BBC Radio 4 programs about education have featured in his work; and participation in the National Oracy Project involved experiments with microphones and cameras. In addition, he works happily with computers and wordprocessors.

Aims

> I want them to be not just watching or listening. I want them to be making decisions
> or judgments on the quality and relevance of what they are looking at—the influence
> it may have. An awareness of audience so that they can be a little more objective ...
> the adverts, billboards, newspapers ... so that there's a more analytical—don't just
> take it for granted—awareness of the 'Big M', media as a whole. I'm very much
> aware of the media as more and more a very powerful influence—if not the most
> important influence—on our kids.

Methods

Kevin's approach to teaching Media is so integral to his view of English teaching
that he found it difficult to isolate the separate parts. Conversation constantly drew
on parallels from drama, poetry, and language study.

All pupils at the school have some Media Education from Year 7, and all English
teachers are actively encouraged to develop ideas and resources. Team-teaching is
used to take advantage of individual strengths, and there are good contacts with the
feeder schools and with the local sixth form college to ensure compatibility of
approach.

Pupils are encouraged to bring in media texts. "The media [have] exploded in
terms of resourcing the work we are doing and it's not just the teacher that's bringing
these resources in."

Favorite Lessons

The department has devised a unit of work, *The Language of Persuasion*, exploring
the language of propaganda about war. Taking as its starting point Wilfred Owen's
lines:

> *The old lie: Dulce et decorum est*
> *Pro patria mori.*

The unit traces "the old lie" in words and images through literature and the
media. The face of Owen's victim:

> *... the white eyes writhing in his face,*
> *His hanging face, like a devil's sick of sin.*

and the photograph of the charred face of an Iraqi soldier published in a Sunday
broadsheet newspaper at the end of the Gulf War are compared with tabloid
headlines. A recording of the Remembrance Sunday commemoration at the Ceno-
taph is listened to: "Below me is a young boy on the shoulders of his father or it
might be his grandfather. I wonder what he makes of all this remembering when
only yesterday is years away."

Year 10 pupils answered the commentator's question with a book of responses of their own, *In Memoriam.*

Pupils show very keen interest in Media work:

> They know the pressures and impact, whether it be the fashions and fads of the time, through to musical influences, through to the pressures pushing them to make decisions which perhaps they're not quite ready to do or they don't feel comfortable about but because they're told to do it or they can see it being done it looks attractive.

Personal Views

Kevin is aware that his own views are developing all the time and hopes that in consequence his pupils are prepared to see him as freethinking, openminded and wishing to encourage independence of thought. Yet there has been a consistent agreement within the department that has put some issues at the heart of their work. In particular, he mentions equal opportunities, gender awareness, and stereotyping.

Key Concepts

Kevin's list was a wide ranging mixture of topics and concepts, including: selectiveness, analysis, questioning, money, sources, different backgrounds, influence, source-practice-process-product, and "coping with alternative opinions."

Resources

The key to Media Education in schools has, Kevin believes, been the VCR. He uses this and the audiocassette recorder extensively to record news, documentaries, plays, and music, helping pupils to recognize the visual and aural challenges that bombard them. He describes how accidents and disasters used to be reported to us first through eye-witness accounts and later by the media of film and videotape. Nowadays, the first reports are often visual so that the imaginative construction of those events by which we previously assimilated their horrors has been replaced. The implications of this are still not understood, but he likes to explore them through works like *Under Milk Wood* in which the blind Captain Cat represents the power of the imagination.

School Policy

Although the school has not produced a curriculum statement on Media Education, the situation is a dynamic one with cooperation between departments. All areas of the curriculum are now influenced by the media, and currently, the school's policy documents on Information Technology and on Language are being rewritten to include media awareness and access to information.

The Humanities Department is well resourced and the Technology Department has just completed a project in which pupils researched the ways Southampton presents itself to the public. This combined research, interviews, photography, video work, and scripting.

Work often develops from tutor sessions. "A few years ago one of our kids died from solvent abuse ... we've looked at the pressures and influences whereby kids at very early ages get little titbits of information, ultimately from the media."

A pupil's myeloid leukamia and the need to search for a bone marrow donor has led to a study of the way the media promote charity awareness, while a grandfather's funeral coinciding with an examination question on Adrian Mitchell's *Old Age Report* inspired discussion of media representations of bereavement. Such issues are often focused in the school assemblies which are seen as central to the school's sense of community, and in which Kevin plays an active part.

The Future

Kevin hopes that schools will be given the chance to "build on the good practice already going on." He fears that the new requirements at KS4 of the National Curriculum may be 'blowing it apart,' and is dismissive of any value the minimal references to media might have. His hope is that media output might eventually be improved because of pressure from a more media-aware audience.

Overview of Lesson Observed

Kevin led a discussion about pupils' recent fortnight of work-experience and its influence on their ideas about the world of work. A video of *The Boy with the Transistor Radio* by Willie Russell was shown and its relevance to the previous discussion debated.

He began the lesson by showing an interest in the pupils' recent work experience. His relaxed questioning had the effect of making the pupils feel that the lesson had not really begun and they talked freely and unself-consciously. The questioning skillfully brought the discussion around to ideas about careers, the conflicting sources of advice, and the danger of unrealistic expectations. By the time Kevin felt ready to show the video, the class was receptive to its fairly difficult theme. Although not all pupils understood its structure, with its mixture of fantasy and reality, they were able to understand the key notion taken by the teacher from the video, and showed enthusiasm for the idea of continuing with the topic in later lessons. A noticeable feature of the discussion throughout had been his willingness to listen, and to show sympathy and understanding for the pupils' concerns.

Although this was a class of 'less able' pupils, they achieved a high level of discussion and, for the most part, appreciated the relevance of the approach. Inevitably, a few wanted to use the reference to television as an excuse to discuss favorite programs et cetera, but Kevin kept them to the point and by the end of the lesson some appeared to have moved a long way from their original positions of hostility to parental and other adult advice. He achieved this in part by the considered way in which he responded to their observations, and the respect he showed them throughout. Discussion of the influence of the media was an integral part of the lesson and provided a useful basis for future work on fantasies about careers. Media concepts included language and representation.

Lesson Aims

The aims of this lesson were:

1. To look at, enjoy and reflect on a play related to pupils' own recent experience.
2. To relate pupils' real work experience to their fantasies about their futures.

The class had recently completed 2 weeks' work experience and in a recent English lesson had worked on a 'Jobs and Responsibilities' worksheet.

Resources

The resources for the lesson were:

1. Video of 25-minute play.
2. Television set and VCR.
3. Worksheet based on play.
4. Jobs and Responsibilities worksheet.

Lesson Introduction (20 minutes)

Kevin reminded pupils of their previous work on jobs and responsibilities, and asked pupils to refer to their notes. Their discussion had centered on how young people make decisions about job value, job importance, and the differences between jobs and careers.

He asked all pupils to write an answer to his question to be discussed at the end of the lesson: "What is the most important job in the world?" He then asked how many intended to look for work as soon as they left school, and what those who had other ideas intended to do. A large group indicated that they hoped to be going on to college, and had taken advantage of careers forums and visits from local sixth form college tutors to obtain information. One boy said that it would be better than ending up in a dead-end job. This gave Kevin the opportunity to develop his theme; he asked what was meant by a 'dead-end job,' and was told that it was one needing no qualifications. Road sweeper was offered as an example.

T: Is that an important job?
B: Quite important.

The class was asked to suggest what qualities a road sweeper needed. Several lighthearted suggestions were offered, an interest in rubbish; enough road sense to avoid being run over, a sweeper's certificate.

T: I expect many of your families are having conversations at home about your future.

G: Lectures!

T: Why lectures?

G: They get carried away.

T: What do you mean?

G: They get big-headed. Try to act big. You say what you want to do and they tell you you've got to do something else.

T: Has that happened to you?

G: Yeah. I want to work with animals, right? And they say I've got to go to college. I didn't want to go to college. I want to work for the RSPCA. You don't need to go to college.

T: How do you know?

G: 'Cos I wrote off to them.

T: But maybe your mum and dad aren't too convinced by that, so what did they say to you?

G: I don't know. They just shut up and let me get on with it.

T: Anyone else?

B: Yeah. I want to take after my dad and go bricklaying. They argued about it and said it's too dangerous for me. He suggested the army (laughter from class).

T: So what happened then?

B: Oh, I went up to army cadets to see what it was like. After about a year I packed it in because I didn't like it.

Others in the group spoke of arguments at home. Kevin asked where these usually took place. Pupils said they happened in the kitchen or when something about a job was seen on TV. One said they happened after parents had been talking to their friends at work. This led to a discussion about the influence of pupils' own friends.

G: They might be doing a job you want to do—they might feel it's not right for you 'cos they know what you're like.

One boy who wanted to be a fireman said his friends had encouraged him because they thought the job would suit him. He admitted that he had also been made interested by the television series *London's Burning*. As he had done his work experience at a fire station, Kevin asked if the program was true-to-life.

B: Some of it.

T: If I say *"Andrex"* to you, what do you say to me?

Pupils realized that he was referring to a commercial in which a fireman rescues a puppy. There was a brief discussion about the image of the job projected by TV and of the idea of the hero figure.

Lesson Development (35 minutes)

T: This time next year some big decisions will have been made for you .... We're going to look at a play about Terry ... the play deals with everything you've talked about this afternoon. Terry's parents are telling him what he's got to do but his mind is made up.

He gave to and got from the pupils some information about Willie Russell, during which he was able to point out the relevance of Russell's work to their own experience and to introduce very casually the idea of reality and fantasy. The video was shown without interruption or comment.

Some of the class were surprised by the conclusion of the play—Sid Vicious singing *My Way*. Most had never heard of the singer and were convulsed by Kevin's brief explanation of punk rock and the *Sex Pistols*. He moved quickly on to the main theme, inviting their reactions to the rest of the program.

Lesson Conclusion (15 minutes)

T: You actually wrote a fair amount of the screenplay before you saw it.

The pupils showed little sympathy for Terry:

B: He's got to get himself sorted out.
B: He's in a different world.
G: The teacher was trying to make him see sense.

At this point, Kevin had to steer the discussion skillfully to keep pupils to the point, as some wanted to digress to details about the structure of the program and its dream sequences (which some had not understood).

B: They want you to believe it to make you buy.

Again, some pupils wanted to discuss advertisements they disliked. The lesson was nearing its end and Kevin asked a final question:

T: Was Terry let down by anyone?

Lesson Analysis

This was both an unconventional and an entirely typical lesson. It was typical of the kind of interactive flexibility that a skilled English teacher brings to the classroom discussion of social issues raised by literary texts, especially with the luxury of a small class who could all be involved simultaneously. This approach enabled Kevin to pursue effectively his second aim, of relating the pupils' real experience of work to their expectations about the future. But it was unconventional as a Media lesson in as much as Kevin's approach was not based on any of the familiar frameworks for Media teaching. His classroom methods were extremely flexible and driven by pupil response rather than predetermined conceptual demands. The pupils' awareness of significant aspects of the media such as language, representation, and modality was enhanced inductively by reference to their own personal work, friendship, and family experiences. The lesson began and ended with discussion of personal and social experience, and the video was used as a development and deepening device rather than simply as a stimulus. At the same time, opportunities for explicit discussion of tele-visual techniques of representation, such as camera work and editing, were not taken up. The emphasis throughout was on social issues in a way that suggested that the media were to be seen as powerful intervening forces operating on the personal lives of pupils. Kevin's second aim, of enabling the pupils to enjoy as well as reflect on the televised play, did not translate into any form of aesthetic discussion of the presentation.

THE AIMS OF ENGLISH AND MEDIA EDUCATION

Many English Departments are currently experiencing high levels of anxiety. They feel unsure of their roles in schools, reluctant to take initiatives, and powerless to defend their present positions. Some have found their time with classes cut to make way for 'new National Curriculum demands' in other sub barely half an hour a day with each class, they feel themselves to be the butt of most of the government and newspaper criticism of declining standards. 'Horror stories' circulate of English Departments amalgamated into Humanities Faculties where they are viewed essentially as servicing agencies, doing the work for which other staff claim to be unqualified (e.g., the marking), and occasionally being permitted to read a poem or short story if it illustrates an historical or social theme.

Media Education occupies an ambivalent position. While some English teachers have always seen it as central to their work, many approach it nervously, fearing that it will be viewed as further evidence that they are not concerned with 'basics.' These teachers feel obliged to justify excursions into the media in terms of the written, (i.e., essay) work they produce. They are inclined to be apologetic, mistrusting the evident enjoyment of their classes and consequently doing less than justice to the many modes of communication the media open up for them.

There is a tension between the desire to assert the value of Literature and the growing awareness of the centrality of the media to most people's lives; a tension made worse by the recent years of debate over the National Curriculum. Few English teachers seem to view the National Curriculum as an enabling document.

To most it merely adds to current practice a demand for assessments (characterized repeatedly as putting ticks in boxes), which many English teachers find alien to themselves and inimical to their relationships with children.

Ideology

Most of the teachers interviewed were implicitly aware of the ideological issues underlying Media Education but found problems in articulating them. Although they tended to talk of the media as manipulators whom children needed to be taught to read, they seemed uncomfortable about discussing *who* was manipulating and for what purpose. Only advertisers were clearly identified in this way, but even here the methods chosen seemed unlikely to meet teachers' declared aims. In terms of *objectives* for a single lesson, teachers described their intentions with clarity, but it was sometimes difficult to match the methods used to their overall aims. Teachers were uncomfortably aware that their own 'necessary' teaching approaches might be seen as closely resembling the methods used by advertisers and propagandists while at the same time their 'exposure of manipulation' often more closely resembled an 'exposition of skills' to be admired and emulated in assignments.

It is by no means certain that exposing an advertiser's means of exploiting our fantasies in any way reduces our susceptibility, particularly when, as often seems to be the case, teachers no longer feel that they have an alternative set of values to offer in their place. In any case, teachers often bring to the study of advertisements and other media texts the techniques learned in literary analysis. It was very noticeable that teachers often spoke of links between poetry and advertising; lessons could be read as explorations of the skill and subtlety of the advertising agencies with no reference to a social context. Just so has poetry commonly been taught, often without recognition of the values of its own age.

At the same time, some teachers seem to have been influenced by the current need to advertise and promote schools. There is a growing interest in the skills of marketing through the media. This interest sometimes seems to be pursued on its own terms without reference to the values that teachers otherwise believe underlie their work.

Invited to indicate their own ideological positions, teachers tended to refer to issues of gender, race and equal opportunity; the agenda set and sanctioned by the media. There was no reference to approaches to ideology in terms, for example, of manipulative, hegemonic or pluralist models. Yet without awareness of the ideological debate it is not clear how teachers hope to meet their own stated aims. Work often seems devoid of a meaningful context.

Virtually all of the teachers interviewed described their unease at the idea of teaching about media institutions. They commonly spoke of this topic as 'dry,' boring, and even irrelevant, a matter merely of factual knowledge about current ownership and profits. They tended to view existing institutions as representing an inevitable hegemony. There was some recognition that bias and distortion might occasionally appear in media texts as they do in literary ones, but there was little sign of any awareness that these distortions might be ideologically determined by institutions rather than personal processes. It is very difficult to see how the media are to be read if their study is devoid of this element.

Teachers' Aims

Teachers tended to describe their aims in instrumental terms relevant to the immediate lesson, that is, objectives. They emphasized understanding (key words were: analyze, deduce, consider, examine, study), and seemed to take for granted many of the aims implicit in the methods used. Often they were in reality *testing* understanding rather than teaching it while the real teaching was of writing skills and oral expression. Some teachers, however, spoke of a shared experience or enjoyment, and believed that their own learning about their pupils' perceptions was a necessary objective.

Although 7 of the 11 lessons observed included group work, only 2 teachers referred directly to the aims of such an approach. Given the place of group and pair work in current GCSE Oral Assessment it is surprising that this was no their stated aims.

Some of the work was arguably at least as valuable for developing the imagination as for understanding but again this was not mentioned. In part, this might be because English teachers are so comfortable with these skills that they take them for granted. But the failure to bring them to the forefront of their consciousness seems likely to mean that they were not given proper weight in planning and differentiating assignments, with the result that such work might be undervalued by the pupils.

Teaching Methods

Because most teachers of English are accustomed to working within the limited space and facilities of a classroom, we expected that lessons would generally focus on front-of-class exposition followed by group work on fairly narrowly prescribed tasks, and concluding with a session in which groups report back or make some form of presentation to the class. These assumptions about method proved to be generally correct. The predominant lesson pattern was indeed teacher introduction followed by group work leading to a brief plenary session. Teachers began with a 15-minute introduction, conducted from a dominant position standing at the front of the class, recapping previous lessons and punctuating an explanation of the work to be done with questions designed to test recall and understanding. The class would then divide into groups to undertake a task, usually reporting back to the whole class and teacher at the end of the lesson.

All used question-and-answer techniques but questions were most often 'closed'. More open responses were sometimes offered by pupils but were rarely allowed to develop. The fact that an observer was present clearly made teachers anxious to complete their lessons as planned, and this could explain reluctance to divert into open-ended discussion. Occasionally, however, there seemed to be anxiety about the evident differences between the media experiences of teacher and pupils. It seems likely that in some cases there had been little past discussion of pupils' own media preferences, and therefore these had not formed part of the planning of the lesson. In three cases, a television text provided the focus of the lesson and the class remained together, though in one of these cases opportunities for discussion with a partner were given.

Most teachers spoke enthusiastically of the response of their pupils to Media work. They often expressed surprise at the insights they had been able to gain into their pupils' perceptions and preferred modes of working. Pupils who were difficult to motivate often showed new strengths, and the pleasant and purposeful atmosphere in the classroom during Media lessons was several times remarked.

It was sometimes apparent that boys' contributions were heeded more than those of girls, especially by women teachers. Boys were usually more direct in their observations while girls' contributions were often tentative and enquiring, demanding a considered response. The knowledge imparted by teachers was often of a 'commonsense' nature, in one or two cases revealing actual misunderstandings about media practice, though never of a kind likely to seriously impede understanding.

Group Work

Given the central importance of teamwork in producing media texts, it is surprising that the variety of approaches to teaching Media that group work provides did not seem to be more widely appreciated. Much has been made in recent literature on Media Education of the value of group work for developing skills of social interaction and expression, but perhaps these benefits should not be taken for granted.

Buckingham (1990a) offers a critical look at the claims made for group work in developing social skills, learning to work under pressure, understanding team structures, providing opportunities for self-reflection, and exploring the idea that reading texts is a process of negotiation. He endorses the view that in sharing their pleasure in texts with their peers pupils are helped to develop understanding. The evidence of our lessons, though, suggests that group discussions led by an adult are of a quite different order from those in which pupils are left to their own devices. In the latter circumstance, conversation was often restricted by hierarchical relationships that coded the conversation, and was sometimes characterized by uncertainty about, and an unwillingness to engage with, the task prescribed. When prompted by an adult though, pupils were much more likely to talk coherently about their perceptions and enthusiasms.

Assignments

The conventional essay continues to be the preferred assignment, though teachers are introducing storyboards, collages, posters, surveys, and other tasks, usually to support a written core. It was noticeable that the essay retained its status in pupil's eyes, partly because teachers find difficulty in assessing other forms. Nonessay forms did receive marks and praise, but informed comment tended to be reserved for the essay, whereas posters and advertisements of very dubious persuasive power were often simply admired. Questions about audience, product appeal, placement, and alternative approaches were sometimes neglected.

Choice and differentiation of assignments were sometimes lacking with the result that groups often carried 'passengers' who might easily have been usefully involved if a range of assignments had been available.

It was apparent that most Media work was classroom-based with little expectation that pupils would refer to alternative texts or sources. In only one classroom did we see pupils using reference works on their own initiative. In general, research skills seemed to be undervalued and it was assumed that pupils' prior knowledge of posters, newspapers, and so fourth, was adequate for them to recall appropriate media conventions.

Classroom Environment

A major surprise was the condition of many English classrooms. It is clear in so many ways that English has not been a main beneficiary of the money apparently poured into schools in recent years. The battered furniture, poor decor, inharmonious jumbles of cupboards, and piles of shabby books were often depressing. Teachers have been resourceful in finding ways to manage overcrowded rooms but the results were seldom attractive.

Furthermore, whereas most rooms could be recognized as English classrooms, very few displayed any evidence that Media Education took place in them. One has only to think one's way around any school to realize how closely subject identity is linked to the appearance of rooms. Only one of the rooms observed was dedicated to Media Education, whereas another three had very good displays of pupils' Media work; mainly storyboards and collages. Judging from the kinds of posters generally on display—images of nature and portraits of poets—English teachers consider film posters and the like garish and unsettling. There was little doubt, though, that where media texts and artefacts were displayed, pupils made use of these as sources and teachers referred to them for illustration.

Learning Resources

Apologies were constantly proffered for video cameras that would have been used if they had not been so 'unreliable.' A main concern about using video camera equipment was its reliability and safety in the hands of groups working away from direct supervision. In addition, because English teachers are interested in selecting from and shaping raw experience (literary skills, in fact), they were inclined to think that little useful work could be done with cameras without the help of editing facilities.

English teachers, even the younger ones, seemed to be most comfortable with sets of books, which they expected to last for ever (and which often looked as if they had). They did not seem to have been accustomed to the regular handling of money for disposable items in the way that some departments take for granted, nor did most seem to be confident with anything requiring maintenance. Many had taken computer courses but still lacked confidence in their own ability to use them, believing that their skills were already out of date. One teacher, however, had made simple but effective use of a computer to generate questions on Media concepts in very large type. These were cut into comic-style bubbles and attached to relevant posters on the walls.

Underlying much of the fear about resources seemed to be a sense of urgency and a reluctance to 'waste time.' Used to receiving English assignments on a regular, often weekly basis, teachers sometimes showed anxiety over work that might not only take much longer but might be produced at widely varying intervals by different groups, thus affecting the continuity of work.

Teachers' Development Needs

Most of the sample had wide and varied teaching experience, usually involving subjects other than English, and several had business or industrial backgrounds prior to teaching. Surprisingly, however, there was very little evidence of any professional experience of the media or of active engagement. They were generally disposed to accept new challenges and inclined to see English as a subject embracing the whole field of communication. Even so, their involvement with Media teaching was sometimes patchy and determined more by accident than by conscious pursuit of a career option.

Eight teachers had taught for at least 10 years and in some cases for more than 20. None of these had any extended training in Media Education but had generally approached the subject from an interest in Literature and a shifting awareness of literary theory toward ideas that place both reader response and a recognition that readers would benefit from reading a range of texts at the center of their approach. The other three teachers, two of whom were in their probationary year, had deliberately chosen degree or PGCE courses with a Media or Communications content. All of them saw the need for further training in a subject they recognized as changing in its concepts and methods, and all valued the work of county advisers and other training agencies. All but one were attending, assisting with, or seeking courses in Media Education.

The teachers believed that their own enthusiasm for teaching had been refreshed by their involvement in Media Education, and that the techniques they were learning were infiltrating their other English teaching. These feelings were strongest where teachers had the security of certain support from other members of their departments. Heads of Departments were particularly important here, and their involvement in the design of teaching packages was especially beneficial. The sympathetic interest of other senior teachers was also much valued, and several teachers were looking forward to a time when there would be leisure to make a long-term appraisal of the place of Media Education in the whole school curriculum (Hart & Hackman 1995).

Teachers frequently expressed a need for much more 'hands-on' experience with computers and video equipment. Training might focus on specific programs and on editing skills. There is also a need for a greater general knowledge of media practices. This might be partly met, for example, by commissioning media practitioners, in cooperation with Media educators, to write monographs about their jobs, and by financing visits to schools. School visits to media studios and workplaces are much valued, although difficult to arrange on any kind of regular basis. An alternative is to involve pupils in media practice through practical English assignments which emphasize the uses of language in the public domain. Such tasks as producing a community newspaper, writing and performing stories for primary children, producing material on safety and health, and investigating local facilities, require pupils to reflect on and communicate actual experience. The need to conduct interviews and make decisions about real social concerns has been shown to transfer understanding to the production and analysis of media texts (Brown, 1990). Work experience placements offer obvious opportunities to extend this kind of work. There is evidence that this has been done successfully with newspaper offices and cinemas.

For the future, it seems that it will not be enough for English teachers to be, as Williams (1976) put it, "determined not to be determined" (pp. 90–91). The critical question for curriculum research and development in Media Education is: How can systematic training and staff development enable English teachers to gain the confidence and expertise to move beyond the limits of the known and familiar territory of English teaching into the more problematic areas of Media Education?

ACKNOWLEDGMENT

An earlier version of parts of this chapter appeared in *Continuum* 9/2, (1996, pp. 146–160). I am grateful to Andy Goodwyn of Reading University for his comments and contributions toward its development.

REFERENCES

Bazalgette, C. (Ed.). (1989) *Primary media education: A curriculum statement.*London: British Film Institute.

Bethell, A. (1981). *Eyeopeners.* Cambridge: Cambridge University Press.

Bowker, J. (Ed.). (1991). *Secondary media education: A curriculum statement.* London: British Film Institute.

British Film Institute. (1993, Autumn). *Media Educaton News Update* (MENU; Issue 4). London: Author.

Brown, J. (1990). *Developing English for TVEI.* Leeds: Leeds University.

Brown, S., & Visocchi, P. (1991). *Hurdles and incentives: Introducing media education into primary and secondary schools.* Edinburgh: Scottish Council for Research in Education.

Buckingham, D. (1990a). *Watching media learning.* London: Falmer.

Buckingham, D. (1990b). English and media studies: Making the difference. *English Magazine, 23,* 8–12.

Buckingham, D. (1990c). English and media studies: Getting together. *English Magazine, 24,* 20–23.

Buckingham, D. (Ed.). (1990d). *Watching media learning.* London: Falmer.

Buckinham, D. (1993). *Children talking television.* London: Falmer.

Buckingham, D., & Sefton-Green, J. (Eds.). (1994). *Cultural studies goes to school: Reading and teaching popular media.* London: Taylor & Francis.

Butts, D. (1986). *Media education in Scottish secondary schools: A research study 1983–1986.* Stirling: University of Stirling.

Davies, C. (1987, 1988) *The Language of the media (*Books 1 & 2). Oxford: Blackwell.

Department of Education and Science. (1989). (The Cox Report) *English for ages 5–16.* London: HMSO.

Department of Education and Science. (1990, March). *English in the National Curriculum* (No.2). London: HMSO.

Department of Education and Science. (1993, April). *English for ages 5–16.* London: HMSO.

Dickson, P. (1994). *A Survey of media education in schools and colleges.* London: British Film Institute.

Hart, A., & Benson, A. (1993). *Media in the classroom.* Southampton: Southampton Media Education Group.

Hart, A., & Benson, A. (1996). Researching media education in English classrooms in the UK. *Continuum, 9*(2), 146–160.

Hart, A., & Hackman, S. (1995). *Developing media in English.* London: Hodder.

McLuhan, M. (1973). *Understanding media.* Falmouth: Abacus.

Murdock, G., & Phelps, G. (1973). *Mass Media and the secondary school.* Basingstoke: Macmillan.

Williams, R. (1976), *Keywords.* London: Fontana.

3

Media Education
in Northern Ireland

Jude Collins
University of Ulster

There has been a significant growth in the development of Media Education in schools in Northern Ireland in recent years. Bodies such as the Education Committee of the Northern Ireland Film Council (NIFC) and the Northern Ireland Media Education Association (NIMEA) have been established to promote the use of media in classrooms and to provide networking and training for teachers. However, this growth in interest has occurred alongside major changes within the Northern Ireland curriculum, which in many cases have been underresourced. As a result, teachers have struggled to keep abreast of many changes forced on them. In some cases, this has led to a sense of overload. So, although a number of teachers have been willing to embrace Media Education, others have avoided the area because they have not had an opportunity to explore its nature fully. Some of those who have become involved in it have not had the kind of time or training to develop the area in ways they would wish. This study tried to incorporate an awareness of these pressures under which many teachers are operating (see Collins & o'Kane, 1994, for a full report of the study).

The Northern Ireland education system consists broadly of two kinds of schools: controlled (Protestant) and Maintained (Catholic) at both primary and secondary levels. The Education Reform (Northern Ireland) Order of 1989 sets out the principal curriculum requirements for pupils. The curriculum consists of six compulsory subject areas (English, Mathematics, Science and Technology, the Environment and Society, Creative and Expressive Studies, and Language Studies), and six compulsory Cross-Curricular Themes (Education for Mutual Understanding, Cultural heritage, Health Education, Economic Awareness, Careers Education, and Information Technology). Cross-curricular themes are to be developed within all subject areas.

57

Reporting as it does on the thinking and practice of a range of teachers, this study raises questions as to what classroom strategies and approaches are best suited to the promotion of Media Education within English, and what the implications are of these for Professional Development.

The Curriculum for English

The Education Reform Order of 1989, following on from the 1988 Education Reform Act in England, marked the start of a major change in the practice of teachers of all subjects. There was a belief that new ways of operating in the classroom and even thinking about each subject must emerge, and quickly. Frustration gripped many teachers. On the one hand, there was a conviction that the new curriculum was introducing many worthwhile emphases and elements. On the other hand, there was an equally widespread belief that the Curriculum had been imposed on teachers, and that the demands of assessment were smothering the possibilities of development within the various subject areas.

Within English at Key Stages (KS) 3 and 4, the Northern Ireland Curriculum marked a coming together of the work of teachers in secondary and grammar schools, with implications for both. In terms of Media Education, teachers in secondary schools were at something of an advantage. The old Certificate of Secondary Education (CSE) program of study had directed attention to study of the media, in particular advertising. Teachers had for some time used the kind of group and practical work which often characterizes Media teaching. Meanwhile, teachers in grammar schools had increasingly been moving to active group work, using drama and the video camera, for example, to clarify and reflect on literary texts. Thus, what the Programs of Study for English required did not represent a complete change, but rather a broadening out into a uniform highway of a path that an increasing number of teachers had already begun to travel.

As with the National Curriculum provisions for English in England, it is clear from the Programs of Study that the media are seen as playing a part in the delivery of the three Attainment Targets for English: *Talking and Listening*, *Reading,* and *Writing*. The media are a means to these ends; they are not seen as representing an area of worth in itself. They act as conduits or vehicles for the delivery of enhanced understanding of literary texts, of more committed and thoughtful writing, of purposeful and enthusiastic listening. Less attention is paid to the ways in which the professional media operate. Such matters as ownership, or organization, or media audiences, for example, are not highlighted.

Research Focus

As with the original research project in England, this study looked at 11 English teachers working with pupils at KS4 (14 ages 16 years old). Interviews were conducted with the teachers to establish their thinking regarding the aims, content, and methods employed in the lessons. The perception of Media Education within the context of the school was also discussed, because the status of such work would clearly affect what teachers attempted to do and how they saw Media Education. Likewise the background of the teacher, the road which had brought her or him to introduce Media Education, was examined.

Teachers willing to take part in the research were identified through the cooperation of English Advisors in the Education and Library Boards. In an attempt to work cooperatively with the teachers, as well as to verify the findings, the written profiles of the teachers were returned to the teachers themselves for comment and, where necessary, addition.

As in the original English study, lesson observation normally preceded the interview, with the observer making audio recordings and taking notes in as unobtrusive a manner as possible. In each case a written account of the lesson was sent to the teacher for her or his comment.

THEMES AND ISSUES

This section offers some general observations that arose from the interviews and lessons.

English Departments

None of the teachers interviewed expressed misgivings regarding the place of Media Education within the English program. This was not surprising, because they were identified in the first instance as having an interest in using Media teaching within English. At the same time, there is an awareness among the teachers that for Media Education to develop successfully, even within the English department, it needs the support of other staff. Several teachers pointed to the fact that the Viceprincipal or Principal of the school was interested in Media Education, and related this to the school's investment in equipment. Beyond enhanced hardware acquisition, this support from management gave a confidence and credibility to the teachers' work. This management goodwill is probably important for any innovation in the school. Given that Media Education comes burdened with a popular sense of the media as an entertainment source rather than a valued subject of study, it is in particular need of acceptance throughout the school.

Teacher acceptance of the media in the curriculum could, of course, be viewed negatively. There might be a degree of unquestioning acquiescence to what is now seen as an established part of the English Curriculum, rather than a considered awareness of its place within the Programs of Study. In either case, it is a source of some satisfaction that in Northern Ireland, where grammar and secondary schools still exist, there appears to be no hankering after a golden age when English was believed to be free from the stain of popular culture and saw its mission as essentially defensive. No doubt the Northern Ireland curriculum, shared by both types of school, has gone some way to bringing about this realistic perception. Within the Programs of Study for English, explicit reference is made repeatedly to the role of the media in the English classroom. In addition, there are several points where the aims of the program—most notably in terms of *Talking and Listening*—provide implicit opportunity for the study of media to contribute to the realization of curricular aims.

Key Areas of Study

The fact that the study found advertising to be one of the most popular areas for consideration within Media Education goes some way toward suggesting the teachers' perspective on the work. In general, the traditional view of advertising is adhered to: The media are seen as 'pernicious', capable of persuading and misleading pupils. Accordingly, pupils need to be armed through classroom work against the wiles of media people.

However, it is unlikely that teachers had only one aspect of advertising in mind. It may be that some chose to work in this area because advertisements are succinct, even in written form use few words, and fit neatly into the 40-minute lesson. There is also the fact (as noted earlier) that teachers in some instances have experience of the old examination. This may have provided a security in approaching this aspect of the media which they might not feel in other areas.

What was notable by its absence throughout all the lessons observed was attention to the way advertising relates to a wider sociopolitical system in a consumer society. Equally, there was little attention to the relationship between program-making and advertisements, or how advertisements relate to program-funding. For the most part, work on advertisements tended to ignore context, focusing largely on what was in front of the pupils, considering examples of stereotyping, emotive language, and a general concern to deceive.

The study found even more frequent attention given by teachers to newspapers. Again, in some cases, this had its origin in the work these teachers did in the old CSE program. Some felt that newspapers were less difficult for pupils to cope with than fiction, perhaps because they appear to be closer to the 'real world'. For the most part, English newspapers were dealt with. In those cases where Irish newspapers were considered, particularly papers in Northern Ireland, attention was drawn to the way they divide along sectarian lines and cater for different sections of the population (although it seems probable that this is something pupils already knew). Again, such papers were not looked at in the wider political context, but rather to draw attention to 'the other side,' and to the fact that a different perspective on events was possible. In this way, one teacher believed, empathy and tolerance could be developed. Beyond that, attention was devoted to alerting pupils to the formal features of layout in the different sections of each newspaper and the tendency of tabloids to employ emotive and sensational language. Pupils were often encouraged to write articles that imitated different newspaper styles.

In general, there were few indications that teachers use local media as matter for examination and reflection. This may be because most Media textbooks tend to be written for pupils in England and thus relate to English media. A further barrier to addressing the local may be the seriousness of the political situation in Northern Ireland. As indicated, newspapers in Northern Ireland divide along political relig- ious lines. Even to engage in consideration of the 'other side's' newspaper could in some instances be seen as a kind of betrayal, whereas critical commentary on the reporting of one's own side might be even less welcome. Such critical work does occur; one of the teachers in the study used two community newspapers, one Protestant and one Catholic, for analysis. But it happens against a current which discourages approaching such work with vigor. Some of the teachers interviewed expressed a reluctance to engage with the local media, or to consider ways in which local media help define (or distort) cultural identity. It was seen as being 'difficult' to do so, because for some people in Northern Ireland cultural identity can be literally a matter of 'life and death'. Teachers did seem aware that pupils might benefit from consideration of such matters but, ironically, it was because of the subject's importance that it was considered too dangerous.

Two further factors may play a part in teacher reluctance to engage with wider issues generally: a sense that they lack the background and training for such work, and a sense that these are 'political' matters and therefore not the province of the English teacher. It is certainly the case that most English teachers do lack a background in media theory. Most come to it accidentally, often through Drama. Thus, their sense of their own inadequacy for the task may be well founded. This said, if teachers can and do develop skills in other aspects of Media Education, it seems reasonable that they should develop understanding in this one as well. The tendency to 'keep politics out of it' is one that runs deep in the psychology of most teachers, particularly in Northern Ireland schools. Principals are on record as defending their schools as places where children are protected physically, emotion- ally, and mentally from the political storms that rage outside. Given this view of education, it is scarcely surprising that teachers do not wish to consider political dimensions of the media. It is not only the displeasure of the principal that may be involved: parents are sensitive to such matters, and beyond parents, perhaps even more intimidating forces. However, the fact that such matters can be life and death issues in Northern Ireland may be all the more reason for addressing them with tact, sympathy, and rigor.

Teachers' Aims

In most cases, teachers were concerned with developing an aspect of the English curriculum—usually *Talking and Listening* or awareness of language— rather than with investigating the media themselves. Films were most often valued for their ability to bring the written text (usually a novel) to life, or to make it more accessible to the pupils. In some instances, teachers spoke of using the film instead of the book. The language of advertisements was seen as worthy of attention in order to expose misleading connotations and to draw parallels between it and the language of poetry. Lessons which involved a lot of talk or looked at talk within the media were seen as helping meet the *Talking and Listening* requirements of the Curriculum for English.

Where the media themselves were directly addressed, teachers' aims in this study resembled those of teachers in the DES' (1983) *Popular Television and Schoolchildren*: The media are all-pervasive and detrimental to the things we value, so an awareness of how they operate must be made plain, to protect pupils and develop their discrimination along lines similar to those of the teacher.

Teaching Methods

Of the 11classes observed, 5 were working on newspapers. In these cases, newspapers or reproductions of newspapers were available to the class. Pupils worked on the materials, focusing on them rather than on the teacher. In the case of the 3 classes who worked on advertisements (2 on magazine advertisements, the other on TV advertisements) the focus was similarly on the materials.

Typically, the lesson began with an introduction by the teacher, the consideration of an aspect of the newspaper or advertisement (sometimes using a worksheet), a discussion within the group, and then a report back to the teacher. In one respect this allowed for a degree of input and thought from the pupils. They were able to exchange ideas within the group, and are responsible for the findings reported to the whole class toward the end of the lesson. On the other hand, the teacher made it quite clear what it is she or was looking for. The questions which pupils were asked to explore tended to be factual in nature—to provide examples of emotive language, to list the different parts of the newspaper. This emerged most obviously in those instances where pupils were using a worksheet, but even when they were not, they were usually working under headings provided by the teacher. This gave the discussion shape, but it may be that aspects which are important to the pupils—perhaps drawn from their own experience—were not included. In addition, it is clear that the materials being considered—newspapers, advertisements—were those of interest to adults. For example, one teacher saw her aim as being the encouragement of newspaper reading. There appeared to be little drawing on the pupils' experience of the world of media in the gathering of materials for analysis. This sits somewhat at odds with one of the most frequently cited reasons for working on the media in classrooms: that it will help pupils become intelligent media consumers.

SELECTED CASE STUDIES:
INTERVIEWS AND OBSERVATIONS

A selection of two lessons and interviews follows. They provide information on the teacher's background, the progress of the lesson, and the teacher's perceptions of the work.

The first lesson described was taught by Helen at Ballymack Collegiate. The class consisted of 21 girls in Year 11. The lesson lasted 75 minutes. Helen was on the Northern Ireland Curriculum Council Working Party for English, and also worked on some of the assessment documentation at KS3. More recently she had been involved in drawing up a new 'A' Level English Syllabus, which involves some continuous assessment through assignments completed during the course. The interview touched on some of these experiences as well as work in school.

Aims: The Programs of Study

A very clear influence on her thinking about Media Education and reading texts in general was her experience on the Working Party. It was a "big step" for them to define text so broadly when the secondary teachers had been conditioned to view 'text' as printed exam texts, and when the primary specialists had "a clear notion of what reading meant… of the processes and strategies included in that." The wider view of comprehension as "making explicit what meaning you have arrived at and how" (whether the text is printed or not) is clearly centered, in her view. Children need to read a full and balanced diet of texts even though there is "a backlog of attitudes" that leads teachers to have an ambivalent attitude toward the use of media texts in the classroom.

She repeatedly stressed how the approach to texts envisaged by the Cox Report in England (DES, 1989) is liberating, and how the approval of media texts can enrich the reading of printed texts. Although she is worried by the term 'critical reading' she aims at a 'critical autonomy' for all readers, which involves making individual responses explicit. She feels that because children are avid viewers of soap opera, a discussion of where its appeal lies could also produce a sophisticated discussion. "Our [Working Party] judgment was that it is a valid way… to use some time to talk about the texts that impinge on their lives. It is indisputable that media texts will be the main part of that." The "articulation of responses," and "the sharpening and honing of reading skills" are central aims of the reading curriculum.

Resources

There are audio recorders and one clanking video recorder, but this lack of resources is not a huge handicap. If specialist Media Studies can be introduced as planned to the Sixth Form (post-16) by one of the English teachers, more resources may be forthcoming. She felt that the study of media was present in many other subject areas, for example in Geography, but particularly in Art. She was acquiring some storyboarding experience with the help of the Art teacher, whose background was performance art.

Method and Content

> Our decision at the beginning was to integrate it so we don't plan separate units of work specifically to look at media texts. That might sometimes happen because of the unit on advertising in the junior school, but mostly the way Media Education has come into our English program is more in the way that we view all texts—which we have borrowed from Media Education—including print texts, and the way that we bring Media Education perspectives into all the units of work. We always had planned units of work around a core text and maybe brought in other fiction, poetry, drama. We would now plan to bring in media texts as well on that particular unit of work, but we try not to think of it in terms of a specific proportion of time to be spent on it.

One teacher in her department "would be able to rattle you off plenty of films that he would think were interesting texts in their own right for pupils at KS3 or KS4, just to look at for purposes of appreciation, in the same way as you might suggest a list of fiction." However, if a media-based canon were to replace the literary canon, the "whole value of the rethink would be undermined." Media texts should be chosen because they, like the printed texts, can provide "a rich experience." A film could be used as a text, though the structure of the school day does present problems, just as it forces the experience of printed texts to be chopped up into lesson-sized bites. However, "we are in a real bind of only using media texts where there exists a print version." She mentioned *Gregory's Girl*, where the film preceded the book.

Most of the Media Education work done in the department has been in response to literary texts. "This has been the trouble—every unit of work that we have would have grown out of literary texts, with all sorts of backup texts, and we have plenty of media texts in the backup area, but what we need to get down to is making media texts central."

> It's interesting that in my last school I can remember somebody saying "Wouldn't it be great if they published the script of the *Billy* plays, because then we could do it as a school text?" There was no notion that you could treat the actual performance as a text.

At KS3 (ages 11–14) there is a unit of work on advertising, the approach being learning through doing. The emphasis in on creativity and the use of appropriate language, not just on manipulation. "Making response explicit" is once again a key element. This emphasis on creativity is something she values at all levels—making a collage, storyboarding, and so on, can reveal complex and sophisticated responses as well as writing essays can. The ability to present a response to a media text for 'A' Level coursework was one of the features of the new 'A' Level syllabus that attracted her.

The Cross-Curricular Themes

The Northern Ireland Curriculum requires the teaching of six Cross-Curricular Themes, but in practice two of these—Education for Mutual Understanding (EMU) and Cultural Heritage (CH)—receive particular attention. EMU aims to develop appreciation of human differences and to deal constructively with conflict. CH aims to foster appreciation of shared and different cultural traditions within Northern Ireland. As Helen explains:

> A lot of things have been thrown up by the new curriculum—for example, Cultural Heritage—[which] make specific demands on you and which concern issues to do with Northern Ireland. The knowledge about language strand is something which is presented very differently in the Northern Ireland Curriculum from the way it is across the water. I just do not know what they [in England] mean by knowledge about language any more at all. It seems to be prescriptive grammar.

She is working on dialect at the moment, and feels that in this area of CH only media, not print, texts can be useful.

In Northern Ireland, the texts for other cross-curricular themes will very often be media texts. In EMU there is an Irish Commission for Justice and Peace (ICJP) pack on 'Conflict in Northern Ireland' that Helen feels could be supplemented by TV drama, "the medium of the troubles."

Helen has an idea that Media approaches have a lot to offer in making pre-20th-century texts accessible. Her class had watched the recent Russian animated version of *Macbeth* (Serebryakov, 1992).

> The animation stylizes and picks out the really quotable quotes, and it was exactly the way to trigger their memories of the texts. So they had this experience of remembering a lot about *Macbeth,* and they were able to decode and read this animation easily. They quite naturally made comments about how Macbeth's face is very blackened somehow; they were spontaneously looking at Lady Macbeth's "malfaisant" eyes, and they were impressed by the way of getting across the whole gist of *Macbeth* in that animation.

> We had spent last term looking at very modern poetry, all of it free verse - a lot of it experimental—and I wanted them to take a 19th-century poem (Tennyson? Rossetti?), something totally different to that, something drawing on completely different traditions, and work on a storyboard, looking at the ways in which the makers of the Shakespeare animation had tried to make that play accessible without losing the spirit of it.

She wants the class to storyboard a pre-20th-century text against this background.

Aims

The aims are as follows:

- To deepen their understanding of the text.
- To examine ways in which printed texts are translated into another medium.
- To motivate (media texts are "their texts").
- To provide an opportunity for a creative (nonessay-type) response to texts.

Resources

The room was an old 'temporary' aluminum structure, but the English Advisor for the Board had cooperated in making the room more convenient for English and more of a 'workshop'—a carpet, black-out curtains, extra sockets, and a studio at the back of the room, which doubled as a book store and a semi sound proofed area. Materials used included: blank A4 and A3 storyboard sheets, plain paper, dictionaries, copies of the poems, Pritt sticks, and colored pens.

Introduction (5 minutes)

The factors to be considered were the target audience, how to capture in visual form the tone of the original, which sound effects were desirable, and especially the script.

Your task is to make the text accessible while preserving the spirit of the original ... You can use the whole text, you can use quotable quotes in the way the Shakespeare animation did. You remember the way you commented on that—how easily you could understand and follow the story of the *Macbeth* animation though it was using the original text. You could, at the other extreme, paraphrase the whole thing, not use any of the words of the original text, retell the story. If you remember when you were wee in First Form you read a book called *Road to Canterbury* which was based on *The Canterbury Tales* and it didn't actually give you any of Chaucer's original language.

Activity (70 minutes)

The teacher moved around the room advising, assisting, and challenging the groups.

T: It's important to think this through....You may use the 'studio' for your
      sound effects tape.

A typical exchange:

T: Right, where are you at? How many frames have you planned ? Talk me
      through those frames then.
P: The first one is ....
T: Right, your long shot?
P: That there—that is the establishing shot, that is the close shot.
T: Right.

Conclusion

According to Helen:

> The bit of it that I'm ashamed of is that there will be no animation produced in the end. What we are going to do then is this. There is a Sixth Year [post–16] group that is working on an animation of Roald Dahl's *Witches* and they have got the Derry Video Group timetabled to come down and work with them. I want to let this class observe that and get the Sixth Form [post-16] group to talk through with them the process, because they have taken it far beyond the storyboard—they make their models and they are actually going through with the animation.

The Lady of Shallott Group

All the groups worked actively on their projects. Most of them, interestingly, began with an establishing shot whether the poem started that way or not. This group had an easier start—the first two stanzas describe the setting. "We have to have this stuff in the poem in the scenery." So they set about storyboarding it.

> The first one is going to be on the landscape. You can have three different angles at the same view. We can do what we like as long as we have the same sort of idea for scenery for the first three.

> You have to have some sort of crop, you have got rivers, islands in the distance.... You can have Camelot in the distance. [ironically] "Welcome to Camelot."

The storyboarding required close textual analysis. For example: "What does 'silent isle embowers' mean?" The group discussed how to present an appropriately 'romantic' picture of Lancelot, and how to present the 'shadows'. They planned long shots, medium shots and closeups, and discussed how to 'frame' the lady in the window and the mirror. A lot of time was spent drawing, and at one point they realized that three of the group were working on pictures of the Lady at the loom. They also planned where the camera should be sited.

Other groups worked on *The Owl and the Pussycat*, *The Highwayman*, and *The Ballad of Dick Turpin*.

The second lesson was taught by Aine at Saint Ultan's High School. The class consisted of 11 girls and 10 boys in Year 11. The subject of the lesson was newspapers, and the lesson lasted for 40 minutes.

Aine started Media Education as part of the CSE syllabus in the 1970s and found that the pupils liked it. Since then the program for Media Education has expanded. From Year 7 onward, the pupils look at advertising and the analysis becomes progressively more sophisticated. In Year 10 there is a 6-week module on the media (see lesson analysis), but work also arises naturally out of the study of texts where, for example, one character will interview another. For General Certificate of Secondary Education (GCSE), the media, especially newspapers and advertising, are thought to fit naturally in English "because in English we are used to looking at texts critically anyway," so an analysis of soap operas could form part of GCSE coursework.

Within the department, one teacher is particularly interested in newspapers and has produced three newspapers for competitions, and used the studios of *Down-Town Radio* to produce a play. One teacher has a special interest in advertising, and does some work with all the Year 11 pupils. Aine herself has worked on a newspaper and other resource packs. However, her main interest is literature and she has recently used Shakespeare's *Animated Tales* (1992, Channel 4) though she commented that the pupils' responses were sometimes colored by their exposure to Disney's animation style. When using the film of a book, she would ask "How does a director decide which bits to leave out, and why?"

> We had Bernard McLaverty [in the school there is an extensive program of visits by local authors]. We would read quite a few of McLaverty's stories and we do his novel.... He told us a bit about how the film production crew worked and how they asked him to change the ending for his novel *Lamb*. And the children were fascinated by that. He said the ending was terribly important because it was the ending that inspired him to write the book in the first place. He told the director, "Whatever else you change, the ending must stay the same."

Aims

There is a general awareness in the department of the power of the media to influence children who are exposed to so many hours of television and music daily. Several references were made to the power of advertisements to manipulate people, and Vance Packard's *The Hidden Persuaders* is sometimes referred to in class.

Also, "since children do believe what they read in the papers" one of the aims is to produce critical readers. This was the focus of the video extract to be used that day from *Hard News*, showing a story that *The Sun* deliberately manipulated to suit their own ends.

> To show them that we must always be critics, we must always look for the truth, and we must always look behind what is printed. It is very difficult to do that because most people only buy one newspaper. They do not buy two newspapers to compare reports.

The lesson was seen as a bridge backwards to a newspaper assignment on a Miller play (the pupils were to write two newspaper stories about events in the play), and a bridge forward to a Media Education module, of which this was the first lesson. The other main topic would be advertising.

Key Concepts

The 'Key Concepts' were mass media, manipulation, bias, and especially editing of news.

Resources

A new extension had just been completed, and the new room had a VCR, computer, and printer. Desks were arranged in rows and easily formed into groups.

Materials used included: a class textbook for each child *(English in Units)*, newspapers brought in by pupils the previous day, a video of *Hard News* showing how a story was changed by *The Sun,* and plain paper.

The main aim was to produce critical readers through:

- Understanding the difference between quality and tabloid newspapers.
- Looking at mastheads, headlines, straplines, and so on.
- Engaging in activities in which the pupils became editors.
- Writing a brief story in a newspaper style.

Introduction (5 minutes)

The class looked briefly with the teacher at definitions of 'mass' and 'media' in the textbook.

T: We are going to start our Media Education this year, with newspapers and how newspapers work, and from there we go on to advertising, television, and so on.

The teacher directed the pupils to open the class text and read a definition of mass media and news.

T: What do they do if they don't have anything new?
P: Make it up, exaggerate, and so on.

The teacher then discussed their choice of newspaper.

T: If you were going on a train journey and you stopped at a newspaper kiosk to buy a newspaper, Eugene, what would you buy?
P: *The Daily Mirror.*
T: What would you buy, John?
P: *The Star.*
T: Supposing *The Irish Times* was all that was available or *The Irish Independent* or *The Irish News* or *The News Letter*, would you buy any of those?
P: No!
T: Why?
P: They are not as interesting.
T: But they are all carrying the news of the day.
P: They do not catch your eye as much. The English papers have a bit of color in them.
T: So it is color you are after?

The teacher indicated the front pages reproduced in this tabloid.

> T: Which one would you buy?
> P: *The Star.*
> T: Why?
> P: The color.
> T: There is another reason, isn't there? It's small, so what does that mean to you on the train? It easier to read. It does not fall apart; sometimes you have to put a newspaper on the floor if you are going to read one of those bigger newspapers.

Activity 1 (15 minutes)

Groups of four were asked to recall recent news items, select 5 from them, and place them in order of importance. Aine gave as an example the novelist Ann Dunlop coming into the school. She stressed that she did not want "world-shattering events," and pointed out that newspapers had printed stories less important than the things they would choose. She then moved around the class, elaborating on the instructions, offering suggestions, and answering questions.

❖*The Ulster News*❖

45p   May 12th 1997

Murdered - Constable **Michael Ferguson, 21,** was shot dead by a lone gunman in Derry yesterday. The IRA have claimed responsibility.

He was shot twice in the head by the gunman outside the busy Richmond Centre at about 2.30pm. His attacker made his getaway by running along Shipquay Street, where he was almost run over by a blue car. Police are searching for the driver of the blue car, as the gunman's fingerprints may be on it.

Constable Ferguson was rushed to Altnagalvin Hospital, but was found dead on arrival.

Witnesses heard his friend, who is also in the Security Services, call out "My mate! Why? Oh why?" Then Michael passed away.

FIG. 3.1.

Report Back

T: Could you very quickly tell me what you left out rather than what you chose and why did you leave it out? I am going to go around you very quickly just to find that out. Declan, what did your group leave out?

P: We left out the Limavady Cinema being built, because it was built a few months ago, and we left out the visitor putting us on tape, because we already had that. We left out Kieran's uncle going to America.

T: You felt that those were not really newsworthy, you had more important things to deal with?

Aine then introduced a focus on specific presentational elements shown in the textbook.

T: Would you open your *English in Units* and go to pages 142–143? On 142 you will notice a very important feature of the newspaper which is called what? [Silence]

T: The masthead. What is the masthead? ... The masthead is the distinctively printed name of the newspaper. Is that an important feature of the newspaper? Why? Is it important that it is the same every day do you think? Do you look for a particular mast head when you buy?

Next, she explained headlines.

T: On page 144 you will see headlines that have done something else to catch your eye: 'Furious Tessa Fires Parting Shot,' 'Yeats Story a Grave Error,' 'The Five Million Storm in a Cereal Bowl,' and 'Stokers' Pay Issue Boils Over,'. Now we will pick first of all the 'Yeats Story a Grave Error.' Can anybody tell me what kind of headline that is? Would you be aware of it? It is what is called a pun. A pun is a play on words. Just over the page again we see how alliteration and assonance are used to sell either newspapers or a product: 'Cork, Cool, Calm and Confident.' What do you notice about that headline? What device or trick did they use there? What trick of language? ...

Activity 2 (15 minutes)

T: I'm going to ask you now to choose one of the five items as your front page story which is going to get pasted up into your newspaper. But remember that it is a front page story, so it will appear at the front of your newspaper after your masthead. It is going to appear so the first thing that you have to do is to design the headline and then your story. We are going to design the masthead and you are going to make up your title and your story. Now, what kind of a paper are each of you going to go for? Are you going to go for a tabloid or quality paper? (Chorus–"A tabloid"). Are you going to make your story sensational? You are going to exaggerate, OK. Away you go and let's see how your headline and your story turns out.

One group discussed how to get attraction into the headline, and worked hard to get an appropriate style. Once again the teacher moved around the groups.

Conclusion (5 minutes)

The class ended with an analysis of what emotion they were trying to engender in the reader.

Comments

There was a constructive and industrious atmosphere in the classroom: Groups formed without fuss, and there was good engagement with the tasks. Pupils clearly showed the ability to mimic newspapers accurately, both in the choice of story and style. Two groups chose as their topic the shooting of a policeman in Derry, even though the teacher's instructions stressed the personal element, and one group dealt indirectly with the decline of the Health Service. Most important of all, they showed that they were capable of reproducing both the style and structure of news stories. The discussion showed that this was deliberate, not just intuitive.

While reading the textbook, introducing the activities, and moving around the groups, Aine's style of teaching was based largely on closed questions to check the pupils' understanding, and to focus attention on important issues. The teacher often elaborated on what pupils said to make the meanings clearer, and very often built on shared experiences.

CONCLUSIONS

Eight of the 11 teachers in the study were women. This may have less to do with Media Education than the teaching of English. In general, as in England, there is a preponderance of women in English teaching in Northern Ireland, and so it is not unexpected that the majority of these teachers should be female. Although popular belief would have it that women are less comfortable with technology than men, this notion is less sustainable when scrutinized. Related research on computers (Collins, 1994) found that women teachers who used computers with their pupils did not perceive themselves at any disadvantage.

However, the classes observed in the study rarely used hardware: Newspapers and magazine advertisements were the most popular points of focus for work. Where hardware was used it was found to be male teachers who used it. There may be some reluctance among women teachers to move into areas of Media Education that would call for some facility with the operation of cameras and recorders.

Teachers appear to come to Media work in very practical ways. To be convinced of its worth, they must see at first hand the possibilities for the subject— a Media course, Drama that evolves into Media, or the development of earlier Media work. There is a wide range of Media Education textbooks now available to teachers, outlining the nature of the work and practical possibilities; but none of the teachers interviewed mentioned a text that led them into Media work. There would appear to be clear implications here for in-service and preservice provision. It may be that such provision should try to find ways of developing thinking as well as practice among teachers. Teacher attitude to Media work seemed somewhat ambiguous. On the one hand, none of those interviewed had any doubt about the worth of Media Education within English. However, some anxiety was communicated. Where teachers had the support of the Department Head, Vice-principal, or Principal, they commented on this— hardly surprising, since it is natural to be pleased when one's superiors seem to support what one is doing. However, there did seem some concern that Media Education within English should receive an official stamp of justification. It would be interesting to see if the same concern would exist if teachers were working on traditional reading or writing. Perhaps old doubts about the validity of studying the media, so closely linked in our minds with entertainment, continue to inhibit some teachers some of the time.

Aims and Topics

There was a general concern among teachers to produce 'critical readers'. This concern focused almost exclusively on the reading of print, particularly newspapers. In practice, this notion became the need to foster an awareness of the shallowness of tabloid papers when set beside quality papers. Where attention was drawn to language, it was for the most part to establish instances of language used in an emotive way to 'manipulate' the feelings of the reader.

A great deal of the work tended to be 'workshop' in nature. Pupils operated in groups and identified aspects of the paper—its different parts, or examples of different kinds of language which had been discussed earlier. Alternatively or in addition, they were asked to produce work of their own that would show these in action—alliterative headlines, emotional stories. There were instances of pupils working so that they became aware of the extent to which news reporting is a matter of priorities and selection, but this sort of discovery was not particularly common.

The tendency to work in terms of general discrimination rather than in terms of Media concepts like ownership, audience, representation, and ideology, may have been influenced by the fact that many teachers were working with an eye to the cultivation of oral skills. From that perspective, what was said about the newspapers was considered less important than that the papers provide a useful stimulus for the kinds of talk that occur in groups and individually. In a lesson of this kind, it is indeed possible that a class may touch on many matters— writing, wordprocessing, desktop publishing, social skills, financial acumen. But besides the danger of attempting to advance all of these within one short lesson, there is a danger that the media under scrutiny will become a springboard rather than an area of investigation, just as literature can sometimes be used as a starting point in ways that show little concern with the literature itself. Perhaps those involved with Media Education in English need to take some clear decisions about the extent to which they want to treat media texts as worthy of scrutiny from a variety of perspectives, rather than solely as a convenient arena into which pupils are shepherded to develop desirable English skills.

What was most surprising was that the one medium to which every person in every classroom devotes several hours each day—television—featured in just one classroom. It may be that electronic media still have not established themselves as legitimate areas of study with the same firmness as print media. (In this connection, it is noticeable that print media which mean something to most adults, such as newspapers, are more likely to receive attention than print media which have appeal and meaning for pupils, such as comics or magazines.) Perhaps print media are considered easier to work with in a classroom. Or perhaps the multiplicity of TV programs makes selection a problem.

The other area notable by its absence was the operation of the media in Northern Ireland/Ireland. There are rich opportunities for the investigation of important issues here. News reporting, representation, ideology—these and others can be considered in a context familiar to the pupils, inviting comparisons with their knowledge of the people and/or events as experienced in life and as they appear in the media. Such local attention would also have implications for Education for Mutual Understanding (EMU) and Cultural Heritage (CH), cross-curricular themes that all teachers are required to address. The avoidance of Northern Ireland/Ireland issues is perhaps due, as one teacher pointed out, to the risk that many teachers associate with such topics. These matters are hot to handle and to address them may have repercussions in terms of parental response. It may also be the case that if teachers were feeling more secure about Media Education generally, they would be less reluctant to embark on such work. But where an uncertainty as to its validity exists, and this is added to by the kind of response that attention to local media may elicit, the anticipated burden could be too much for most. Finally, there was considerable dependence on the beneficial effects of practical work. For the most part, pupils seem to enjoy such work, but there may be more need for a balance between focus on those aspects of the topic that the teacher wishes to deepen understanding of, and concern for pupil initiative when working in groups.

Facilities and Resources

There was little sign that classrooms had been designed to accommodate Media Education work. Because in fact they were English classrooms, this is not surprising. At the same time, if the classrooms had reflected the importance attached to Media Education within the English Programs of Study through their layout or displays, this might have had a positive effect on pupil thinking. There did not appear to be a resource center in any of the departments visited. In some there were film posters on the wall or displays of work done by pupils. Where a VCR was needed it was available, and in one case the teacher had access to and used four TVs and monitors, as well as prerecorded tapes. A number of teachers used pre-recorded video tapes (e.g., from *The Media File*).

But because the majority of classes looked at newspapers, these formed the focus of most of the work. Teachers had multiple copies of local papers, photocopies of selected items, and advertisements from magazines. In conversation none of the teachers expressed dissatisfaction with the facilities, except perhaps indirectly. Thus, although there did not appear to be a great deal of support in the way of hardware provision, there seems to have been enough to leave teachers confident to tackle the work they had decided on. Several classes used *The Media File,* and one used copies of the *Daily Telegraph* pack. These appeared to give teachers a sense of the work's legitimacy.

There is no sign that a particular textbook or pack has emerged as a hub around which teachers structure their work. This probably leaves more room for individual choice and teacher initiative. It also may enhance the chances that Media Education becomes knitted into the English Curriculum, rather than emerging as a specialized subject. However, the observations do show a somewhat predictable and unchallenging approach to the media that might benefit from more systematic structure. A central textbook/pack of high quality might have a role to play here.

There is a refreshing enthusiasm for and belief in Media Education among the English teachers in the study. A range of approaches to the work has been devised, and in many cases pupils are arriving at important insights about media texts and/or constructing their own in effective ways. Media work is providing new ways of looking at traditional aspects of the English curriculum, particularly literature. It is also providing an attractive area for purposeful speaking and listening, and for group work that has particular audiences in mind.

Ways Forward

This study found that there is room for the development of a fuller and more focused view of what Media Education has to offer the English teacher. It may be that the vastness and looseness of the world of media encourages teachers to disregard the wider issues in favor of attention to particular detail. Helen touches on this when she says that much of her work tends to use media texts as a supplement to the written text rather than as meriting study in their own right. If pupils are to be helped to discern order and pattern in their study of different media texts and in the construction of their own, a set of broad guiding principles might well add to the quality and opportunities offered by the work, as appears to have happened to a greater extent in England with the BFI's 'Signpost Questions.'

Further attention to the nature of media in Northern Ireland would be desirable. Pupil distaste for Irish papers emerges in Aine's lesson, but is simply accepted: "So it is color you are after?" Perhaps because most textbooks concern themselves with the operation of the media in Britain, teachers tend to forget that the media across the Irish Sea have distinguishing characteristics which merit study. To fail to address these is to ignore a rich vein of experience, one which plays an important part in young people's thinking.

There is a need for Media Education to look beyond the classroom in its practical work. The professional media operate beyond the school. Pupils too, should be provided with opportunities to collect their material there, and to locate wider audiences for their work. Ways might be devised where pupils make greater use of portable recorders and video cameras to tape interviews as part of documentary packages on selected issues. Likewise, more opportunities could be provided for pupils to visit those places where Media work is under way—advertising agencies, radio stations, TV stations, newspaper offices, recording studios. There is little emphasis on bringing the world of the professional into the classroom. Significantly, when Aine speaks of a visiting writer, it is a novelist, not a journalist.

Teachers need to be helped to develop confidence both in their planning and execution of Media work, and in assessing its worth. Where Media Education emerges in endproducts that are themselves media texts, or where understanding of professional media processes and products shows in the ways pupils themselves work in nonwritten forms, the teacher needs to know what it is she or he is aiming at. Is the storyboard good because it would form the basis for a successful video production, or is it good because it shows signs of thought regarding the text which it is working on? Or is it—can it be—both? Helen felt "ashamed" that her storyboard work did not become animation, even though the purpose of the work was to provide understanding of poetry. Only where such matters have been thought through and resolved will the teacher and pupils gain from the work as they might.

Particular attention needs to be paid to progression. Advertising is a case in point. This kind of work often starts at KS3, or even KS2. It is not always clear how such study has developed in depth and complexity by the time it reaches KS4. This suggests the importance of an integrated Media Education policy and program of work in schools and English Departments. In the lessons observed, teachers appeared to be working as relatively isolated individuals. If a whole-school policy is not developed, the alternative may be repetitious attention to some aspects of the media, and the relative neglect of others.

Language is central to any consideration of the media. This might be dealt with in a more thorough way. Such matters as representation of women should have developed to a reasonably sophisticated level by the time pupils reach KS4, and certainly beyond a simplistic attention to sexism-spotting. Attention to aspects of language other than the media's tendency to use emotive and manipulative phraseology would be helpful. More sustained focus on such matters as language and genre, language and speaker, and language and audience would widen the span of media analysis. It is noteworthy that Aine's approach to newspapers is in terms of 'color' rather than representation, ownership, or editorial line.

Finally, the role of nonprint media texts in English requires further consideration. What priority are they to have? Should they receive the same amount of time and attention as printed texts? Greater depth in approach to media texts would be helpful: consideration of editing, framing, lighting, as well as the forms that plot and characterization take in film and television. Reference has already been made to the uneasiness felt by Helen about not developing animation. Until the importance attached to media texts by English teachers is made clear, in terms of number studied and depth to which they are studied, the position of Media Education within English will continue to be uncertain.

REFERENCES

Channel 4. (1992). *Shakespeare: The animated tales*. Cardiff: Channel 4 Wales.

Collins, J. (1994). Computers in classroom and college, *Computer Education, 77*, 30–33.

Collins, J., & O'Kane, J. (1994). *Media education in English: Teachers at work*. Belfast: University of Ulster.

Department of Education and Science. (1983). *Popular television and schoolchildren*. London: Her Majesty's Stationery Office.

Department of Education and Science. (1989). (The Cox Report). *English for ages 5–16*. London: Her Majesty's Stationery Office.

Serebryakov, N. (Director). (1992). *Macbeth*. Cardiff: Channel 4 Wales.

4

Media Education in an Emergent Democracy: KwaZulu–Natal, South Africa

Sue Court
Costas Criticos
University of Natal

At this time of transition, at the dawn of a new democratic order in South Africa, Media Education has the potential to contribute significantly to the development of a critical citizenry. This was the generally agreed view of the teachers who were interviewed and whose practice was observed in the project conducted in KwaZulu–Natal in South Africa over a 2-year period, from mid-1993 to 1995.

Although the research design was based on the *Models of Media Education* project in England, the findings of this survey point to some important areas for future research and development that are unique to South Africa.[1] Most notably, these are: Media Education policy; curriculum design; Teacher Education and support, and the design of learning materials. Although this all sounds optimistic and encouraging, it is necessary however, to sound a note of caution. As is elaborated later in this chapter, Media Education is not perceived to be a priority issue by the current national curriculum planners. In order to understand the unique contribution that Media Education can make in South Africa at this particular historical juncture, it is helpful to have an overview of the historical and educational context.

---

[1] An earlier version of parts of this chapter was presented as a paper at the La Coruna Pedagoxia da Imaxe conference in 1995 and subsequently appeared in *Continuum*, 9/2 (Court, 1996, pp. 86–93).

Context

Media Education cannot be seen in isolation from the context in which it occurs and the educational philosophy which informs that context. As in England, different paradigms or educational traditions have informed education in South Africa. Three are generally acknowledged: a 'Positivist' or 'Transmission' tradition, 'Liberal Humanism,' and 'Progressive' education. There is a further distinction in 'Progressive' education between 'resistance/oppositional' and 'critical/radical' educational practices. An understanding of these educational traditions is necessary in order to make sense of the findings of this survey into models of Media Education in South Africa. Before embarking on an investigation of these paradigms, it is helpful to give a brief overview of the history of education in South Africa.

Overview of the History of South African Education[2]

The colonial history of South Africa differed from that of the rest of Africa in that there was conflict between the early European colonists, the Dutch settlers (the Boers), and the British colonial authorities, which culminated in the Anglo–Boer War at the end of the 19th century. From the earliest times, there was division between the English and the Dutch with respect to the philosophy, aims, and content of education. Whereas the British colonial government developed a system of education that rested on notions of European culture and civilization, with a deliberate policy of Anglicization, the Boers formulated their own ideology of Christian National Education that found expression in the foundation of schools in the Transvaal and the Orange Free State during the immediate postwar period.

In 1948 the Instituut vir Christelike Nasionale Onderwys (Institute for Christian National Education) produced a document of some 15 articles that summarized the ideology, aims, content, and methods of Christian National Education. In essence, this ideology linked the state, church, home, and the school in an indissoluble network resting cozily on ethnic separation. This document was to provide a blueprint for education when the Nationalist party was elected to power in 1948 and Apartheid was born. Race was legitimized and entrenched as the defining category that enforced separate development in all areas of society: residence, occupation, social services, health, and the system of education. Apartheid education eventually spawned a cumbersome bureaucracy with 19th educational authorities, defined by race and geography.

In the province of Natal there were, until April 1994, five separate educational authorities: the White Natal Education Department (NED) under the House of Assembly (HOA); Indian education under the House of Delegates (HOD); 'Colored' education under the House of Representatives (HOR); Black education administered by the KwaZulu homeland; and Black education outside the homeland administered by the Department of Education and Training (DET), which was

---

[2]For a comprehensive account of Apartheid Education, see Kallaway (1984).

responsible to the national cabinet. This separation was accompanied by inferior educational provision and selective curricula for 'non-Whites'.

In the wake of the Soweto uprising of 1976, developments in the 1980s heralded a period of unprecedented change in South African politics, and the 1990s opened with the historic announcement that inaugurated the transition to majority rule. Schools that had been established to cater for particular race groups were now legally permitted to admit a quota of pupils from different ethnic origins.

In 1996, nearly 2 years after South Africa's first democratic elections, the educational system is in the process of transition. The old Apartheid provinces and homelands have been replaced by nine new regional political structures with their own educational authorities, and new educational policies and curricula are being drawn up. KwaZulu–Natal forms a single region and the five departments are being amalgamated into one educational authority.

EDUCATIONAL PARADIGMS

This political history is reflected in the four different traditions of education referred to earlier.

Transmission Education

Transmission education characterized formal education in South Africa during the Apartheid regime. The ideology of Christian National Education was dominant and decreed that education for Whites should have both a 'Christian character' and a 'national character.' Both 'Christian' and 'national' had a particular meaning that pertained to one minority group: the white Afrikaner. Black education under the Bantu Education Act of 1954 was directed to provide a subservient work force which did not threaten the existing relations of power. This was clearly articulated by the then Minister of Education, Hendrik Verwoerd in his speech to the Senate June 7, 1954: "There is no place for the Bantu[3] in the European community above the level of certain forms of labour" (Behr, 1988, p. 36). Education contents and methods encouraged passive learners who did not engage in the process of the construction of knowledge.

Liberal Humanism

Liberal Humanism's emphasis on the uniqueness of the individual and the eternal verities of the human condition, was embedded in the English-speaking colonial tradition. Educators in the English schools enjoyed greater autonomy than in the

---

[3]The traditional South African term for Black Africans.

other educational authorities. As might be expected, Liberal Humanism was most clearly expressed in disciplines from the humanities, and it is perhaps predictable that Media Education entered the secondary school curriculum through English (First Language) in White education, and was subsequently appropriated by Indian education.

Media Education was strongly influenced by the Leavisite tradition in the United Kingdom. Consonant with the concern that mass culture had a degenerative effect, early Media educators distinguished between 'high' culture and 'low' or 'mass' culture, drawing parallels between literary and nonliterary texts. Literary or high culture was perceived as being under siege before a mass culture propelled by the might of industrial mass production. As in the United Kingdom, the justification for teaching Media in the classroom was to provide a defense (or inoculation) against the demoralizing effects of the media.

There is an interesting parallel between early Media Education and the way in which literature was taught along the lines of practical criticism and the Leavisite 'Great Tradition'. In the same way that the terminology of literary criticism was taught in the English literature classroom, so the terminology of filmic devices was taught in the Media lesson. In both, the focus was on the intentions of the author/producer with an underlying moral dimension.

Resistance Education

The Soweto uprising of 1976 was a catalyst for change in South African politics. The students demonstrated against the bureaucratic dictum that Afrikaans be the medium of instruction for half the secondary school subjects in Black schools. The rejection of Afrikaans symbolized a rejection of Apartheid political structures in general and the system of education in particular.

The 1980s were characterized by popular resistance to the domesticating education of Apartheid. The cultural struggle was rooted in Freirian notions of the process of 'conscientization'. Media activists criticized the pervasive ideologies inscribed in mainstream media. By 1986, People's Education was formally defined at a national alternative education conference. People's Education linked education and politics. The struggle for an alternative educational system could not be separated from the struggle for a nonracial democratic South Africa. As Prinsloo (1995) pointed out, resistance education marked opposition to the state and should not be conflated with the pedagogic concerns of critical education. Mass mobilization did not equate to critical reflection.

The changing approach to Media Education emerged as part of the 'struggle' against the homogenous adversary of apartheid. It is based within a paradigm of media understanding that adopts a particular interpretation of the work of the earlier Frankfurt school theorists and the power of the 'culture industry' to domesticate and placate the population by producing 'false' consciousness. With the shift of consideration of institutional context and the notion of agency, teachers in this department

(HOD) incorporated concepts derived from semiotics, in which signification focused attention on representations and mediation of meaning, how codes and conventions work and are used, and how cultural 'myths' operate. They adopted a conspiracist approach to the media and this overtly oppositional approach related to South African identity politics. (Prinsloo, 1995, p. 19)

Critical Education

The current political transition has allowed space for the introduction of a critical approach to Media Education. Critical pedagogy rests on postmodern or poststructuralist understandings which reject the notion of a single truth and emphasize the social construction of knowledge and the deconstruction of text.

Regarding texts as cultural representations, Media Education raises questions about who is represented, how they are represented, who is omitted, who has made the message, and whose interests are being served through the discourse. It aspires to create learners who are able to cross borders and locate knowledge historically, socially, and critically. It proposes that learners need to construct their own narratives and histories, while recognizing that they are themselves located by narratives.

Media Education Initiatives in South Africa

In 1990, the first national Media Education conference, entitled *Developing Media Education in the 1990s*, was held at the University of Natal. What was particularly noticeable was the similarity of approach among the different education authorities toward Media Education. The commonly held view rested on Leavisite concerns that mass culture had a degenerative effect. The aim was to provide an inoculation against the debilitating effects of the media. Film was privileged as an extension of the 'Great Tradition'. This position is reflected in the following statement of the White Transvaal Education Department.

Film Study ... raises the consciousness of pupils and enables them to discriminate and resist manipulation; the traditional skills of writing, language study and literary criticism are advanced by film study; the film has been shown as a valid medium by which literary themes and preoccupations are conveyed ... (Prinsloo & Criticos, 1991, p. 34)

Similar aims were expressed by the White Cape Education Department, which spoke of the need to combine "aesthetic appreciation of the medium as 'communication art form' and critical awareness of the techniques employed by its creation to achieve specific or implicit intentions" (Faasen, 1991, p. 30).

The White NED was also preoccupied with film study and notions of 'high' culture, but there was more flexibility with regard to teaching approaches and support for teacher research. The Leavisite echo also reverberated in the Indian

HOD where, once again, Media Education was largely restricted to a literary approach to film.

At the conference there were no representatives from the HOR (the 'Colored' authority), the two Black education authorities, the DET, or the KwaZulu education authority. None of these authorities had considered the possibility of teaching Media Education. Outside the formal education authorities, academics and media activists resisted the high cultural emphasis. In spite of the Leavisite preoccupations represented in many of the papers, in the end the conference recommended that Media Education should not "be confined to those media forms generally associated with high technology and sophisticated electronic media such as film and television, but that educators should use those media resources readily available to them to engender critical discussion" (Prinsloo & Criticos, 1991, p. 300).

The 1990 conference influenced a shift of focus within the White and Indian Education Departments toward Media Education and away from Film Studies. Although the DET expressed interest in these initiatives, the other education authorities remained indifferent. Beyond the White and Indian schools, it has made no significant inroads in Black schools, which constitute the largest number of schools in the country.

The Origins of the Study

Following the original methodology of the study in England (Hart & Benson, 1993) 12 teachers in schools in the Durban functional region were interviewed for the Media Education survey during the period from July 1993 to September 1995. Five of the teachers were recommended by the English subject advisor for the NED; four were students in the Department of Education of the University of Natal, and the remaining three were recommended, either by academics within the Department of Education, or other teachers involved in the survey. Of the 12 teachers interviewed, 1 was a student teacher, 1 was a teacher in an independent school, 3 were teaching in Indian schools and the remaining 7 were teachers in the NED. One of these NED schools was founded in the early 1990s to cater exclusively for Black, mainly Zulu-speaking pupils.

Nine of the teachers were White and the remaining three were Indian. It is not surprising that there were no Black African teachers as Media Education has not been part of the curriculum for African schools. Under the Apartheid system of education different educational authorities were established for the different population groups. Within these authorities, not only was there a grossly unequal provision of educational resources, but an educational ideology prevailed that was inimical to the critical pedagogy appropriate to Media Education.

All of the teachers were specialist English teachers with three teaching Drama as well and an additional two having either a great interest or a qualification in Drama. When questioned, eight of the teachers claimed to be most interested in the teaching of English Literature, whereas three preferred teaching Media, and one stated that he was most interested in teaching life skills that would be useful to the children in later life.

RESEARCH METHODS

The research methods employed closely followed the original Southampton, England, study. Twelve teachers were interviewed: Eight of these interviews took place in the schools where they were employed and the other four took place in the Department of Education at the University of Natal. The interviews were recorded on audiocassette but notes were taken for future reference. The interviews were conducted in an informal manner, and many questions outside of the structured schedule arose spontaneously and provided fruitful direction for future research and communication. The teachers were, without exception, cooperative about being interviewed, and regarded the contact as an affirmation of their teaching and creativity.

The 35 questions posed were the same as those used in the Southampton study and covered the teachers' background, both educational and experiential; the support available to teachers, both inside and outside of the school; the aims and broad expectations of teachers of Media Education; the methods and contents of the media work done by teachers in the school; and the focus of individual lessons observed.

However, it was not always possible to observe a lesson and, in the end, only 10 lessons were observed. Where lessons were not observed teachers were asked to discuss a lesson that they might teach or to describe a Media Education program that they had devised and taught. As it happened, this strategy of 'making a virtue of necessity' brought out some interesting observations. Although structured questions provide for useful comparisons, and observed lessons are illuminating indicators of procedure, the unstructured questions prompted teachers to expand on their own beliefs in Media Education. In general, these teachers had formulated their own philosophies of education, and Media Education played a central role in that. In other words, the beliefs that underpinned their teaching in general were focused on their Media Education work.

Teachers spoke enthusiastically about their engagement in Media Education and their particular programs. They had designed teaching materials that they had used in the classroom and were willing to share these with other teachers. They saw themselves as a small group of professionals, beleaguered in an alien bureaucracy, committed to helping each other. One of the teaching programs which had been implemented with considerable success and used by fellow Media Education teachers was *Super Heroes* (see Fig. 4.1).

It was intended that the interviews should last for 1 hour. In practice, they often turned out to last for 2 hours or more, with many of the questions giving rise to dialogue on issues relating to Media Education but not recorded on the interview

FIG. 4.1. Super Heroes figure (reproduced by permission of Russell Untiedt of Westville Girls' High School).

sheet. Again, this seems to point to a general observation that teachers who teach Media Education are committed teachers who are vitally involved in the educational enterprise, and it is often their own enthusiasm that has given birth to the meaningful practice of Media Education in their schools.

MAIN FINDINGS

One of the first and most obvious findings is that the sample fell neatly into equal gender divisions: 6 men and 6 women. This provides an interesting contrast to the Southampton and Northern Ireland studies, where 8 of the 11 teachers interviewed were women. Apparently, the early years of Media Education in the United Kingdom were dominated by men, but nowadays the majority of the English teachers are women who have manifested an interest and engagement with Media Education. This appears not to be the case in KwaZulu–Natal although it needs to be emphasized that the situation here is not necessarily representative of South Africa as a whole. Certainly there are more women than men teachers of English in the schools that previously fell under the NED and the HOD, but the teaching of Media Education does not appear to be dominated by women.

Another observation is the comparative youth and inexperience of the teachers interviewed, which is again a contrast to the Southampton study where "eight of the teachers had taught for at least ten years and in some cases for more than twenty" (Hart & Benson, 1993, p. 116). The average number of years of teaching experience in the South African study is 7.8, whereas the average period of teaching Media Education is 5.3 years. What this seems to reflect is the recent emergence of the discipline of Media Education in South Africa, which has been discussed earlier in this chapter. Those teachers who have most recently qualified for or have studied for a Bachelor of Education degree have the advantage of formal education in Media. Seven of the teachers acknowledged that they had had formal training in Media: Three of them had studied for the Bachelor of Education degree with Media Education as an option; one had an Honors degree in Drama and Education that included a component on Film Studies; one had completed a Technikon diploma in Television Arts, and one was reading for a Master's degree in Media Education. Three of the teachers had been introduced to Media Education during their initial teacher education course. All of them had attended in-service courses in Media Education.

Again, this provokes an interesting and unexpected finding when compared with the Southampton study, where eight of the teachers had no training in Media Education. Taking into account the considerable period of time that Media Education has been established in the United Kingdom in comparison to South Africa, the expectation was that more of the British teachers would have had formal training than would the South African teachers.

When asked how they became interested in Media Education, four of the teachers stated that Media had been part of their formal education, while two said that it was due to the incorporation of Media Education into the syllabus or that the school had a policy of Media Education. Five of them claimed that their interest in Media Education was generated by the pupils themselves. Generally, it was their desire to take as a starting point for the teaching of English the world that the children knew. One of the teachers pointed out that as a citizen in a society that is framed by the media, Media has to be included in the educational program in order to prepare pupils to participate in the society. Interestingly, three of the teachers were involved with the formulation of a Media Education policy for their particular schools.

In all cases, the teachers interviewed had a passion for Media Education. It was something in which they fervently believed and it was reflected in their teaching. Although the enthusiasm of individuals appears to be responsible for the development of Media Education programs in schools, it would seem desirable to broaden the exposure to Media Education in all the previously segregated education authorities that are in the process of being amalgamated into one department. The view that is promoted here is that Media Education provides for the development of critical literacy in children. This, in turn, is formative in the evolution of a critical citizenry better able to dismantle the legacy of Apartheid ideology.

Teachers referred to a range of useful and influential readings, but common to half of them was *Media Matters in South Africa* (Prinsloo & Criticos, 1991) the publication that contains the proceedings of the first Media Education conference in South Africa: Developing Media Education in the 1990s. Others mentioned works by Alvarado and Gutch, Masterman, Foucault, and Fiske and Hartley. Two mentioned pedagogic texts like the *Gemini Reading Scheme* and an Australian series; one spoke vaguely of books recommended by academics in the Department of Education at Natal University; another asserted "nothing in particular," and one claimed that she did not refer to academic texts but "worked on instinct". While this kind of variety may be common to many Media Education teachers, references to *Media Matters in South Africa* suggest that teachers are aware of the important movements in Media Education in the region.

There was a considerable range in the percentage of time that teachers devoted to Media Education. At one end of the spectrum a teacher claimed that "most of (her) teaching related to Media in some way," three claimed that 50% of their time was devoted to Media Education, with the others ranging from 30% down to 10%.[4]

Nine of the teachers did not teach Media Education outside of the English classroom because they were exclusively English teachers, although one of them uttered the proviso that some of the texts that he used might appear to have nothing to do with English. One said that her school supported cross-curricular approaches,

---

[4]Unfortunately, the study gives no data on commitment to Media work as a proportion of total timetable.

and that Media provided opportunities for collaboration. She also taught Drama and employed media in the teaching of that subject. Another referred to the role of Media in the source-based approach to the teaching of history. These kinds of responses indicate that teachers had not learned the discourse of Media Education, and had a limited understanding of the subject. Using the media in teaching does not constitute Media Education.

The question about the exposure of pupils to Media Education during the primary phase drew a variety of responses. One teacher admitted that she did not know. Four of the interviewees claimed that "very few" of their pupils had been exposed to Media Education in primary school; two said "some"; two guessed 50% to 60%, one said 80%, another 90%, and one claimed that all his pupils had some experience in Media Education because they studied the newspaper in Standard 6 (the first year of secondary schooling in South Africa) at his school. It would seem that the teaching of Media Education in primary school in South Africa is a random affair but no details were given about this. As indicated earlier, there is some confusion about what Media Education means, some teachers understanding it to mean "how to use the media" rather than a critical understanding of media.

Apart from one teacher, all the respondents claimed that some other Media work was done in their schools. In the school that has implemented a cross-curricular approach (an Indian school), Media materials were employed in the teaching of Drama, History, Afrikaans, and Geography, but it needs to be emphasized that this does not constitute Media Education. In the school that takes a source-based approach to the teaching of History, Media is also part of extracurricular activities like the Photographic Society. This kind of involvement was also reported in four other schools, but no link was made between these extracurricular involvements and classroom activities. Two schools had comprehensive Media courses run by the teacher–librarian. In one other school, Media was used extensively in History teaching but no details were offered as to the approach to the subject. Two teachers stated that many teachers use video in teaching but pointed out that a clear distinction needs to be made between teaching the Media and using the media to teach.

Nine of the respondents asserted that they collaborated with colleagues both within their own schools and at other schools. Three of these also had contact, independent of the project with academics at the University of Natal. An interesting development was the working group on narrative, coordinated by a lecturer in the Department of Education at the University of Natal, to which one of the teachers belonged. Two of the teachers reported that they enjoyed support from outside commercial advertising agencies, and one had access to a Media Resource Unit. Also of interest is the fact that a number of teachers were working together informally, sharing ideas and materials for Media Education.

With regard to a policy for Media Education in the school, five of the schools had no policy at all. Of the other seven, one school had had a Media Education

Policy in place for some time. This had been researched and written up. The staff had a great interest in Media Education; they collaborated in team-teaching and were constantly engaged in the design and production of new teaching materials. Another teacher spoke of a policy that was a very general guideline on how to use the media rather than Media Education. Three of the schools were either working on new policies for Media Education or were revising old ones. In one case, a teacher had been asked to rework the Media Education policy, which was perceived as being too technicist. One of the interviewees, a full-time Bachelor of Education student, was devising a Media Education policy for his school as part of his academic studies, and hoped to implement the policy when he returned to the school the following year. In addition, three of the teachers were themselves involved in the construction of a Media Education policy for their schools. Again, this points to the enthusiasm and commitment of this particular sample of teachers.

The majority of the teachers (seven) asserted that their aim for their pupils was that they should become critical thinkers. What is of interest here is what the teachers understand by the word 'critical' which does not necessarily accord with notions of critical pedagogy as discussed earlier in this chapter. This is illustrated by what the interviewees perceived to be the key concepts in Media Education. Only four of the teachers revealed that they had any understanding of the concepts which underpin critical pedagogy as evidenced by their responses, which revealed an understanding of the social construction of reality and the notions of representation and agency. Perhaps predictably, all four teachers had a formal background in Media Education (two were currently Bachelor of Education students, one had an Honor's degree that included a component on Media Studies, and the fourth was reading for a Master's degree in Media Education).

Other responses indicated that teachers were coming from different educational paradigms. For example, one teacher stated that for him the two key concepts in Media Education were intention and a consideration of how that intention was expressed in the work. Whether consciously or unconsciously, it would seem that he was operating from a Liberal–Humanist position in which the intention of the author is paramount. Another offered a generalized and unspecific answer about the nature of communication and the effectiveness of communication; whereas yet another spoke of key concepts as being "to use the life experience that the children have." Knowledge of the British Film Institute's 'Signpost Questions' was limited to those who had experienced a formal course of study in Media Education.

Other aims isolated for pupils in Media Education were "self-development of pupils and upliftment of their state of being," lofty goals indeed, but the precise meaning and implications were not clear. Another's aims were to encourage pupils to become more literate and to be able to use comparative texts and nonverbal texts. Another spoke of learning broad life skills and developing effective users of English. A young Indian teacher at a multicultural school stated that her aim was to get her pupils to respond, interact, and communicate, and to update them with current information. One teacher who was teaching second-language pupils had straightforward and a pragmatic aim: she wanted her pupils to compete with mother-tongue speakers of English and to pass the matriculation examination (the final school-leaving examination in South Africa). Her second aim was that they should grow as individuals and develop their own viewpoint. Interestingly, she stated as a key concept that media are all around children's lives and that they should learn to be critical.

Most of the teachers reported that their pupils responded very well to Media work, although one teacher qualified her comment by saying that her lessons were not always successful in the way that she expected them to be. One teacher reported that pupils initially regarded Media Education lessons as being free periods, then when they realized that they were expected to put in a considerable amount themselves, there was resistance and finally, when they engaged fully with the subject, real interest was generated. Several teachers commented that their pupils reacted positively because the material was familiar to them: It was relevant and part of their everyday lives. The general consensus was that pupils were never apathetic about the work.

All of the teachers agreed that their teaching was influenced by their own views about media and society. Two teachers cautioned that they had to be careful not to impose their own views on their pupils. One teacher at a large, formerly White middle-class boys' high school confessed that before embarking on his Bachelor of Education studies his main motivation had been to protect his pupils against undesirable media.

In response to the question about difficulty with regard to concepts, four teachers replied that they had none. Two reported difficulty with semiology and another that she was not very good at theory. An Indian teacher reported difficulty with race because "prejudices go deep." One teacher expressed a problem with the word 'Media', which he felt was "a bit broad," and that one was really looking at communication. He commented that there were different perceptions of what is meant by Media and that perhaps there should be a more specific frame of reference.

The teachers were, without exception, convinced that Media Education had a very important role to play in South Africa over the next 10 years. They emphasized different aspects and values of Media Education: it is a life skill that is an ongoing process beyond formal education; It helps pupils to understand themselves and society; literature should be de-emphasized, and Media Education should be given more space; it should play a central role in the English curriculum, not a peripheral one as it does at present; it will provide common ground for communication in the new multilingual, multicultural educational dispensation in South Africa; it makes connections with the modern world, and it is fundamentally important for the survival of English.

Teachers varied with regard to the areas of Media work in which they felt most comfortable. One teacher claimed to have no uncomfortable zone. Six of them expressed a preference for film, although one included advertising, newspapers, and posters as well, and another included comics and comparative studies of media.

One teacher stated that she avoided film because "it takes too much time," one concentrated on television, another on advertisements, and three focused on cartoons, comic strips, newspapers, and magazines. One teacher at a multicultural school stated that she avoided television because many children do not have it at home.

As to content, three of the teachers claimed that there were no topics which they avoided. Two steered clear of political issues; two Indian teachers avoided religion because their pupils were sensitive to religious issues; another male teacher in a church school avoided religion because he is agnostic and "it didn't go down too well"; another balked at explicitly sexual content and a male teacher at a boys' high school avoided religion and sex. There were two original replies. One teacher avoided whatever the pupils are exposed to at home and attempted to bring in new material, whereas another avoided discussing Agency as in the British Film Institute ' Signpost Questions!'

Approaches to the teaching of Media were different in every case. The following is a summary of the various categories of aims, activities, curricular approaches, and classroom methods that teachers identified:

- The teaching of concepts, drawing on pupils' experiences, and facilitating a critical understanding of texts.
- A thematic approach using media wherever possible.
- An introduction to emotive language, moving on to radio and television commercials and film: focus on the director's intentions and how these are expressed in film.
- Teacher presentation followed by group work concentrating on familiar media.
- Examination of a range of media and working toward a comparative analysis of media.
- Whole class discussion followed by some activity.
- Pupils bringing their own material to the classroom as a starting point for lessons.
- Attempting to integrate Media with all English teaching, making explicit connections with the world around.

With regard to teachers new to Media Education, four of the participants suggested that teachers should become aware of the Media around them and explore creative ways of teaching it. "Pay attention to your children's voices," said one, "and go for variety, avoiding whole texts." Two recommended developing a framework of concepts as a basis, and one suggested watching a lot of film and persuasive material and analyzing how persuasion works. Two advocated reading seminal texts like *Media Matters in South Africa* (Prinsloo & Criticos, 1991). One would give advice on courses and libraries, and two suggested a 'jump-in-the-deep-end' approach, taking risks and learning from mistakes.

Most of the teachers felt that their work in Media Education had influenced the way in which they taught other subjects, but they were sharply divided as to whether their background in literary studies had influenced the way in which they taught Media. Four of them were adamant that their studies in English Literature had not prepared them for teaching Media Education: Indeed, two of these stated that the reverse was true, that the teaching of Media influenced the way in which they teach English literature. The remaining eight acknowledged that their English studies had informed their teaching of Media in various ways. It was pointed out that a number of aspects of literary theory can be applied to Media texts.

Teachers had different understandings of what was meant by "useful resources." Two teachers referred to hardware like the camera and the videocassette recorder. One mentioned key introductory texts. Another preferred published materials specifically designed for classroom use. Six teachers articulated a preference for the print media, especially newspapers. One teacher stated that his resources were determined by the teaching context, but that he would use any popular culture media text and found music videos an interesting resource. A teacher who had worked in the advertising business for a number of years said that the commercial world provided him with most of his resources.

As has already been mentioned, all of the teachers stated that they produced their own resources. They felt that they were more comfortable with material that they had designed themselves, even if they had derived the concept from elsewhere. It was important to renew resources all the time. The teachers' working groups provided a valuable opportunity for the sharing of ideas and resources. One notable case was a teacher at an independent school who had produced a 15-minute video entitled *Imagery and Meaning in Film.* During the interview the teacher explained: "It begins with an analysis of what art tries to do, and tries to differentiate between written and visual expression." It is designed for teaching purposes and, according to the producer, "fills a 40-minute period nicely." He poses questions and then the idea is that it allows for teachers to pause and discuss various aspects with pupils. The focus is on the director's intention and how he achieves that intention, using filmic devices. The aim of the video is to prepare pupils for the study of a full-length feature film. The teacher admitted that he "teach(es) film like a book essentially," and that ultimately the pupils will be writing a literary essay on the film itself.

This particular teacher comes from a commercial background. His 11 years of teaching were interrupted by a stint of 8 years working for an advertising agency. His own views on Media Education are articulated in a document written for a national competition to find "the best teacher in South Africa," in which he gained second place and in which he said:

If the pupil can take with him [*sic*] clarity and precision in speaking, reading and writing; an appreciation of the manipulative power of language and the media; an enrichment of his understanding of literature and its insights into the human condition, he will have acquired a small basis by which to comprehend and control his world.

In the lesson observed, this teacher's stated aim was to demonstrate the combined power of words and images on the screen and the emotive power of the visual image, through an analysis of television commercials and the music video *In the Living Years*. The lesson was a clear reflection of this teacher's stated position in the interview and his document on education. He isolated two key concepts in Media Education—intention, and how that intention is expressed. It is clear that this teacher, whether consciously or unconsciously, was teaching from a Liberal–Humanist position, so his own notion of a critical pedagogy or what he refers to as "living consciously" resides in that paradigm.

The majority of the teachers interviewed supported the notion of a teachers' resource center that was accessible in time and space. This should house a library of reference texts, teaching materials, and the facilities to produce materials. Space should be provided for the meeting of teacher support groups. Personnel with the relevant expertise should be available for guidance and consultation. One suggestion was for a recognized national policy of Media Education. A need was expressed for a professional body to promote Media Education, and a suggestion was made that a Media Education association be formed. The value of teachers' working groups was also articulated. There was general consensus that there should be more dialogue among those parties with an interest in Media Education: education departments, schools, teacher education colleges, and universities. In this way a climate of sharing could be created, enabling teachers to empower each other in the face of the new educational dispensation.

LESSON OBSERVATIONS

In addition to the lesson referred to above, advertising was the topic of two other lessons that were observed. One focused on the development of pupils' awareness of the different aspects of an advertisement through a group activity. The other aimed to raise pupils' awareness of emotive language in magazine advertising. In another lesson the teacher aimed to raise the consciousness about the pupils of the working conditions of domestic workers, through the use of constructed material (a slave-sale poster), advertisements, cartoons, and video (see Fig. 4.2).

He employed group work and worksheets. Another teacher concentrated on the development of verbal and nonverbal communication skills using excerpts from a film, *The Breakfast Club*, overhead transparencies illustrating body language, and small-group discussion in order to enable her pupils to make the ideas their own.

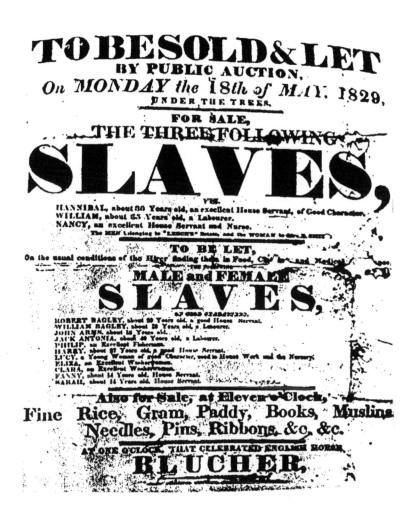

Ciskei Manpower Development Centre advertisement, Daily Dispatch, January 30 1981

FIG. 4.2. Two examples of slave sale posters.

Another teacher devised a Media Education program based on a text of short stories called *Deep Cuts* (see Fig. 4.3).

FIG. 4.3. *Deep Cuts* Comic figure (reproduced with permission of Neil Napper of the Storyteller Group, Johannesburg, South Africa).

The text also appears in comic form. The teacher was employed at an NED school[5] in which all of the pupils were Black second-language speakers of English. The teacher chose this text for three reasons: It appears in both print and comic form; the subject matter is accessible to second-language learners of English; and the book is relatively inexpensive. The program is designed to last five weeks and the stated aims are:

- To teach the pupils how to read the text.
- To introduce pupils to new terminology.
- To enjoy the printed text as well as the comic form.

It is important to register that her overall aim was to use the cartoon text in order to facilitate the transition to the written text. In this particular case, the pupils were second-language pupils of English who were learning through the medium of English, and would be writing the same final school-leaving examination as mother-tongue speakers of English. The teacher was determined that they would be able to compete effectively. This was her overall stated aim, but in pursuing it, she also attempted to facilitate critical thinking in her pupils by encouraging them to think about the differences between the verbal and the visual text; why certain images had been chosen, and what the stories were saying about the role of women in society. Interestingly, this teacher was one who declared that she had no knowledge of theory and works "very much on instinct." Although she was not familiar with the dominant discourse of Media Education, she had a clear practical sense of the processes of representation and the construction of reality.

A Media program on myths and Super Heroes, which was developed at a previously white boys' high school, is aimed at a Standard 9 group (the penultimate year of school in South Africa). The School's stated aims for this program[6] are:

- To facilitate an awareness of the manner in which one's sense of reality is manipulated by a sophisticated machinery of mass media which bombards one with value systems entrenched in an ideology which is essentially escapist, sexist and orientated toward an extreme and supposedly justifiable use of violence.
- The focus of the program is not on 'teaching' per se, but, instead, on allowing the pupil to observe, to interpret and to arrive at his [sic!] own conclusions and thereby to become a critical consumer of film.

---

[5]At the time of the interview, this was the only secondary school of this nature in the Durban Functional Region, and its establishment arose from the initiatives of the government to open schools to children of other ethnic groups after the announcement by the then State President at the beginning of 1990, which opened the was to majority rule.

[6]'Cedarwood' Boys' High School: Standard 9 Media Program, 1993.

• The success of this program will evolve out of the nonimposition of a viewpoint—the teacher is there purely to guide or facilitate the process.

The idea underlying this material is the study of myth looking at the way in which comics are used in creating Super Hero myths. The teacher adopts a sociological stance in examining how comics are used in the creation of these myths. This is then related to issues such as stereotype, propaganda, and the phenomenon of political cartoons. His aims are to facilitate an awareness of the way in which the reader's sense of reality is manipulated, and to make pupils critically conscious of film, to be able to see what the producers of the film have chosen to exclude. This teacher is very clear about his teaching aims. Learning cannot take place through transmission: It is only through the pupils' active engagement that learning can take place. Teaching is about teaching children how to think and to shake them out of complacency.

In the observed lesson, which was designed to instill an awareness of the paradigms operating behind films, the teacher showed a series of film clips that illustrated the development of the Super Hero by examining the processes of selection and the construction of reality. This was a 'one-off' lesson designed to demonstrate the material, aims, and objectives of the program. By the teacher's own admission this was a teacher-directed lesson. Ideally, he claimed, he would have employed a more participatory, facilitative mode of teaching and learning in which the pupils would arrive at an awareness themselves. "I have a strong perception of what I want to achieve but I like to facilitate rather than impose. Often I don't know what is going to come out of a lesson. That is what happened with the Super Hero program—I come back to things later."

Various aims, objectives, methods, and materials were employed in the lessons observed. In one case a teacher aimed to develop his pupils' awareness of representation and the construction of reality in the media, particularly the press. He chose a controversial local topic on conservation, and by means of overhead transparencies of press cuttings and careful questioning of his pupils he facilitated their understanding of the process of selection and the construction of reality in newspaper journalism.

> Pupils are going to look at a particular issue which has been reported in the newspaper. They are going to focus on representation and reconstruction of reality and visual text—look at their positions and that of the newspaper—how it has constructed its stance.
>
> … This is a one-off lesson but I would have given a series of lessons on representation—would look at other media—magazines, cartoons, radio, TV, and film.

In another lesson, which focused on representation and the construction of reality, the teacher chose a political cartoon (see Fig. 4.4). In this lesson, the teacher

FIG. 4.4. Political cartoon figure (reproduced by permission of the *Daily News* newspaper, Durban, KwaZulu-Natal).

focused on the selection of visual images and language. Through means of judicious questioning, the teacher guided the pupils to an understanding of the positioning of figures in the cartoon, and the connotations of the images and the language, which led to a discussion on stereotyping. The teacher emphasized that the cartoon was somebody's idea of reality. In another lesson, the teacher's aim was to develop the pupils' skills in argumentative writing with reference to newspaper reportage of the Rugby Union World Cup. She focused on the concepts of bias, agency, audience, and message.

Another teacher aimed to explore meaning in photographs, and to develop in her pupils a critical reading of photographic texts. This involved teacher presentation in which technical and symbolic codes were explained and illustrated, followed by the pupils engagement in a task to facilitate their understanding of these codes.

This selection of lessons and materials revealed a group of teachers who are dynamically engaged in the negotiation of meaning with their pupils; who are concerned that in their teaching of English they are facilitating their learners' critical understanding of the world around them. In some instances they approach the task with a consciousness of the theoretical paradigms and concepts that inform the work. In other cases it would appear to be an intuitive approach that achieves the intended outcome without an explicit knowledge of theory.

CONCLUSIONS

Media Education in the Development
of a Critical Citizenry

In South Africa, the African National Congress (ANC) Draft Policy Framework for Education and Training statement on Goals and Values states that:

> The education and training system under apartheid has been characterized by frag-
> mentation along racial and ethnic lines, widespread inequalities in access to education
> services and lack of democratic control by participants in the system. This situation
> has resulted in the destruction of human potential and has had harmful consequences
> for social and economic development. The challenge facing us now is to create an
> education and training system that will develop human resources and potential to the
> full and empower all citizens by opening the doors of learning and culture to all.
> (Education Policy Unit, 1994, p. 1)

In the face of this challenge to create an education and training system that will develop human potential and bring about a democratic citizenry, Media Education has a potentially valuable role to play. It is pertinent to note the views of the Media Education teachers in the survey. Their overwhelming response was that Media Education is a potentially liberating force. They were conscious of the need to escape from the dominant paradigm of Transmission Education that has informed much teaching in South Africa. In their desire to facilitate in their pupils a broader understanding of the world around them, beyond the prescribed syllabus, they have found Media to be a rich vein of resources.

The teachers identified a range of different aspects and values of Media Education: It helps pupils understand themselves and society, echoing Bob Ferguson's description of Media Education as "an endless enquiry into the way we make sense of the world and the ways others makes sense of the world for us" (Prinsloo & Criticos, 1991, p. 20). It is a life skill that is an ongoing process beyond formal education: teaching pupils to be critical thinkers; to be critically literate.

It is generally recognized that Media Education has a formative role to play in developing countries. At the Toulouse Colloquy in 1990, international media educationists attempted to explore *New Directions in Media Education*, and the task of one of the three Commissions was to investigate Media Education in developing countries. Among their recommendations, they acknowledged that Media Education outside the formal education system deserves particular attention, and that organizations have an important function. They stressed "those aspects of Media Education which enable individuals and groups to contribute actively to endogenous cultural development" (Bazalgette et al., 1992 p. 233).

There is no doubt of the value of Media Education in developing a critical citizenry for the new South Africa. The problem is that very nearly 80% of the school population have not been exposed to Media Education at all, which leads to a consideration of its place in the curriculum.

Media Education in the Curriculum

In the interviews, the teachers recommended that literature from the canon of high culture should be de-emphasized and Media Education, which by its very nature includes a wide variety of popular texts, should be given more space; indeed, it should be central to the English curriculum, not peripheral as it is at present.

Within the previously White education authority (the NED), the initiatives for introducing Media Education have rested largely with enthusiastic teachers. This is partly because Film Study is an option in the Senior Certificate syllabus and is perceived as being a luxury. In 1993 the English Subject Advisor in the NED gathered together a group of concerned teachers to confront the problem of teaching English to rapidly growing multilingual, multicultural classes consisting of mother-tongue and second-language learners. A draft document was drawn up that proposes narrative as the common textual experience of all the learners. It argues for a wide range of textual materials in a variety of forms, and diverts attention from the content to the process of narrative construction by the narrator and the receiver.

Understanding Media Education

This study draws attention to the fact that there are different understandings of Media Education. What teachers understand by the word 'critical' does not neces-sarily accord with the notions of critical pedagogy as discussed earlier in this chapter. This is illustrated by what the interviewees perceived to be the key concepts in Media Education. The responses revealed that only those teachers who had a formal background in Media Education had an understanding of the concepts that underpin critical pedagogy. Other responses indicated that teachers were rooted in different educational paradigms, particularly Liberal Humanism.

If Media Education is to take root in any significant way, it will have to be implemented by teachers. This means that there is an urgent need to incorporate Media Education into teacher education programs at both preservice and in-service levels. The findings of the survey highlighted that seven of the teachers interviewed had had formal training in Media Education. This is, however, a select group chosen because they are themselves concerned and committed practitioners of Media Education. They are not representative of the majority of the English teachers in either the region or the country. At this time of educational transition it is crucial for curriculum planners to take cognizance of Media Education.

Pedagogical Implications

It follows from this that Media Education requires a different approach to education that is opposed to the Transmission content-based approach described by Paulo

Freire as "banking education." It is pupil-centered and engages learners in their own construction of knowledge. All of this needs to be incorporated into teacher education programs. It involves important shifts in the perceptions of teachers with regard to their own role, not as purveyors of knowledge but as participants with their pupils in the enterprise of the negotiation of meaning.

Teachers' Support Groups and Resource Centers

Teachers emphasized the importance of being able to collaborate with other teachers in the promotion of Media Education. This is already happening informally, as is evidenced by the teachers' support groups, like the working group on narrative at the University of Natal. Teachers felt, however, that there should be other formal structures like the establishment of a teachers' resource center that offers a library of texts, facilities to produce materials and space for teachers to meet. Media Education teachers, who are very often working in isolation, feel keenly the need to have some recognized central point.

Media Education Policy

To date there has been no uniform policy of Media Education in South Africa. There is clearly a need for a policy at the level of both formal educational structures and the school. It is not clear at this juncture how Media Education will be included in either national or regional educational policy. However, there is nothing to prevent schools from formulating their own policies, as some of them are already doing. One school had had a Media Education policy in place for some time. In three other schools, teachers were either working on new policies or were revising old ones. In two of the schools teacher-librarians were already offering comprehensive Media Education courses. This is an initiative that might well be pursued by other schools, although it does presuppose appropriate resources in terms of expertise and equipment. It is an area that might well be examined in further research.

The study demonstrated convincingly that materials from elsewhere cannot be applied indiscriminately in the South African context. South Africa is in a unique position in its history, and although ideas may be borrowed from other countries, they will need to be adapted to the local situation. All of the teachers had developed their own materials: videos to introduce an approach to the study of film; Afro-centric narratives, that are represented in both comic strips and printed text in order to facilitate the reading competence of second-language speakers of English; comic strips and video clips of Super Hero characters as an entrée to a study of myth and stereotypes, and press cuttings from local newspapers in order to illustrate notions of representation and agency. Other media included photographs, advertisements, political cartoons, propaganda and specially constructed texts directed toward developing a critical consciousness of the construction of reality.

Teaching Media Education means, among other things, teaching Critical Language Awareness (CLA). Language can be used, and is used, to maintain and challenge existing forms of power. "What makes CLA critical is its concern with the politics of meaning; the ways in which dominant meanings are maintained, challenged and changed." (Janks, 1993, p. iii). *The Critical Language Awareness* series is an example of texts that have been locally produced, and that provide interesting and relevant material for the South African student. It is pertinent to note that none of the teachers interviewed referred to these books. Presumably they had not encountered them.

LIMITATIONS OF RESEARCH AND DIRECTIONS FOR THE FUTURE

Any hope that Media Education might be introduced in all schools through the ongoing curriculum reform process has dissipated—it has not been picked up as a priority issue in the national curriculum debates. The demands of national reconstruction and redress will have taken attention away from curricular initiatives such as Media Education. These demands include the need to address urgently the critical shortage of classrooms, an illiteracy rate as high as 60% in some provinces, grossly underqualified teachers, and pressure to replicate the Asian economies that have reaped the benefits of technological education.

Given these major preoccupations, Media Education may either be shelved as a peripheral curriculum initiative or acknowledged as an essential weapon to improve education and prepare citizens for democracy. If the latter is to be realized, then those who are promoting it need to acknowledge its current weak status and begin to work out how to popularize it through association with curriculum priorities, and by demonstrating its utility across the curriculum.[7]

There are several implications for future research. The first point is the limitation imposed by the size of the sample. It is a relatively homogenous grouping of nine White and three Indian teachers, all of whom speak English as their first language and who cannot be seen as representative of the English teaching population of the country. In a country where only 8.6% of the population are mother-tongue speakers of English, the reality is that the majority of the English teachers speak English as a second language. Second, the sample is drawn from one geographical area, one

---

[7]One exemplary case of advancing the ideals of Media Education through an integrated curriculum is the *Integrated Approach Series* published Sacred Heart College. These materials,which were developed and given a trial run at the college, incorporate Media Education in an integrated way. In Unit 5 of *Going Places*, one of the books in a series, the students become enmeshed in the debate between conservation and mining. Part of the evidence that students consider relate to media reports on the debate. They are also directed to exercises in which they produce media texts on the issue. For these authors Media Education in analytical, creative, and integrated.

of the nine new provinces of South Africa, KwaZulu–Natal, which is again not representative of the ethnic and linguistic variety of the rest of South Africa. A third point, which was discussed at length in the overview of the history of South African education, is that the teachers are drawn from the previous White and Indian education authorities. There are cogent reasons for this: It is in the NED where Media Education has first taken root in the region, followed by the Indian education authority, the HOD.

It might be helpful in the future to widen the sample to include more Indian teachers who have been involved in Media Education. Older, more experienced teachers from the ex-HOA schools might also be interviewed. However, it needs to be remembered that the White NED and the Indian HOD together constitute only 22% of the region's school population. Perhaps the study should be broadened out to involve teachers from other regions as well.

Collaboration with other Teacher Education institutions in the region as well as in the nation could be pursued fruitfully. The new norms and standards for teacher education in South Africa are currently being implemented. Whereas the new document unfortunately makes no specific reference to Media Education, the new policy focuses on competencies and outcomes, and allows for far greater autonomy on the part of teacher education institutions to draw up their own curricula appropriate to their own constituencies and unique visions of education. This is an opportune moment to investigate the possibilities of introducing Media Education into the curricula.

As noted earlier, because Media Education has not been part of the curriculum in Black schools to date, there were no teachers to interview in this survey. One research program that has grown out of this particular project is an investigation into the acquisition of visual literacy among second-language speakers of English at preprimary level.

This research points to a pressing need to involve African teachers to facilitate an awareness of the role that Media Education can play in the development of a new educational dispensation in South Africa. This in turn, will contribute to the growth of a new generation of citizens able to think critically about the world in which they live, empowering them to participate creatively, morally and responsibly in the new democratic society of South Africa. The way forward is located in the children and their world. As one teacher commented poignantly: "Pay attention to your children's voices."

REFERENCES

Bazalgette, C., Bévort, E., & Savino, J. (Eds.). (1992). *New directions in Media Education*. London/Paris: BFI/CLEMI.

Behr, A. L. (1988). *Education in South Africa. Origins, issues and trends: 1652–1988*. Cape Town: Academia.

Court, S. (1996). Listen to the childrens' voices: The role of media education in developing critical literacy in South African school children. *Continuum, 9*(2), 86–93.

Education Policy Unit. (1994). *Summary of ANC draft policy framework for education and training.* Johannesburg: Author.

Faasen, N. (1991). Media and film studies in schools of the Cape Education Department. In J. Prinsloo & C. Criticos (Eds.), *Media matters in South Africa* (pp. 29–31). Durban: University of Natal, Media Resource Center.

Hart, A., & Benson, A. (1993). *Media in the classroom.* Southampton: Southampton Media Education Group.

Instituut vir Christelike Nasionale Onderwys. (1948). Federation of Afrikaans Cultural Societies: Johannesburg.

Janks, H. (1993). General Introduction to *The critical language awareness series.* Johannesburg: Hodder & Stoughton in association with Witwatersrand University Press.

Kallaway, P. (Ed.). (1984). *Apartheid and education: The education of black South Africans.* Cape Town: Galvin & Sales.

Prinsloo, J. (1995). Media education and the reconstruction of South Africa. *Media Development, 42*(2), 18–20.

Prinsloo, J., & Criticos, C. (Eds.). (1991). *Media matters in South Africa.* Durban: University of Natal, Media Resource Centre.

5

Media Education in Western Australia

Robyn Quin
Edith Cowan University

THE CONTEXT

In 1972, television was 11 years old in Western Australia, broadcast radio had been available for 50 years, the capital Perth had (and continues to have) one of the highest ratios of cinemas to population in the world, and newspapers had played a significant role in social and political life since the founding of the colony. The term Media Education, however, was never heard nor would it have been understood by teachers, students, or the public. And yet by 1988 study of the media had become a normal part of the curriculum for all Western Australian students. Today, Media Education is a mandated part of the curriculum in every Australian state, and teaching about the media constitutes one quarter of the English syllabus from Years 1 to 12 in Western Australia. In addition to the study of the media within the compulsory subject of English, secondary students may choose to take the discrete subject Media Studies.[1] Three factors contributed to the rapid and widespread development of Media Education in Australian schools. First, the change to the school cohort in the early 1970s and related demands from teachers for relevant curriculum. Second, the timely availability of commonwealth government funds for teachers' professional development, and third a major reconception in the 1970s of the purpose and nature of English teaching.

Although educators and educational administrators frequently boast that Australia is at the forefront in the implementation of Media Education, its introduction

---

[1]Although English is one of the eight 'learning areas' established by the Australian Education Council in 1991 and accepted by all states, the discrete subject Media Studies is taught within the learning areas of The Arts and Technology.

has not been uncontested by teachers, administrators, or parents, and there is not complete agreement among its adherents as to what constitutes Media Education. A secondary teacher at a large independent boys school said in response to the publication of *A National Statement on English for Australian Schools* (Curriculum Corporation) in 1994:

> While the document does acknowledge the category of 'classic literature,' this is seriously compromised by the inclusion of such texts as films and 'expository texts in disciplines such as history and science' in this definition. The effect is to place Patrick White's *Fringe of Leaves* or Jane Austen's *Emma* on the same footing as *Sylvania Waters*.

In contrast, a teacher at a government secondary school said: "For those educationalists and academics who fought for the inclusion of media analysis in mainstream English courses this recognition of the mass media as a legitimate sphere of study is long overdue."

The interviews with teachers and classroom observations discussed later in this chapter illustrate the different interpretations of Media Education and the some-times contradictory philosophies that underpin the teaching about the media in the English classroom in Western Australian schools.

In 1970, school curricula were rigidly controlled, unabashedly traditional, externally examined, and marked by a strict hierarchy of disciplines. Teachers were becoming increasingly dissatisfied with the existing curricula, a dissatisfaction fueled by the problems of dealing with the growing number of students remaining at school beyond the compulsory leaving age. Between 1955 and 1965, the retention rate to Year 10 in government schools increased from 40% to 75%. In the next 3 years, following the raising of the school leaving age from 14 to 15, it jumped to almost 90% (Dettman, 1969, p. 32). The increase in retention rates led to a questioning of the relevance of the traditional curriculum and its teaching methods. The dissatisfaction was both with the content of the curriculum and the individu-alistic desk-bound, pen-and-paper approach to learning which the public examina-tion system fostered (Quin & Quin, 1994, p. 112). As in other parts of the world, Australian teachers began to search for ways to make curricula and learning methods more relevant not only to the 'new type' of secondary student, but to all students who would live their lives in the second part of the 20th century and the first part of the 21st.

A particular focus of interest for many lay in the potential offered by the new (at that time) technologies of communication. In particular they were attracted by the relatively cheap technologies of Super 8 film making and VHS portable VCRs. Barrie McMahon, a secondary English department head in the early 1970s, recalls his initial interest in Media Studies:

> I was organizing an English camp at Hamilton Senior High School and searching for
> something to do that did not involve sitting down at a desk and writing. It was obvious
> that the traditional English activities of drama, spoken English and debating were not
> going to be a big attraction. One of the first-year-out teachers said that she knew of
> someone at another school who taught film making in his drama class. I invited Ray
> (the teacher) to the camp and we took turns shadowing him as he introduced each
> group to Super 8 film making. At the usual postmortem review of the camp activities
> the film exercises were the ones that had captured the students' interest.

McMahon went on to organize after-hours film-making workshops for teachers,
and a loose, informal network of teachers focused on promoting film making was
established. This group was the genesis of the short-lived Screen Education Society
that aimed to expand the focus from film making to include film criticism and
television. The formation of the Screen Education Society marks a significant shift
in the early Media Studies movement in Western Australia away from a concern
with amateur film production toward an interest in the wider educational implications of the media.

At the same time that a wider conception of Media Education was developing,
some of the major barriers to the modernization of the curriculum were being
dismantled. In 1971 external examinations for 15-year-olds were abolished to be
replaced by cumulative\continuous assessment at the school level. Control over the
lower secondary curriculum was taken away from the university-dominated Public
Examinations Board and given to the school systems. Procedures were put in place
to enable schools or groups of schools to develop their own syllabuses and submit
them for accreditation to the Board of Secondary Education. Opportunities were
created for the development of new conceptions of knowledge.

In Higher Education, similar spaces were opening up, with the expansion of the
university system to include new universities offering courses in mass communications, Media Studies and Cultural Studies. For the first time, people training as
English teachers could study courses not based entirely on literature. University
academics working in Cultural Studies and Media Studies were appointed to
syllabus committees and participated in teacher in-service courses.

At the national level, the Labor government was elected in 1972 with a mandate
to increase substantially the level of commonwealth funds for education. At the
federal level, it established the Schools Commission, gave it enormous resources
and the brief to devolve control for curriculum development and innovation to the
local level. Priority in the allocation of funds was given to projects originating in
schools. Media-interested teachers were able to access these funds for physical
resources and teacher Professional Development. In Western Australia a program
of extended, live-in, fully funded Professional Development workshops was established. This program of Professional Development in Media Education ran for 8
years. The participating teachers (the vast majority of whom were English teachers)

became the media specialists in their schools, and were able to access further funds through the Schools Commission's Innovation program to get the subject off the ground in their own institutions.

The growth in popularity and respectability of Media Studies courses in schools, the changes to English teaching at the tertiary level and the challenge to traditional conceptions of English teaching posed by the emergent 'personal growth' model of English had a significant effect on the English curriculum. Until the late 1960s the English curriculum in Australia, in both content and pedagogical practice, reflected a 'cultural heritage' model (Milner, 1993, p. 13). As discussed in earlier chapters (see especially chapter 2), this approach to the teaching of English is familiar to anyone educated in the 1950s or 1960s in Britain, Australia, New Zealand, or Canada. It was marked by an emphasis on taste and critical discrimination; a belief in the power of great works of literature to teach universal truths and maintain cultural and moral values; an insistence on the responsibility of English teachers to train pupils to resist mass culture, and an adherence to a canon of worthwhile texts. It was a legacy of Matthew Arnold and F.R. Leavis, and entered English teaching through the works of Denys Thompson and David Holbrook. It did not matter that most English teachers had never read their books because the tradition was naturalized through their own school and university education, and the demands of the external examination system. The 'cultural heritage' model of English teaching was not necessarily something Australian teachers consciously chose to adopt, but rather they simply did not recognize the possibility of an alternative approach.

This 'cultural heritage' model of English teaching drew, in fact, on a British 'cultural heritage,' and most Australian literature was denied a place in the canon of works to be studied in schools. Australian literature was seen as simply not good enough. There was, however, significant opposition from English teachers to the narrow conception of literature embodied in the 'cultural heritage' model, and this opposition articulated its position in an insistence on the inclusion of Australian literary texts in the curriculum. Thus, Henry Lawson and Banjo Paterson, both populists, were given a place in the canon of this much less exclusive Australian version of the 'cultural heritage' model. The Australian variant laid the foundation for the study of Australian popular culture and Australian cultural analysis.

Developments in English teaching in Britain in the mid-1960s, and the publication of John Dixon's *Growth Through English* (1967) and James Britton's *Language and Learning* (1970) significantly affected English teaching in Australia. 'New English' or the 'personal growth' model, as it was known, successfully crossed two oceans and captured the hearts and minds of English teachers in Australia. The focus shifted from cultural transmission to language acquisition. Teachers were exhorted to begin 'where the students are at,' to negotiate the choice of texts with the class, to value and stimulate children's own written and spoken language, and to provide a range of language activities that were both developmentally appropriate and central to students' interests. The 'personal growth' model of English was actively promoted in Western Australia by the English superintendents, and widely disseminated through the English Teachers' Association publications *Backchat* and *Interpretations.*

The 'personal growth' model for English did not decrease the focus on literature, but it did use literary texts in a different way. It used literature as a springboard for personal growth and as a motivational device for eliciting personal responses. Although literary texts remained predominant, the approach allowed for the inclusion of texts, both print and visual, from outside the literary canon. Media texts, usually feature films and documentaries, were employed as motivational tools to encourage discussion and to provide the stimulus for writing. There was no encouragement from the English superintendents to make media texts in themselves objects of analysis. Those few English teachers who taught film criticism and aesthetics tended to use a methodology similar to that of literary criticism to study the film classics. But not all teachers were happy with the 'personal growth' model. Of course, there were those that believed it undermined the traditional 'cultural heritage' goals of English. Others however, criticized the 'personal growth' model on political grounds, arguing that the reading of the text was confined in this model to a view of the world that supported the *status quo.* A teacher recalling her own experience of this approach to English said:

> I began to wonder whether or not 'personal growth' meant growth away from the class, cultural and ethnic locations which my students already occupied and towards a position that assumed the values of white, masculine, middle class society; this in spite of the fact that the rhetoric of my classrooms explicitly valued what I viewed as the unique locations of individual students. (Patterson, 1992, p. 137)

Alongside and occasionally in competition with the 'personal growth' approach to English there has developed a Cultural Studies approach in Australian English education.[2] From the evidence of interviews with teachers the motivation for the introduction of Cultural Studies into English teaching has come from teachers' own experience of the discipline in their tertiary studies, and has been reinforced by their subsequent experiences in schools. This approach essentially rejects English as literature (a view shared by both 'cultural heritage' and 'personal growth models) and posits in its place English as cultural analysis. This view of English opens up spaces for popular texts and nonprint texts. It emphasizes the social processes of reading and the plurality of readings. The focus is on analysis rather than appreciation, relevance rather than worth. Language in this approach is seen as a social construct, the meaning of which is a negotiated process on the part of those who produce texts and those who 'read' them. The Cultural Studies approach to English

---

[2]This approach roughly corresponds with the 'critical' approach described in South Africa and is almost identical with the 'cultural analysis' approach described by the English Cox Report (DES, 1989) discussed in chap. 2.

does not apologize for the inclusion of visual texts as objects of study, nor does it seek to legitimize them as motivational tools. Media texts in the Cultural Studies approach are as essential to the study of English as print texts. Cultural Studies does indeed seek to place *Sylvania Waters* and *Emma* on the same footing, but for different reasons.

THE CURRENT SITUATION

Current policy statements, curriculum documents, support materials, and professional teacher publications show traces of the 'cultural heritage', the 'personal growth' and the Cultural Studies approaches to English teaching. The official documents are a compromise between the three approaches although 'personal growth' and Cultural Studies models are arguably more strongly represented. The following excerpts from *A National Statement on English for Australian Schools* (1994) and the Western Australian *Secondary Education English Syllabus* (1994) exemplify the types of incorporations and compromises that have occurred:

> Literature is fundamental to the English curriculum, although opinions differ on what distinguishes literature from other texts. Typically, literature involves the use of language and the imagination to represent, recreate, shape and explore human experience. Through composing, comprehending and responding to literature, students extend their understanding of the world and of themselves and come to see how cultural beliefs and values have been formed. (*A National Statement on English for Australian Schools*, 1994, p. 10)

> Effective teaching is based on what children already know and can do. The teaching of English will achieve most where the considerable informal language knowledge and competence of students, whatever their cultural or language backgrounds, is acknowledged, used and extended. (*A National Statement on English for Australian Schools*, 1994, p. 8)

> Many students spend more leisure time listening to, reading or viewing mass media texts than in any other activity. The English curriculum provides for critical analysis and understanding of these texts. (*A National Statement on English for Australian Schools*, 1994, p. 10)

> A key principle of this course is the principle of shaping. Making meaning with texts is an active process of shaping on the part of writers (including speakers, presenters, directors, etc.) and readers. Writers create texts in particular contexts but rely on readers to make sense of them. All texts, whether they be non-fiction, literature or non-print texts, reflect the particular attitudes and values of their writer … meanings, therefore arise out of the relationships between and among the writer, reader, text and context. (*Secondary English Syllabus*, 1995, p. 36)

Currently in Western Australia the teaching of viewing within English is mandatory in Years 1 through 10 of schooling. The upper secondary (Years 11 and 12) English syllabus requires students to study a range of popular media texts and this strand of the syllabus is externally examined. The situation is similar in other states although the study of viewing is not compulsory in the early years of schooling in two other states, Victoria and New South Wales.

The next section of this chapter examines teachers' aims, views about, and practices in Media Education. It demonstrates that teachers in Western Australian schools are generally receptive to the inclusion of viewing in English, and confident of their own ability to teach about the media. The material was gathered for the international extension of the *Models of Media Education* project conducted in the School of Education at the University of Southampton (Hart & Benson, 1993). The ways in which the data were collected in Western Australia need some explanation because the methodology was not as systematic as in the original project. During 1994 and 1995, 23 teachers of English were interviewed about their opinions on, and classroom applications of, the Media strand in the English syllabus at lower high school level. In the selection of the interviewees, there was no attempt to randomize the sample nor make it representative. The subjects were chosen primarily on the basis of ease of access. Most of the 23 teachers worked nearby, were involved in the teacher training program of the researcher's own university, or were personally known to the researcher. The approach could be kindly described as eclectic. Of the original group, 10 were selected for further investigation in the form of interviews and lesson observations. Again, there was no consistent selection criterion applied in the choice of the 10 teachers for follow-up sessions. Generally, as in the England, Northern Ireland, and South Africa studies, they were chosen on the basis of their willingness to participate in the project, although there was an attempt to include males and females, government and nongovernment school teachers.

The arbitrariness of the method of selection meant that no teachers from outside the metropolitan area were included in the sample. The noninclusion of teachers from the country areas has implications for the age and experience of the teachers in the sample.[3] The teachers included in the case studies that follow are not, therefore, representative of Western Australian teachers. Although the sample group were, in general, enthusiastic about Media Education, their views are not shared by all in the system. There continues to be resistance from some teachers to the teaching of viewing and visual texts, and resentment about its place as a compulsory part of English. For example, a lecturer responsible for English teacher education at Edith Cowan University in Perth, says:

> The visual literacy pendulum, like all pendulums, has swung too far. Certainly there was a time when English teachers paid too little attention to the messages of the picture. We needed to have helpful Media Studies colleagues teach us the basics of reading pictures. But let's not go overboard on this as seems to have happened when English teachers who feel perfectly confident in approaching *Dons' Party* or *The Club*

---

[3]In Western Australia, young teachers are sent to the country and a city posting is a reward for years of service.

as stage performances suddenly, apparently, feel incapable of studying those same narratives in film. Pictures add something, but they are not that important. Language, that is verbal language, is still king. In a television news story it is language that comes first; with pictures added later. In documentary it is the language of voice-over that tells us how to read a montage. And in a film it is dialogue that does the main job of establishing character, theme and plot.... The only problems I have found in teaching film and television arise from the purely practical difficulties of studying something that is visual and so ruthlessly linear. It is so much easier to study when we have something on paper which we can read and re-read. Obviously it is easier to study the dialogue and the visual if you have information about them on the page in front of you.

SELECTED CASE STUDIES

The following material is drawn from the study just described. Ten teachers were interviewed and then observed teaching one or more media lessons. All of the teachers were English teachers with more than 5 years experience and, without exception, all supported the inclusion of viewing skills and nonprint texts in the curriculum. Some of the teachers saw themselves as primarily teachers of English Literature in that literature was their first love, but the scarcity of literature classes in upper school meant that for the most part they were forced to teach the subject English. Others, although appointed as English teachers, saw themselves as Media teachers and either had taught, or were currently teaching, the subject Media Studies in addition to their teaching of English.[4]

The teachers currently spend, according to their own estimates, between 20% and 33% of their teaching time in English on the study of nonprint texts. The majority argued that more time should be spent teaching about the media but felt that the syllabus did not allow for this. Their reasons for promoting the study of the media in English were similar and referred frequently to students' enjoyment of this aspect of English and positive student responses to media texts. One teacher said she felt "the need to take advantage of children's willingness to 'read' visual texts," whereas another argued the need for more time to be spent on study of the media "because students are immersed in the visual culture all the time and have a good knowledge of it—we need to teach them to interpret and discriminate what they are watching" [sic]. The view that children had a good knowledge of the media was expressed by a number of the respondents and is best summed up by:

> For a change they can prove they know something. When I am teaching print texts it is always the same. They know nothing and I know everything. At my school they are viewers, not readers, and already know a lot about films and television. Media

---

[4]In Western Australia, Media Studies specialist teachers are required to have English as their second teaching area. Structurally, the Media Studies teaches are responsible to the Head of Department of English in the school. In Years 11 and 12 students may choose to study Senior English, English, or English Literature. Only the latter two subjects qualify for inclusion in a tertiary entrance score.

classes give them the chance to demonstrate their knowledge and so I exploit it heavily. The students really tap into it.

The media texts selected by the 10 teachers for inclusion in their English program were an eclectic mix. The teachers used extensively popular magazines such as *Dolly* and *Girlfriend*, television, surfing and motorbike magazines and used more occasionally serious magazines like *Time* and *The Bulletin*. Popular television choices included the American series *Roseanne* and *The Simpsons*, Australian programs such as *G.P.*, *Blue Heelers* and *Neighbours*, and current affairs and advertising. Although they are available for off-air recording, none of the teachers mentioned that they used British television programs (although, in fact, one teacher was using British texts). When pressed on this issue one of the teachers recalled using an episode of *Yes, Prime Minister* to demonstrate a point about irony, but felt that it was too sophisticated for the 14-year-old students. The teachers' criteria for using specific television programs appeared to be based primarily on the popular appeal of the program, and secondarily on the suitability of the text for the particular concepts they wished to teach. The source of the text, British, Australian, or American, or commercial/noncommercial broadcasting, played no part in teachers' considerations in choosing television texts for study purposes.

The interviews and discussions with teachers about their film choices produced a different story. They seemed to use a different set of criteria in deciding which feature films to analyze in the classroom. Issues of quality were mentioned by all 10 teachers as a concern in their choices of feature films. Quality, however, meant different things to different people. One teacher defined quality features as "ones that have some ideological basis or ones that you can use to comment on some aspects of society," and gave the examples of *Platoon, Dances With Wolves, Gallipoli,* and *Pretty Woman* as quality films. Another teacher listed the 'quality' films that she liked to use as *Dances With Wolves, Witness, Educating Rita, Aladdin, The Lion King, The Man From Snowy River, Stand By Me, The Glass Menagerie,* and Polanski's *MacBeth*. One respondent equated quality with "the films that have strong themes like growing up or dealing with conflict." Two of the teachers stressed that they liked to use Australian films and named *Gallipoli, The Man From Snowy River,* and *Crocodile Dundee* as favorites. It was interesting to note in these two instances that the teachers assumed their decision to use Australian material demonstrated their commitment to quality in their choice of texts for teaching.

All of the teachers participating in the study had a strong background in literature, and all stated that they felt this background was a help in preparing them to teach about media texts. As evidence they cited the importance of understanding narrative and characterization although one teacher said: "As I see it, concepts such as representation and ideology that modern literary theory is emphasizing apply to all texts, including media."

An English department head described his literature background as both a help and a hindrance to his ability to teach media texts. On the positive side, he believed it had given him "skills in close textual analysis and the understanding that apparently transparent texts are complex constructions." But he felt that his educational background in "New Criticism and unthinking British 'cultural heritage'" had failed him in that "it did not articulate the reasons for the study of language and literature" and "did not ground the study of language and literature in a wider social context."

Five of the 10 participating teachers had studied Communications/Cultural Studies at a university and of these, two had quite extensive experience in teaching the subject Media Studies. All five had been teaching for some years and were familiar with, but to different extents, the three approaches to English outlined earlier in the chapter. Their description of their own approach, was in their words, "a mixture of 'growth' and Cultural Studies' approaches." They regarded their own knowledge of the media as their prime resource for teaching about it. The other five teachers, those without formal training in Media Studies or Media pedagogy, claimed to be comfortable with teaching about the media. They cited other teachers, Professional Development programs, and student media resource books, in that order, as their major sources of information for teaching about the media. Only one teacher cited the media themselves as major sources of information and knowledge about film and television: "I always watch *Media Watch* and *Review*, and I read the film reviews in the newspaper." This same teacher was the only person to mention the Internet as a resource in teaching about the media. She regularly used it to search for background material, stills, and reviews.

> There is a lot of high quality material on the internet if you know how to find it. There is information about current television programs, summaries of all the episodes, information about actors, reviews and pictures from features. I recently searched the Net for material on Robin Hood and I found a list of all the films that had ever been made about the legend, a copy of the lyrics from the old TV series and printed versions of the story. There was enough there for a whole unit of work.

The resources used by teachers in their media classes were books and videos. The books were invariably student resource books containing minimal amounts of discursive information and a large number of student activities. The teachers tended to use the discursive material in the textbooks as the basis for their own lessons and used only the activity sections directly with the students. The most frequently used books focused on textual analysis and included exercises on editing, composition, narrative analysis, characterization, and plot. The teachers had access to a wide range of off-air recordings and purchased feature films, although many complained that their major need was for edited pieces which could be used in a 40-minute lesson. None of the teachers in the study placed any emphasis on student practical work and rarely, if ever, involved students in making a visual production.

Lesson observations revealed differences in focus and approach to Media Education among the 10 teachers. These differences are highlighted by five case studies. These five examples are selected because they are representative of the group in terms of gender, background, and seniority. They also reflect, with the exception of the third teacher, the range of views and approaches identified through interview and observation of the 10 participants. They cited lack of equipment, lack of technical skills, and lack of time as their reasons for not involving students in production.

The first case study is of Miss Smith, a teacher of English and English Literature. She expressed in her interview the belief that her training in literature was very helpful in teaching about media texts. She saw a fair degree of overlap in the skills required to analyze a prose text and the skills needed for the analysis of a feature film. It was for this reason, she said, that she concentrated on feature films in her teaching about the media rather than television or documentary, which she considered much more difficult to deal with in the classroom.

In the interview, Miss Smith described her aims as giving her students "an understanding and appreciation of what it was the director wanted the audience to feel." She therefore devoted a major proportion of the class discussion time to aspects of theme and students' personal responses to the issues raised by the film. She, in turn, shared her understandings and interpretations of the film with the students. Questions about and reflections on authorial intent (with the director treated as author) figured prominently in the discussion. Aspects of the *mise en scène* such as lighting, framing, camera movement, and editing were ignored. A series of two lessons on a feature film focused on the narrative structure, character development, plot, and theme. Most of the discussion about the theme related to how values and attitudes had changed over time specifically with reference to attitudes to women, women in employment, and social attitudes to single women. (The film under discussion was *My Brilliant Career*.) The teacher did not attempt to theorize her own position nor did she link the students' responses to a theoretical position, although a number of the students' remarks reflected a feminist reading of the text.

A second teacher, Mr. Jones, described himself as "using a Cultural Studies approach," describing it as one that gave "students the opportunity to think critically." His aim was to "give students an understanding of the processes of meaning, discourse, and ideology." Mr. Jones said that he relied heavily on concepts from semiotics (which he had studied at the university), although he did not use the term with the students nor did he see himself as teaching semiotics. The concepts of sign, signifier and signified, connotation, and myth he felt to be accessible to students and useful tools for visual analysis. Mr. Jones also had a background in literature but felt that issues of characterization, plot, and theme were secondary in his teaching of visual texts. He criticized other English teachers for treating visual texts "as books of pictures" and thereby limiting their teaching to concerns about the narrative at the expense of exploration of the constructed nature of visual texts. He described his approach as one that looked at "cultural values, institutions, and ideology." In his lessons he dealt with a wide range of media texts and print texts, often treating them intertextually and making comparisons between the value positions shown in different types of texts. In the lesson, his students closely analyzed selected scenes from a television drama, a current affairs program, and a feature film. The discussion focused on such aspects as the television presenter's eyeline, the iconography in the television drama, the length of shots, and the relationship between the length and the sense of pace. This teacher repeatedly stressed issues of how meaning was created in the text and spent little time on discussion of what the meaning was.

The third teacher seemed to take a rather idiosyncratic approach to the teaching of visual texts. This teacher argued that visual texts must be taught from both "an ideological and an aesthetic position." He argued that the emphasis on deconstructing the text in the English syllabus was unfortunate, and believed that greater attention should be paid to the affective and subjective aspects of the visual media. He described his approach as one that:

> ... seeks to draw out students' real feelings and emotional responses to films. I am not interested in right answers or politically correct answers. The whole reason we go to films is for the emotional pleasure they give us, but this aspect is usually ignored when it comes to teaching about film. If you listen to what the students say about a film outside of the classroom you will hear them talking about their own responses to characters and situations, not about codes of representation. This is why kids love horror movies—they can give free rein to their emotions and revel in their own feelings.

Although he did not show horror movies in the classroom, he chose visual texts that depicted what he considered to be highly emotive issues. Films that dealt with violence, jealousy, family breakdown, and gender relations were, he felt, the ideal stimuli for discussion about the self and one's feelings about, and attitudes towards, life. Favored film titles for teaching were *The War Game* (a dramatized documentary about nuclear war), *The Outsiders*, *Ordinary People*, and *The Breakfast Club*. He claimed to teach as little about television as possible, believing that film was "intrinsically a superior medium of communication." To the lesson observer, however, there seemed to be little difference in lesson content, or the manner in which it was conducted, between the lesson taught by this teacher and that of Miss Smith in the first case study described above. Both teachers focused on issues of theme at the expense of questions of structure; both encouraged and valued the personal responses of students; both gave their personal opinion on the material at some length and tended to treat the text as a stimulus rather than an object of study.

Miss Allen was the subject of the fourth case study and probably the most typical of all the teachers interviewed in the course of the project. She was enthusiastic about teaching visual media, confident of her own abilities in the area, and supportive of an expansion of this strand within the English syllabus. (This teacher had no formal background in media or communications studies.) Miss Allen stressed in the interview the importance of valuing students' own knowledge of the media, and claimed that she chose the texts for classroom study in consultation with the students.

Her approach to the actual teaching of a visual text was more highly structured than the previous three examples. Before viewing, she gave each student a worksheet containing pointers on what to look for in a few scenes, some questions on theme, character, and structure, and instructions about drawing a diagram of the plot. After viewing, the students formed small groups to complete the worksheets and develop group responses to a series of questions about narrative, representation, and point of view. Each group had to choose a short section from the video to support and exemplify their responses. The groups made notes on an overhead transparency, and a group spokesperson delivered the group's response with reference to the overhead transparency summary and the selected excerpt. Class discussion and teacher input happened frequently during the feedback sessions.

Miss Allen's lesson on representation in *Dances With Wolves* highlighted a problem perceived by nearly all the teachers in the sample. The problem seemed to be that, although the students are heavy viewers of film and television, the range of texts with which they are familiar is very narrow. Their understanding of genre is limited, in Miss Allen's words, "to the list of shelf titles in the video shop." Before she could explore the alternative representations of Indians offered by *Dances With Wolves* she felt she had to teach the students the content of the traditional representations. None of the students was familiar with old Westerns, they had no preconceived notions about how Indians were depicted and did not recognize nor respond to, the political correctness of the representations in *Dances With Wolves*. In an attempt to demonstrate the ways in which this film broke with the traditions of the genre she struggled with a few comparisons between this film and earlier Westerns. The students remained unenlightened until she introduced the issue of the army's treatment of Dunbar's animals. The shooting of the wolf convinced the students that the army were the bad guys and the Indians the good guys.

The last example is of a Head of Department. Only one head of an English department was included in the study, and he is not typical in that he has published a textbook for teachers on viewing in the English classroom. He described his aims in teaching about the media as "giving students an understanding of texts as complex constructions which are sites for the construction of particular ways of thinking about the world and that these ways of thinking are strongly connected with social conditions."

He felt that the staff in his own department, although happy to comply with the syllabus demands, were not necessarily either clear or in agreement with each other as to the reasons why they were studying media texts other than because of the syllabus requirements. He saw his own role as a modeling one, whereby he would share his understanding about Media Education with his staff through models of best practice provided by himself. Of all the teachers interviewed and observed in the study, this Head of Department was the only person who articulated conceptual links between contemporary literary theory, English pedagogy, Cultural Studies, and Media Education. His choice of media texts for teaching purposes is illustrative of his approach to Media Education, an approach that focuses sharply on a set of concepts and understandings about the media, and emphasizes written responses to visual texts. He used, for example, a 1955 black-and-white film called *The Night of the Hunter* with his class of 15-year-olds to illustrate changes in textual conventions over time and the concept of *film noir*. He was the only teacher observed to use a noncontemporary text. At another time he used *The Journey of Natty Gann* as the vehicle for illustrating the archetypal journey as a growth narrative and the ways in which the representation of gender was contested. His class handouts on *The Night of the Hunter* are reproduced in Figs. 5.1 and 5.2.

This teacher's approach to the teaching of *Gallipoli* is illustrative of the limits to Media Education that arise from its positioning within the subject of English. He regarded *Gallipoli* as an appropriate tool for teaching about the context of the production and consumption of a media text. His approach was to teach *Gallipoli* as a product of the New Wave of Australian film of the 1970s and 1980s, a period in which film makers made deliberate attempts to appeal to a broad Australian audience through their filmic representations of particular expressions of Australian national identity. His concern for teaching about the context of the film, however, is limited to concerns with the social context. In his teaching about the text of *Gallipoli* no attention was paid to the political economy surrounding the text—the commodity status of the film, the orchestrated media campaigns that accompanied release of the film, the fact that Rupert Murdoch was one of the producers or that it was his paper *The Australian* that gave it rave reviews, that Murdoch owned Channel 10 and it was this channel that devoted a special program of *Movie Scene* (a weekly entertainment review) to *Gallipoli* (King, 1983, p. 51). Wider issues about cross-media ownership, marketing, and power relations are not included in the syllabus, and are considered by most teachers to be inappropriate to Media Education in the English classroom. His class notes on *Gallipoli* are reproduced in Figs. 5.3 and 5.4.

CONCLUSIONS

The case studies represent a continuum at one end of which we find visual texts treated as a stimuli for teaching about something else entirely, and at the other the text as the object of study. Regardless of where they were on this continuum teachers felt justified in their approaches to Media Education, and on occasion, critical of those using alternative approaches or having different conceptions about teaching visual texts. It is interesting to note that, apart from the Head of Department, none of the teachers made any explicit references to the syllabus require-

Year 10 English

The Night of the Hunter

Preparation for Film Review

The Night of the Hunter is very different from most other films you have seen. It would therefore be wrong to judge it by the standards which you would apply to other films.

The following exercises are designed to help you think about how the film is different from other films and thus develop a framework for reporting on and evaluating the film.

Write answers to the following questions in your journal. Each answer should be *at least* a page long. Single sentence answers are not acceptable and nor are answers which mention only one point. You need to show evidence of considered thought in your answers.

The Nature of the Film

1. What aspects of the film seem to indicate that the film makers did not intend the audience to treat this as a realistic story? What aspects of the film are *obviously* unrealistic or *obviously* unlike real life?

   Consider such things as the plot, some of the characters, some of the scenery and camera angles.

2. What similarities are there between this film and many fairy tales, such as Hansel and Gretel and Snow White for example?

3. Write about the character of Preacher Powell as portrayed by Robert Mitchum, describing how you think the audience is intended to think about and respond to the character.

FIG. 5.1. Hand-out 1 for *The Night of the Hunter.*

Year 10 English

Film Review

Background

We have read a number of film reviews and discussed their content to give you an idea of how film reviews are written.

We have watched *The Night of the Hunter* and I have gone through and pointed out aspects of how the film has been made.

The Task

You are required to produce an extended review of *The Night of the Hunter*.

Your review may be positive or negative or a combination of both but it should show an understanding of the way the film has been made. You will be both reporting on the film and evaluating aspects of it.

Your review should mention, among other things:
• the way the film draws on aspects of the fairy tale or bible story tradition;
• the way the film draws on the film noir tradition;
• the film's use of light and dark to create atmosphere, convey character and communicate ideas on a symbolic level;
• its surrealist approach to film narrative.

Remember: a review should also be interesting to read in its own right and have a sense of personal voice.

Length: At least 800 words

Due date: Friday 24 March

FIG. 5.2. Hand-out 2 for *The Night of the Hunter.*

Gallipoli

Pre-viewing Notes

This is an Australian film made in 1981. The two main characters are Archy (Mark Lee) and Frank (Mel Gibson).

In studying the film our focus is on the influence of context and target audience, in comparison with *The Overlanders*. In doing this there are two main points to keep in mind.

The first is a similarity: both films are Australian (even though *The Overlanders* was made by a British company) and designed to appeal to Australian audiences.

The second is a difference: the films were made 35 years apart, so there is also a difference in their target audience.

The process of study we will use is as follows:

Step 1

I. Identify those aspects of the construction of *Gallipoli* designed to appeal to Australian audiences of the early 1980s.

Step 2

Draw comparisons and contrasts with *The Overlanders*.

You will begin step 1 today. After reading these notes, you will watch 45 minutes of *Gallipoli* and then make notes on the following question: What aspects of the film are intended to appeal to Australian audiences of the early 1980s?

Answer the question by writing at least a couple of sentences explaining how each of the following have been used:

I.	Choice of subject matter	II.	Plot
III.	Characterisation	IV.	Film language
V.	Setting/s	VI.	Any other points you notice

This work is to be completed by the end of the period and handed in for me to check before our next lesson.

FIG. 5.3. Hand-out 1 for *Gallipoli*.

Context	*Gallipoli* 1981:	*The Overlanders* 1946:
	Time of growth of Australian nationalism. Questioning of history. Search for an independent identity.	National pride as a result of the war.
Subject Matter	Significant event in Australian history.	Significant event in Australian history.
Attitudes Toward the subject matter.	Critical approach - asks the audience to question the traditional view of the Gallipoli campaign by presenting the deaths as a waste.	Celebratory approach.
Toward Australians.	Presents Australians as rather naive and innocent but heroic.	Presents Australians as heroic.
Toward the British.	Presents the British as arrogant snobs who treat the Australians with contempt and use them for their own purposes.	British are shown as comrades of the Australians.
Toward Aboriginal people.	Disapproves of racism - the only directly racist comment comes from a character the audience disapproves of.	Implicitly racist I. Aboriginal people are treated as unimportant in the exposition. The north of Australia is described as "inhabited by only 5000 white people." II. Aboriginal people are portrayed, humorously, as easy-going to the point of irresponsibility. III. Traditional Aboriginal people are treated as objects of curiosity and almost on the same level as strange animals by being referred to as "wild blacks."
Methods of Construction Character	Creates characters that Australian audiences can relate to by drawing on characteristics seen as typical of Australians: appearance, language, background, sense of humour, sportsmanship, belief in mateship, contempt for authority.	
Setting	Extensive use of outback scenery to signal the film's Australian-ness.	
Resolution	Ends in tragedy.	Ends in triumph and success.
Film language	Extensive use of close-ups early in the film to establish audience identification with main characters and to highlight dramatic moments.	Use of voice overs to establish exposition.

FIG. 5.4. Hand-out 2 for *Gallipoli*.

ments, nor did they attempt to justify their approach in terms of the syllabus. The official written documents seem to have little impact on what is taught or how it is taught.

A second finding from the study is that the presence or absence of, a background in Media Studies/Communication Studies makes little or no difference as to whether or not teachers are confident in their ability to teach film and television. No teacher expressed doubts about their competencies in the area, nor did those without formal training express resentment at having to teach something they were not trained to do. Whether this confidence might be misplaced is another question.

Third, the 'personal growth' approach to English teaching appears to be somewhat more in evidence than a Cultural Studies approach although, arguably, a number of the teachers exhibited elements from both schools of thought. The majority of lessons focused on concepts derived from literature such as characterization, plot, and theme. The differences among the teachers was mainly in where these issues led them in the discussion, toward personal responses or ideological analysis. Two of the teachers firmly placed themselves within the 'personal growth' model with their use of film texts as stimuli for discussion of personal beliefs and attitudes. Two teachers consciously rejected the 'personal growth' model and focused on issues of cultural analysis. One teacher drifted between the two positions in the space of a single lesson.

The syllabus for English in Australia requires that media texts be included along with literary and transactional texts as objects of study. It was clear that although all of the teachers in the study (with perhaps one exception) were following the syllabus, their interpretation of what constitutes Media Education varied widely, and in practice teaching about the media seemed to be restricted to teaching textual analysis. A 1992 study of the nature and level of 15-year-old students' understanding of the media in Western Australia found that students were skilled in textual analysis. It showed that students exhibited well developed understandings about visual codes, connotation, narrative, and characterization, but little understanding of the relationship among these textual elements to wider issues of representation and ideology (McMahon & Quin, 1993, p. 194). Three years later, the situation remains the same. Media Education as it is currently taught in English maintains the focus on textual analysis and largely ignores the role of the media as consciousness industries.

This study has highlighted a couple of areas that need further research and action. The syllabus and its articulation in the classroom reflect a strong bias toward the text as the single object of study. The academic research of the 1980s into the ethnography of audiences and the complex relationships among producers, texts, and audiences seems to have made no impact on Media Education in the English classroom. There is a need for work on ways of making these often complex ideas accessible to teachers and students. Finally, further research is needed into the outcomes of Media Education in Western Australia. In the current situation the emphasis is on inputs, on the texts, and the content that will be taught. There are assumptions being made about the outputs, and about what students know and are able to do, but little evidence to support these assumptions.

REFERENCES

Britton, J., (1970) *Language and learning.* Hammondsworth: Penguin.

Curriculum Corporation. (1994). *National Statement on English for Australian schools.* Carlton, Victoria: Author.

Dettman, H. W. (1969) *Secondary education in Western Australia.* Perth: Education Department of Western Australia

Department of Education and Science. (1989). (Cox Report) *English 5–16.* London: Her Majesty's Stationary Office.

Dixon, J. (1967) *Growth through English.* Huddersfield: National Association for the Teaching of English.

Hart, A., & Benson, A. (1993). *Media in the classroom.* Southampton: Southampton Media Education Group.

King, N. (1983). Changing the curriculum: The place of film in a department of English. *Australian Journal of Cultural Studies, 1*(1), 51.

McMahon, B., & Quin, R. (1993). Monitoring standards in media studies: Problems and strategies. *Australian Journal of Education, 37*(2), 194.

Milner, A. (1993). *Cultural materialism.* Carlton, Victoria: Melbourne University Press.

Patterson, A. (1996). Setting some limits to English. In P. Freebody, A. Luke, & S. Muspratt (Eds.), *Constructing critical literacies.* Cresskill, NJ: Hampton Press.

Quin, R., & Quin, R. (1994). Media education: The development of media education in Western Australian schools. In B. Shoesmith (Ed.), *Media, politics and identity.* Perth: University of Western Australia

6

Media Literacy in Massachusetts

Renee Hobbs
Clark University

When the phrase 'Media Education' is used in the United States, most educators think of public television broadcasting, or else they think the reference is to video production classes at the secondary level, usually designed as nonacademic vocational-style coursework for students who are about to drop out of school, or at the very least, are "not college bound". Few spontaneously identify Media Education with the process of learning about media industries or actively analyzing media messages. When U. S. educators and advocates got together at a national leadership conference on media literacy sponsored by the Aspen Institute in 1992, much attention to definitional concerns was present. Because it did not restrict itself to audio–visual media, the phrase, 'Media Literacy' was recognized as superior to the concept of 'Critical Viewing Skills' that had been visible since the mid-1970s, when the first rush of interest in Media Literacy was fueled by increasing concerns about the impact of media violence on young people.

A working definition of Media Literacy was established by U. S. educators, as documented in Firestone (1992): "Media Literacy is the ability to access, analyze, evaluate, and communicate messages in a wide variety of forms."

This definition represents an expanded conceptualization of literacy, so that reading, speaking, listening, writing, critical viewing, and media production are all included under this umbrella definition. Strategically, the definition was aimed to help educators recognize the connections between media access, analysis, and production skills, and the larger aims of kindergarten through Grade 12 (K–12) education, because the lack of connection between Media Literacy educators and the mainstream K–12 community continues to be an important obstacle to implementing Media Education in the curriculum.

The operating principles of Media Literacy seem consistent with perspectives on Media Education that are identified by other contributors to this volume. U. S. educators have adopted a set of concepts, borrowed from Canadian and British educators, which recognize that all media are constructed representations, that meaning is derived from the intersection of reader, text, and culture, and that messages have economic, political, social, and historical contexts. Media Literacy educators also generally recognize that good classroom practice includes a balance between media analysis and media production activities, that student-centered inquiry approaches to learning and teaching are most effective, and that a wide range of media forms and genres, not just audio–visual media, should be formally included as study objects.

THE CONTEXT

Educators are coming to recognize that, in a world saturated with media messages, it is important for students to be able to access, critically examine, and communicate using print, images, video, and other forms of expression. In addition, it is no longer adequate to pretend that the information received from television is peripheral to a student's life: mass-mediated messages are now central to our political system, our understanding of global issues, and the ways in which we perceive ourselves in relation to others. In part because of its ubiquity and pervasiveness, teaching about the media can be relevant to a number of curricular areas, including language arts, social studies, health, vocational education, journalism, science and technology, and the arts.

In the United States, Media Literacy initiatives have often been based on the efforts of a single teacher in a school or district, working alone. Teachers in the subject areas of language arts, video production, or social studies (most usually at the middle-school level and above) frequently become attracted to issues relevant to Media Literacy, for one or more of a wide spectrum of reasons ranging from the desire to protect children from media manipulation to an interest in promoting social change (Hobbs, 1994). Teachers who begin to experiment with Media Literacy in the K–12 classroom are often unaware that there exists a network of educational resources and educators who share their interests, or a theoretical literature that examines the pedagogy of Media Studies. Frequently, these individuals will have devoted significant self-study to the issue and developed their own approaches to teaching Media Literacy before they ever become aware of others engaged in similar work.[1] Occasionally, their backgrounds in Media Studies and Media pedagogy come from reading TV criticism and reports on the media business in the pages of the local newspaper, reporting on Hollywood and the media business

---

[1]These informal claims are based on personal experience of introducing teachers to Media Literacy in communities across the United States.

as part of entertainment TV, and critics, scholars, and popular writers including Marie Winn, Neil Postman, Jerry Mander, David Bianculli, and Ken Aulettta. Also, teachers with interests in Media Literacy come with a range of different types of academic training, from degree programs in education, the arts, literature, history and politics, and journalism and communication.[2]

It is important to recognize that the decentralized educational system of the United States promotes such diversity of approaches. With 15,000 different school districts and more than 2.5 million teachers, political and community leaders in the United States have an antipathy toward national models for education policy. Each of the 50 states sets its own curriculum frameworks, and each school district interprets those frameworks and develops a program of instruction, staff development, and student assessment. This approach to education ensures large differences in the funding of local education, and as a result, there is wide stratification in the quality of education between communities. Some U. S. schools have made huge investments in computer and video technologies, for example, whereas others have barely enough money for paper, pencils, and supplies. Reverence for community-centered education policies and hostility toward any attempt to develop coherent national programs is demonstrated by the near-constant efforts of political conservatives to recommend the abolition of the U.S. Department of Education.

The wide diversity of approaches used by teachers of Media Literacy in the United States has led to a number of schisms among media educators, most notably between those who view Media Literacy as a form of protection for children to help them resist the lures of commercial culture, and those who view Media Literacy as a discipline in its own right, often on the grounds that Media Literacy empowers young people to make their own interpretations and strengthen their communication skills (Fehlman, 1995).

At the elementary levels and in the field of health education, where critical analysis of alcohol and tobacco advertising is increasingly common in U. S. schools, the 'protectionist' stance is dominant. The *'empowerment'* model is common in both poor urban and wealthy suburban and private schools, where politically active, younger, and intellectually engaged teachers are comfortable straying from the packaged materials provided by textbook publishers, which serve as the defacto curriculum for most schools.

Recently, Media Literacy programs have begun to take hold in some schools and school districts as a result of increased educational opportunities for teachers. Because staff development opportunities are usually controlled at the district level, Media Literacy advocates have attempted to reach educators not through teacher education, but through the creation of resource materials, videotapes, curriculum guides, and other material designed for in-classroom use (Brown, 1991). Media Literacy staff development programs have often been aimed at teachers within a

---

[2]Based on interviews with a sample of 12 teachers of the 90 who attended the Harvard Institute on Media Education, Cambridge, Massachusetts, August 1–5, 1994.

metropolitan region or school district, initiated by a faculty member at a nearby university, using methods composed of lectures, discussions, viewing activities, model lessons accompanied by analysis and critique, production activities, and time and resources for strategic planning to help teachers develop new ideas to implement in the classroom.

Until the 1990s, few formal training programs were available to educators, particularly in the United States. In 1993, the Harvard Institute on Media Education was initiated at Harvard Graduate School of Education.[3] It was the first of a number of staff development programs that began to emerge in the United States in the 1990s. In 1993 and 1994, the Harvard experience provided an opportunity for nearly 200 teachers and academics to identify the motives and priorities each brought to the enterprise of involving students in media analysis and production.

During the 1990s, as education reform efforts at the state level encouraged the development of new standards, curriculum frameworks, and innovative assessment models, a number of states explicitly called for the inclusion of skills of media analysis and production. The State of New Mexico, for example, mandated a course in communication for all high school students (McCannon, personal communication, 1995); the State of Massachusetts included media analysis and communication skills not as a separate subject, but within language arts, social studies, health, science, and the arts.[4] More than 15 states have curriculum frameworks that support Media Literacy goals. In 1996, the State of North Carolina embarked on the development of an optional end-of-year assessment of Media Literacy skills for students in Grades 3 and 4, 7 and 8, and 11 and 12.[5]

Teachers who embrace Media Literacy often take on increasingly active roles in their school districts, even though most tend to focus their energies on their own classroom practice. In 1995, I distributed a questionnaire to the 200 educators who had completed the Harvard Institute on Media Education in 1993 and 1994, with questions designed to identify the behaviors they had engaged in since returning from the Institute, as well as items measuring their attitudes about the possibility of expanding Media Literacy programs to reach all students in their schools. Of the 40% of participants who returned the questionnaire, 87% of the full-time teachers

---

[3]The Harvard Institute on Media Education began as a week-long residential program of professional development for educators from across the United States. In 1994, a number of Media Literacy summer programs at other universities were implemented in addition to the Harvard program, including at New York University, Columbia Teachers' College, the University of Dayton, and Ryerson Institute in Toronto. Media Literacy teacher education programs sponsored by public television stations, art museums, cable television programmers, and newspaper publishers have also proliferated.

[4]Drafts dated March 1995 of the Massachusetts Language Arts Health, Social Studies, and Art Education curriculum were being widely circulated to educational leaders across the state, although at the time of writing, a final document has not been approved by the Massachusetts Department of Education.

[5]Personal communication from D. Vickers, June 15, 1996.

who participated in the Institute continued to work primarily as individuals in the classroom, with only about 13% engaging in collaborative activities with other teachers. However, more than 65% of teachers have shared the materials they received at the Institute, and more than 50% of the teachers have led in-service programs, mentored other teachers, or shared their resource materials, videotapes, and lesson plans. Only about 8% of respondents have developed models that promote the learning of media analysis and production skills across an entire school, aiming to bring these practices into widespread use by many teachers across multiple grades and subject areas (Hobbs, 1996).

The purpose of this chapter is to profile a small sample of the 26 teachers who participated in the Master's Degree program within the Billerica Initiative. By examining the process by which teachers create their own approaches to curriculum in Media Literacy, we aim to identify how teachers' attitudes toward education, youth, culture, and media shape their curriculum choices and interpersonal behavior in the classroom. By examining the ways they see themselves in relationship to their students and their peers, this chapter describes some factors that predict a teacher's willingness to take on the task of becoming knowledgeable about media and skilled in using Media Literacy pedagogy in the classroom. Using profiles of teachers working with students ages 12 to 17, the chapter explores the range of teacher attitudes, behaviors, and philosophies in order to better understand the characteristics of Media Literacy as it is practiced among some teachers in U.S. public schools today. The chapter concludes with some observations, hypotheses, and critical questions about the application of the district-based model of Media Literacy education that was employed in Billerica.

THE BILLERICA INITIATIVE

The Billerica Initiative is an ongoing effort by the Billerica, Massachusetts Public Schools to develop Media Education training in a comprehensive program aimed to integrate Media Literacy concepts into Grades K–12 in a working-class community northwest of Boston. Through staff development, community outreach, curriculum development, and performance assessment the Billerica Initiative attempted to introduce the skills of Media Literacy to 340 teachers and 7,000 students. The most important component of the initiative was a long-term staff development program consisting of a graduate-level program of courses that led to a Master's Degree in Media Literacy, sponsored by Fitchburg State College and the Merrimack Education Center, a cooperative staff development program which serves 22 school districts in the communities northwest of Boston, Massachusetts. The program resulted in the creation of a group of Media Literacy experts within the school district, a number of ongoing cross-curricular programs, and a substantial amount of media analysis and production activities which are integrated within the day-to-day lives of students and teachers.

Billerica was one of the first sites in the United States to receive *Channel One,* a commercially supported current events television program for teenagers, now in place in more than 12,000 schools, with a reach of more than 7 million students each day. Schools receive television equipment for use in classrooms in exchange for broadcasting the program, which contains 10 minutes of teen-oriented news programming and 2 minutes of advertising each day. At the introduction of *Channel One,* educators in Billerica were deluged with public criticism from academics and educational leaders, including the National Education Association who charged them with selling their students to advertisers and wasting valuable minutes of the school day. Nevertheless, school officials in Billerica believed that the program offered them the opportunity to improve their students' understanding of current events, enhance the use of media technology in the schools, and promote a sense of community through the broadcast of student-produced news and information programming.

Since 1989, when *Channel One* was first introduced in Billerica, educators within the district have become increasingly sensitive to the need to help strengthen students' ability to analyze and evaluate media messages. In addition, increased availability of hardware in the classrooms has made it easier for some teachers to increase their use of video materials as resources for teaching and created a climate of interest among teachers about strategies for using video production activities for educational purposes.

When Middle School teachers voted unanimously to receive *Channel One* in 1992, they did so primarily because they wanted the opportunity to have a television monitor in every classroom. But some teachers and parents were also strongly concerned about the perceived vulnerability of Middle School students to advertising and news content, with a number of teachers noting that younger students often lack the reasoning and critical thinking skills to analyze sophisticated, slickly produced advertisements, and lack the world knowledge to appreciate the current events information provided on *Channel One*, which is largely aimed at high school students.

In Billerica, Media Literacy was initially understood by school officials to serve as a form of 'protection' for students who were about to be exposed to *Channel One* each day. Only gradually did educators and leaders in the school administration recognize the possibility that Media Literacy could enrich the curriculum in Grades K–12 across a range of subject areas.

Before *Channel One* was turned on in the district's two Middle Schools, all teachers attended a 2-hour presentation introducing them to the concept of Media Literacy, where teachers practiced analyzing news and advertising and learned of some simple activities and discussions to engage students' critical viewing skills. A group of middle-school teachers also attended a 1-day seminar on Media Literacy, which was designed to introduce teachers to media analysis skills, and to discuss connections between Media Literacy and the middle-school curriculum. The program was enthusiastically received. Teachers noted that the high level of engagement and enthusiasm among colleagues was in startling contrast to the usual ambivalence, skepticism, and mild hostility that was often a part of staff development efforts.

As a result of the success of this program, in the Spring of 1993, 30 teachers (representing each of the faculty teaching teams in the Middle Schools) enrolled in a 30-hour in-service course, *Introduction to Media Literacy*, with some teachers enrolling through Fitchburg State College to receive graduate credit. This course provided a broad overview of the issues involved in the analysis of print, imagery, and electronic media. Teachers regularly engaged in analysis of a variety of different media, including newspapers, magazines, TV entertainment and news programming, and episodes of *Channel One*. In addition, they wrote critical reviews of existing resource materials and curricula for Media Literacy, and designed their own lesson plans for integrating Media Literacy concepts in their classrooms.

RESEARCH METHODOLOGY

The data reported here were collected as part of the teachers' coursework, required for completion of the Master's Degree in Media Literacy. Teachers had the option of interviewing and observing a colleague as one of two possible course assignments. In one course, teachers studied the profiles and classroom descriptions developed in the original *Models of Media Education* project (Hart & Benson, 1993). To participate in this project, teachers had to volunteer to be observed and find a partner who could schedule time to watch one or two classroom lessons and conduct a detailed interview. Twelve teachers chose to engage in this project, and in this chapter we report only 4 of the teachers who work with students ages 11 to 16, excluding from the sample those teachers working at other grade levels, or those whose work is in subject areas other than language arts or social studies. These profiles make it possible for the reader to gain a set of mental pictures about the practice of Media Literacy education at a specific moment in time. Teachers' articulations of their rationales are distilled from a 40-minute interview based on the original U.K. *Models of Media Education* project (Hart & Benson, 1993). The accounts of practice were written as descriptive observations of one or two classroom periods by those teachers with primary responsibility for students in the middle-school grades (ages 11–14) and the first 2 years of high school (ages 14–16).

Teachers selected a colleague to observe, negotiated a specific date and time, arranged with the Superintendent and the Principal for coverage of the observers' classes for the observation time, and carried out their observation. Then, after school, within a week of the observation, the teacher-observer interviewed the colleague using the structured schedule of questions developed in the original project in England. The reports were written up, shared among the entire class of 26 teachers and served as data for classroom discussion.

Teachers discussed with the author the experience of having a colleague make an observation. In Billerica, classroom observations are exclusively reserved for purposes of evaluation, and educators in Billerica have relatively little exposure to educational research on site. Teachers noted that this tradition created an expectancy that caused some tension on both the part of the observer and the part of the teacher being observed. Although teachers agreed about the importance of capturing authentic classroom experience, the novelty of the experience created at least two distinct methodological effects which could be labeled the 'safe' lesson and the 'teacher focus'.

As noted in the Introduction to this book, teachers being observed sometimes chose to engage in practices they considered 'safe.' Although Billerica teachers frequently noted that were increasingly comfortable developing more spontaneous approaches to media study based on the 'teachable moment,' the act of a colleague observing and writing a report about one classroom period led to the tendency for teachers to choose a 'sure fire' activity that carried little risk of failure. As a result of the Master's Degree coursework, teachers had a lot of exposure to the use and analysis of 'found' media texts from current newspapers, television programs, popular music, and other sources. Many teachers gained increased comfort with using such spontaneously collected materials within their own classrooms. The techniques and pitfalls of the use of 'teachable moments' were a recurring theme in the staff development program. In some instances, this also created a more artificial learning experience for students, who in a few cases had been exposed to the same lesson earlier in the school year.

SELECTED CASE STUDIES

The four examples that follow illustrate something of the range of approaches found among the teachers in the study. They also illustrate the limitations of using teachers rather than researchers to interview their colleagues and observe their lessons.

Examining Families on Television: Jean

Jean is at Franklin Middle School, where she teaches both language arts and social studies, possessing an undergraduate degree in education and more than 20 years of experience in the classroom. Her motivation to teach Media Literacy comes primarily from her interest in helping students make connections between the humanities and social studies, her interests in the representation of gender, race, class, and ethnicity in the mass media, and her concern that students become engaged in the learning process and personally responsible for their own education. Jean commented on the tension at work in wanting to include more Media Literacy activities but feeling tied down by the demand to 'cover content' in terms of the specific content she is responsible for addressing in her social studies class. For example, she tries to include Media Literacy concepts even when she is teaching about the Renaissance, as she invites students to examine critically images and points of view.

Her lesson on TV families was taught to seventh graders for two separate 40-minute periods. The general approach for the lesson involved brainstorming of key ideas about being a critical viewer, with some media research being done by the students during class time and at home, and some discussion about the perceived realism of different prime-time situation comedies. Jean identified three broad goals for the learning experience:

1. Students should gain the experience of watching television actively and to appreciate that the media's representation of families was constructed;
2. Students should gain skills of critical decision making based on evidence from a range of sources;
3. Students should gain an appreciation and respect for their own (and others') opinions and choices.

Before the first session, the students were given a sheet which outlined a 'pre-viewing assignment,' to be completed the night before the first class presentation. The assignment required students to make a list of films or TV shows that portrayed families. The students then had to evaluate each of these families on the basis of their being 'realistic' or 'unrealistic,' and they had to provide specific evidence to support their choices.

Jean began the session by asking students to define 'media' and the idea of being a 'critical viewer' in their own words. They brainstormed a list of different types of media and agreed that all media offer messages that may include both print and visual components. Students in this classroom quickly identified that 'critical' didn't necessarily have a negative connotation, but that being critical had more to do with understanding messages rather than assigning labels like 'good' and 'bad.' In a carefully guided discussion, Jean led the students through a process of generating a set of elements that 'critical viewers' use to make their judgments about various mass media. The list that was generated including the following concepts: realism, entertainment value, age appropriateness, credibility, and quality of construction.

To further the concept of being a critical viewer, Jean asked the students to make use of their pre-viewing assignment to examine those programs that were identified as 'realistic.' The development of this list was vigorous and was punctuated by the spontaneous singing and humming of theme songs associated with the TV shows the pupils were suggesting. The session ended with a list of programs that students identified as 'realistic' for the 1990s. These programs included *Family Matters, The Simpsons, Murphy Brown, Fresh Prince of Bel Air, Step by Step, Family Ties,* and *Full House.*

VIEWING ANALYSIS SHEET

Student Name:

Name of Program

List all Characters   Occupation   Approximate Age   Gender

Choose one character and write three adjectives to describe the person's personality.

Describe the major problem or conflict in the episode.

Describe any other problems or conflicts in the episode.

Describe the solution presented in the episode.

Who resolved the problem?

What action happens before each pod of commercials?

List all commercials and TV promotions shown during the episode.

FIG. 6.1. Viewing Analysis Sheet.

On the second day, the session began by looking in more depth at family shows. Jean led the students through a step-by-step process of analyzing the shows with a greater attention to specific details outlined on a 'Viewing Analysis' sheet (see Fig. 6.1).

After discussing some of these questions in terms of specific shows, students concluded that many of the family problems presented in the programs they had watched earlier in the week could not, in fact, be solved satisfactorily in the 30-minute airtime for the show.

One student was adamant about the fact that many of the problems and relationships depicted on these shows are realistic and that the situations could really happen. For example, after the teacher showed students a short clip from *The Simpsons,* one student recognized that Homer Simpson's beer drinking may reflect some fathers. In *Full House,* the students also felt that the ability of the characters to help each other solve their problems with sensitivity and caring was also an accurate portrayal of many families. In the follow-up interview, Jean commented on the importance of being sensitive to the developmental levels of her students, noting that in her classroom, different students demonstrated different kinds of ability in making modality judgments. In this case, the teacher is echoing similar arguments by Dorr (1983) who pointed out age trends in children's strategies for making judgements about a television program's realism, showing that by about the sixth grade, children define "real" as "something that could possibly happen" (p. 92).

The classroom session concluded with the discussion of relationships between characters. Jean noted that the children were actively involved in debating the perceived realism of different programs, and they discovered that different students make different judgments about the same characters, depending on their own particular experiences and backgrounds. The lesson established the idea that perception of realism is an interpretive judgement, not an intrinsic characteristic of a message. It seemed to fulfill the general aims identified by Jean as the overall goals for the lesson, because the activity depended on students' active use of television viewing in the home, the discussion about realism introduced the idea that multiple criteria are used in making reality judgements, and the classroom discussion gave a number of students the opportunity to share ideas in a climate where different points of view were valued.

Analyzing Broadcast News: Gina

Gina is a journalism teacher at Lincoln Memorial High School, where she teaches journalism to mixed age groups of students aged 14 to 18. She is a journalism educator who has considerable experience in integrating both media analysis and media production within her courses. She is also comfortable adapting the activities to students with a wide range of abilities, because she has both younger and older students together in her classes. She identifies a range of goals in her own approach to integrating Media Literacy within journalism education. She identifies the following as goals for her students in reading or viewing news:

1. To realize that all messages are constructions that are created for a specific purpose and effect that is determined by the news organization.
2. To learn that messages represent the social realities of the times and places far removed from the students' own world;
3. To understand that a skillful viewer should examine many different stylistic features of a medium and should pay careful attention to the context in which the message occurs.
4. To recognize that each form of communication has unique characteristics, for example, television news differs in many ways from print news.
5. To learn to recognize the concept of 'audience' when using news media.

On the day of the observation, Gina handed out a survey form that was to be completed at home. The survey asked questions about the news consumption patterns of various family members. Gina later used the surveys as a framework for discussion and analysis about family patterns of news media usage. This survey included questions like: What news programs are watched at home? Who watches? How are programs selected? Is a newspaper part of home life? How frequently does the newspaper arrive? If so, who reads it? Do any family members read a news magazine? If so, why was that particular one selected? Which medium do you use to get information about current events?

After introducing the assignment, Gina and her students examined an episode of *CBS Evening News* that had been shown two days earlier. The class was divided up into groups of six or seven. Each student in the group had to watch the broadcast with a specific target task in mind. For those analyzing news, one student was in charge of looking at the relationship between the visual images and the verbal messages to see which stories had a close connection between image and sound, and which stories had images used to 'wallpaper' over a story where the images were essentially decorative. Another student's task was to identify the various points of view that were characterized in the segment elements; another examined the time elapsed for each story; another identified the placement within the program.

For those students who were analyzing the advertising within the news program, one student had the task of logging all ads. Another had to identify the target audience for each ad. Another team of students examined the techniques of persuasion used in each ad. Students watched the broadcast in its entirety, and reviewed specific segments in order to complete their tasks.

In the following class, small groups worked to determine patterns and relationships between the data collected. Students discussed the news organization's decisions about story importance; they identified various target audiences, including the elderly, affluent males, and busy professionals. They discussed what information was missing from the nightly news and made a list of where a viewer could go to get more information about various issues.

The observer for this classroom session noted how well this specific activity allowed for differences in cognitive and writing abilities, and generally made use of the diverse age grouping of the class. Some students were assigned the more concrete tasks, like counting and naming, while others were assigned tasks which involved more complex skills of analysis. Both teacher and observer recognized that this activity helped to create interest in news among students, and that it served to orient students to the idea of an 'author' in the news-making process, which is not always a transparent concept for adolescents.

It is worth noting that Gina makes use of 'key concepts' in identifying her general aims. Many other teachers found the articulation of overarching principles to be valuable in helping them recognize the different dimensions of learning about media in the classroom. However, there is a danger that the 'key concepts' may be used as a kind of specialized language that serves teachers well for the writing of educational objectives but has very little practical purpose aside from satisfying supervisors, faculty, and school officials because they have not been made truly operational in the classroom.

Newspapers and Violence: Dave

Dave is a former middle-school English teacher who has developed expertise in computer literacy and is now is responsible for the computer classes that are a part of the middle-school curriculum. He has 20 years of experience as a teacher and is very comfortable with technology. Dave sees connections between Media Literacy education and technology education. His general goals for integrating Media Literacy concepts within his 'skills-oriented' computer literacy class are embodied in this statement:

> If students can leave my program understanding that all media, including the software that they use, are constructions, that media production is motivated by special interest, and that media can affect them without their conscious knowledge, then I have successfully conveyed some important media concepts.

In one lesson, Dave introduced Media Literacy concepts by asking his students to demonstrate their ability to use word processing and publishing software in the preparation of a mock-up of the front page of a newspaper. The front page would contain the various elements common to most newspapers: banners, headline, multicolumn articles, graphics, and images.

In a previous class, Dave had asked students to create a news story suitable for the publication. Their story categories included human interest, sports, politics, accidents, baby stories, alien encounters, stories about violence, and advertisements. Students seemed surprised when Dave pointed out the similarities and differences between their topics and the contents of a newspaper. He commented outside of class on his dismay to find that students' general familiarity with newspapers was low and that their major contact with newspapers was mainly through the sports pages.

Students recognized their own application of the concepts of 'Who, what, where, when, why, and how,' and were then led into a discussion focused not simply on what was told, but also on what or whose story was not told. Dave noted, "I could tell by the responses of students and their level of animation that they were coming in contact with an area that they had never encountered."

On the following day, Dave explored the content of the articles students had written, many of which contained violence, either through exposition or through graphics. He asked the students whether the violence was characteristic or reflective of the culture they live in or whether their selection of violent material originated in the desire to appeal to audience interest in order to sell newspapers. He used discussion with the whole class to help students recognize that their choice of content originated from a number of different news and 'reality TV' programs featuring police, victims, and criminals rather than from their own life experience or experience with print media.

Dave invited students to analyze why violence was so popular. Students created a list:

- It was easier to write about.
- The themes were familiar and predictable.
- Violence is part of life.
- Violence is contained in a large part of the information we receive from mass media.

Dave concluded the lesson by commenting on how, because of media messages, our society may be reaching a level of 'comfort violence,' which makes the presence of violence invisible, ordinary, and normal, and that to tolerate violence in this manner is to create a culture where everyone is at risk. Afterward, Dave recognized that he was "standing on his soap box in front of the kids" by concluding with a little speech about the evils of violence, but he feels passionately that his students need to know that he finds the culture of violence to be reprehensible. He is careful not to blame his students for their own interest in violence, but he is burdened with a concern that his students are "tuned in to the cultural priorities of the media, and turned off by the priorities and values of the school."

Dave's concern about the physical, social, and intellectual health of his students is evident in the energy he devotes to his work, and he attributes many of the cultural changes in the United States to the media's impact on cultural norms and values. Clearly, Dave recognizes that his 'protectionist' stance towards the issue of media violence represents contested terrain, but his work illustrates an important, widespread, and pervasive dimension of Media Literacy education in the United States.

Teaching About Film: Vic

Vic teaches English at Lincoln High School in Billerica, and has a life-long interest in film and mass media. He graduated from Emerson College, the first college in the United States devoted exclusively to the study of communication, and he has been teaching for almost 20 years. His aims in teaching Media Literacy include:

1. Helping students visualize both real and figurative images as derived from literary sources.
2. Showing students how one's personal experience is part of the process of connecting to a written 'story'.

3. Helping students apply key conventions of storytelling to the genres of literature and film.
4. Helping students analyze the construction of film images.
5. Strengthening students' interpretation and imagination in the reading process.

In this class of ninth graders, Vic has been reading *A Separate Peace* with the students. Working on Chapter 3, he began the class with a 'quickie quiz', a series of questions for students to answer in writing. These questions were concerned with the characters in the novel, and the questions encouraged students to reflect on the connections between the story and their personal experiences. After students finished writing, Vic invited students to respond to the questions orally. Few responded. He read a selected passage from the novel that illustrated a particular relationship between two characters and asked the class if anyone had experienced a similar situation. Again, few responded.

Vic then showed a segment of the film, *A Separate Peace*. He selected an image of a tree that was central to the narrative theme. The students readily offered their analysis of how the director used camera angles and other techniques to convey the story's meaning. The 'tree' image was shot to create the feeling of a loss of balance through camera movement. Discussion of this scene and the development of the characters at this point in the film suggested that students were connecting the story to their own experience.

When Vic asked students to compare and contrast the literary work to the film, students were clearly more uncomfortable with the visual scene of the boys diving beyond the river bank, into the water, as compared with their emotional disengagement from the same scene in the novel. According to the teacher-observer, the "literary version of the story elicited less spontaneous and emotional responses than the film." Students seemed unwilling or unable to reflect on the figurative elements of the novel and the film. One key scene from the film seemed less accessible to students, and Vic noted that this scene is dependent on language, not images.

Vic commented on his own observations about students' skills in analyzing literary works and film works. His concern after this class was that students' increasing reliance on content that is 'real' and 'visual' may work to the detriment of their ability to deal with content that is figurative, not literal, and imaginative. This comment underlines Vic's aim of helping students to develop an appreciation of figurative language , and stems from his anxiety that these skills are compromised in some way by the dominance of audio–visual media.

COMMENTARY AND ANALYSIS

Although many variables are involved in a teacher's adoption of teaching strategies and processes, the teachers in Billerica shared similar resources, including limitations in time, space, and materials. Since all have been working in the same district

for more than 10 years, their day-to-day experiences as well as their staff development experience is shared. While working within a common cultural environment
of the school district, their curriculum frameworks are distinctly different, due to
the differences in student age, intellectual ability, and subject areas. Their teaching
methods vary widely, and most critically, their motivations, aims, and goals for their
students differ in important ways. Some teachers understand Media Literacy to be
powerful because of its ability to elucidate the ways in which media institutions
have the power to shape young people's understanding of the world and themselves
as actors in it. Some teachers understand Media Literacy as a useful expansion of
the powers of analysis and inquiry that are central to understanding how knowledge
is created and used in society. These underlying motivations shape the choices
teachers make about what to teach and how to teach it.

Several teachers in the study observed that projects that involved collaboration
did receive more attention and support from school administrators than projects
developed by teachers individually. However, it also appeared that as the team of
Media Literacy teachers grew stronger within the school community, a number of
factors served to diminish or reduce their influence. For example, during the 3 years
in which 26 teachers received intensive Media Literacy training, none of the
administrative staff including principals, department heads and school curriculum
specialists received any training whatsoever. Only one department head was a
regular observer in the course of 3 years of weekly meetings. As a result, teachers
often found little support and occasionally great hostility to their efforts. Many
teachers complained that although they had the 'official' support of the superintendent, their direct supervisors would dismiss or trivialize Media Literacy, withhold
the small resources they would request, or otherwise put roadblocks in their efforts
to develop new activities and programs for students.

Another phenomenon identified through interviews with teachers in the Billerica
Initiative is that teachers who chose to continue their professional development in
Media Literacy perceived the processes or skills involved in media analysis and
production as directly relevant to the subjects and skills that they already teach. The
cases presented in this chapter show how teachers with various content responsibilities manage to integrate Media Literacy concepts and activities into their
teaching, and how such practices fuel their confidence in the value of these choices.
For a conversation about media violence in the context of a word processing and
desktop publishing skills development course for middle-school students to happen, a teacher needs to have a high level of comfort with trying new ideas, a sense
of his or her own perspective, values, and ideology, and an appreciation for how
students will manage these ideas when they get exposed to them. Without the
confidence that such activities have substantial merit and value to students, it is
unlikely that teachers could sustain these practices as a regular part of classroom
work.

Several teachers voiced concerns about the difficulty of building connections
between Media Literacy and various subject areas. They asked themselves whether

Media Literacy, as a set of concepts and practices, should be integrated into every class where literacy skills are called on, or should Media Literacy have the legitimacy to stand by itself, as a set of knowledge and skills that deserves attention independent of its connection to literature, history, technology education or the arts. The tension around this issue reflects Michael Apple's (1990) observations about the relationship between ideology and curriculum, because Billerica teachers noted that, as a domain, 'mass media' is considered far too trivial, secondary and minor in relation to traditional subject areas. Hence integrating Media Literacy within the curriculum is a survival strategy, because "schools preserve and distribute what is perceived to be 'legitimate knowledge.' Schools confer cultural legitimacy on the knowledge of specific groups" (Apple, 1990, pp. 63–64). It seems unlikely that schools as cultural institutions will be willing to recognize the legitimacy of knowing about and analyzing mass media as long as high-ranking education officials persist on blaming 'evil media' for lower reading scores, or demonizing media and promoting the image of the helpless innocent, manipulated by capitalistic media barons.

Billerica educators received an enormous amount of negative pressure when they chose to accept Whittle's *Channel One* as a classroom resource, even when in doing so, educators recognized its potential as a tool to create opportunities to strengthen students' skills of critical analysis. The established paradigm among educational elites, that television is inadequate, dangerous, and inferior, means that Media Literacy educators cannot, at present, make claims that appear to shift or challenge the current distribution of 'legitimate knowledge.'

Most of the teachers who make use of Media Literacy concepts in their curriculum describe their own high levels of concern about their students' relationships with media culture. Teachers who do not perceive Media Literacy's connection to their curriculum, who believed that media study was displacing the study of more important subjects, or who are not personally worried about children and the influence of media were more likely to use media as a tool for accessing information, or documenting student performance on traditional tasks, and unlikely to continue professional development in Media Literacy.

CONCLUSION

Teachers' choices about what to do in the classroom are motivated by their own underlying philosophies about the subject area, the processes of learning, and their assessment of their own and their students' skills and talents. For many teachers, the dominant application of Media Literacy is in textual analysis, not creative production. The instructional technique of 'textual reading' is a familiar and comfortable process for most teachers. Few teachers in the United States have the access to production technology or the flexibility in their curriculum to involve students in media production, and many are sensitive to the historical contexts in which media production has occurred in schools. They implicitly recognize that they work in a culture where media production activities have been "variously exploited to motivate alienated under-achievers, to extend self-expression and to develop individual creativity as ends in themselves" (Grahame, 1991, p. 148). Even when teachers have the skills to implement a media production activity, large class sizes and the 45-minute period limits teachers' ability to provide students with effective and meaningful hands-on experience in creating, designing, and producing media projects.

Media Literacy will probably continue to grow as a result of the individual efforts of teachers as they discover the resource materials, professional groups and networks of educators with shared interests, and emerging scholarly literature. Work within individual classrooms will always be at the heart of Media Literacy pedagogy. But if Media Literacy is to emerge as a new vision of literacy for the Information Age, then a high degree of coordination will be required from among a wide range of shareholders: the scholarly community, educators in K–12 environments, school administrators and educational leaders, parents, the technology, publishing, and media production industries, and the standardized testing industry. Given the decentralized and politicized nature of U.S. schools, it is unlikely that such coordination will receive the national or even meaningful state-level support it needs, and more likely that Media Literacy initiatives will develop as a result of innovation and experimentation in the diverse 'laboratories' of individual districts, schools, and classrooms.

REFERENCES

Apple, M. W. (1990). *Ideology and curriculum* (2nd ed.). New York: Routledge.

Brown, J. A. (1991). *Television "critical viewing skills" education.* Hillsdale, NJ: Lawrence Erlbaum Associates.

Dorr, A. (1983). No shortcuts to judging reality. In J. Bryant & R. Anderson (Eds.), *Children's understanding of television: Research on attention and comprehension.* New York: Academic Press.

Fehlman, R. (1995, Fall). Editor's note. *Media matters newsletter of the assembly on media arts.* Madison, WI: National Council of Teachers of English.

Firestone, C. (1992). *National leadership conference on media literacy.* Washington, DC: Aspen Institute.

Grahame, J. (1991). The production process. In D. Lusted (Ed.), *The media studies book* (pp. 146–170). London: Routledge.

Hart, A., & Benson, T. (1993). *Media in the classroom.* Southampton: Southhampton Media Education Group.

Hobbs, R. (1994). Pedagogical issues in U.S. Media Education. In S. Deetz (Ed.), *Communication Yearbook 17* (pp. 453–466) London: Sage.

Hobbs, R. (1996). *Harvard institute on media education: Teacher questionnaire results.* Unpublished manuscript.

7

Media Education in Ontario: Generational Differences in Approach

Robert Morgan
University of Toronto

'Media Literacy' has been a required part of the secondary curriculum in Ontario for a decade. Previously, individual teachers, on their own initiative, developed units on newspapers, films, and less frequently, video production within their English practice, whereas arts teachers might include units on "electronic imaging" and photography (Ministry of Education, 1986). However, in 1987 the *English Curriculum Guideline* for Intermediate and Senior levels (ages 12–16+) stipulated media study was to become an official "category of study for one third of scheduled classroom time in one mandatory English credit at each of the Intermediate and Senior Divisions levels" (Ministry of Education, 1987). More recently, a government document entitled *Broad-based Technological Education* (Ministry of Education and Training, 1995) empowered schools to offer courses in "communications technologies" of which "print" is just one. This led to ground-breaking projects in a few schools between the Technology department and English teachers. Nevertheless, for the past 10 years and into the foreseeable future English departments are likely to remain the principal site of Media work.

RESEARCH METHOD AND PROCESS

The Ontario research into teachers' conceptions of media teaching took two complementary forms: interviews with 40 High School teachers as well as a subsequent province-wide survey. The interviews were conducted one-to-one in settings chosen by the teachers and at their convenience. Averaging more than 2 hours in length, they followed a set agenda of some 70 questions that included but extended the original Southampton schedule. These were intended to cover the following topics: life history, teaching background, current work context, espoused aims of Media Education, understanding of the relationship between Media Education and English teaching, curricular choices and teaching methods, the nature and extent of available resources and institutional support; relations with students and sense of their prior media knowledge; and relations to parents and local community. The following section on teachers' generational experiences of media and its impact on their teaching is based on a reading of these interviews. A follow-up survey, employing a revised and more selective set of questions, was designed and sent out to 500 Secondary Schools. The surveys were used as a means of cross-checking patterns emergent in the interviews, but contained some surprising results on their own. One consequence was a closer look at teachers' stated aims for Media Education and its intended impact on students.

Durant (1991) described Media teachers as straddling a number of analytic frameworks, thus employing a "contradictory debris of discursive fragments" (p. 408). The primary focus of this study of 'Media Literacy' in Ontario was to explore the principal discourses teachers drew on in implementing what was, for most of them, new educational territory. For example, 87% of the teachers surveyed had received no preparatory work in this area at the Faculty of Education they attended, whereas the remaining 11% percent typically gestured to an Instructional Media course (which was intended to familiarize teachers with the use of film strips, the making of overheads, etc.) as the sole basis of their training. The starting point of the research project was therefore to chart the discursive resources teachers made use of in thinking about their work in this area. What were the dominant discourses, patterns of talk, and metaphors that structured their sense of Media pedagogy? 'Discourse' is defined here in the Focauldian sense of regularized, institutionally sustained ways of talking, perceiving, and acting in the world. It also carries the connotation of ways of speaking/thinking that are not simply a matter of conscious intention and expression. Discourses are therefore public language forms that are naturalized yet nevertheless remain vested with sociopolitical value. Furthermore, a discursive practice is "constitutive in both conventional and creative ways"; that is, it can contribute to the reproduction of social relationships, systems of knowledge and belief, yet it may also provoke and support delimited social transformations (Fairclough, 1992, p. 65). As a signifying practice, discourse is therefore implicated in the social "exercise of power and struggle(s) over power" (p. 67). This interest in the discourses employed by Media educators is appropriate since Media pedagogy itself, in both English (cf. Masterman, 1985) and Canadian contexts (*Media Literacy Resource Guide*, 1989), could fairly be described as preoccupied with the ideological dimensions of media discourse.

The multiplicity of discourses at work in everyday conversation, however, meant that individual teachers were not expected to produce fully elaborated, totally coherent explanations of 'Media Literacy' in an interview. Instead, their accounts of Media teaching were regarded as being constructed from and reflective of a range of experiential, professional, and public discourses. Finally, there was no assumption that what teachers told researchers about their practices was identical with what they actually did in their classrooms. Although their remarks during interview sessions were sometimes compared to their classroom practices or curriculum outlines, their comments were mainly treated as evidence of the conceptual resources they drew on in making sense to themselves and others of what 'Media Literacy,' a new subject area, was about.

Also relevant to this approach is Hall's (1986) conception of *articulation* (53–54), the idea that any teacher's presentation produces a unique combination and realignment of the discourses it employs. Thus, in building an image of Media pedagogy from the interviews in this study, it became clear that a teacher might access a variety of discourses, some of which were adjacent or complementary in nature, whereas others were likely to be conflictual or contradictory bedfellows. At the level of an individual teacher's response, these diverse elements were typically fused, and provided with a gloss of consistency and homogeneity. In other words, teachers' representations of 'Media Literacy' are treated as intertextual creations, the strands of which originate from a plurality of sources: their own life histories, past and current media uses, formal educational training, the rhetoric of official guidelines and media texts, popular sentiment about the media (e.g., panics about media violence), implicit teacher lore about what works in the classroom (Downing, Harkin & Sosnoski, 1994), departmental policy (if any) regarding Media Education, and especially teachers' own beliefs about their students' media habits and interests. Additionally, the discourses available from any one of these sources is also likely to be multiple, unstable, and contradictory, for example, competing versions of Media Education embodied in different classroom texts.

HOW MEDIA TEACHERS' EXPERIENCES OF MEDIA RELATE TO THEIR TEACHING

This section explores the discursive intersections between teachers' media biographies, their acquired professional vocabularies as teachers of English/Media, and their perceptions of the nature of students' media experience. Most of the teachers we spoke to originally came from small towns, growing up in an era when the configuration of media, their status, and various social functions, were substantially different than they are today. The extracts presented here from teacher interviews have been organized into three clusters, reflecting roughly three different generations of teaching experience. There is, then, approximately a 7-year gap between each group's entry into teaching. The teachers are responding to questions that attempt to get at the relationships noted previously, and their answers reveal interweaving of biography, professional discourse, and their sense of the contemporary moment.

The first group consists of two senior teachers. Alice has taught for 33 years and is the head of the English department in what one of her colleagues describes as a 'Fifties School': an older, conservative staff with a predominantly 'White' and homogeneous student population.[1] Brendan has taught English for 26 years. He is the Head of English in a school that provides mainly academic course work for a multicultural student population.

Alice

Interviewer: What role did the media play in your own childhood and adolescence?

Alice: We didn't have television until I was in Grade 13 because my father thought it was bad for you, so in fact very little. It's true that the newspaper played some role in my adolescence and childhood. Music did. And popular music certainly and radio played a very large part. Popular music ... certainly in my ... adolescence in the 50s; my childhood in the 40s ... books and magazines, particularly books, played a large part. And certainly when I was a teenager ... popular music on the radio was very important.

Interviewer: What are your current media preferences and habits?

Alice: I watch some television. I tend to watch ... predictably I tend to watch *Masterpiece Theatre* and some A and E [Arts and Entertainment channel], some public television, a little bit of CBC—those tend to be my preferences. There are a lot of things I like on television but it's a matter of time. I have to make choices and it's often ... if I'm choosing between reading a book and watching television, I'll choose the book because it's my preferred medium, actually....Although I watch more now and I watch a little bit more widely simply because I'm teaching it. I mean I really need to know what's going on television if I'm going to try to teach it. Of course, I read newspapers regularly. I don't as far as the other kind of things, video and video games, ... I would have no interest in video games [laughs], computer games, and all that kind of stuff. I have watched them because my kids used to play them but it's just not my thing.... Most people who grew up in my generation.... the movies were very important and, in fact, most of us are *very* interested in film.

---

[1]The names and locations used in the extracts have been altered to ensure the anonymity of respondents, because this was a condition of their participation. I would like to thank the Social Science and Humanities Research Council of Canada for their generous support of this work, and also the graduate students who conducted most of the interviews: James Fowlie, Victoria Littman, Carol McBride, Robert Pritchard, Arleen Schenke, and Michael Hoechsmann.

Interviewer: What roles do the media play in the lives of the students you teach?

Alice: Well … a very big role if you're talking about electronic media, if you're talking about television and … video games…. We had one presentation on CDs that I learned a great deal from. And this kid knows, as far as I could tell, everything about them, knows how they were developed, knows the technology, knows the future. You know, many of them know far more about certain aspects of that than I. I think they watch a lot of television … at least many of them do. If you're talking about things like newspapers you find that there are fewer students that pay attention. Television plays a large part in their lives … a much larger part than it does in mine for example, and certainly some aspects of it, video games for example, the whole popular culture part of it, is very, very important in their lives. They are aware of it, much, much more than I am.

Brendan

Interviewer: What role did the media play in your childhood and adolescence?

Brendan: Well, I went to an English public school which meant that there was very little media that penetrated those walls. So, I would say relatively little. I didn't even see television till I came over [to Canada] in '59. Prior to that it was newspapers almost exclusively and magazines. But I would say a fairly small part, probably.

Interviewer: Would you briefly describe your current media preferences and habits?

Brendan: Well, preferences? Every week a group of English teachers goes to see a movie … an art house movie usually and spend most of the evening in going over it, and looking at and trashing it. Or analyzing it, or whatever. A lot of reading of newspapers, a lot of reading of books. I don't get to see theatre that much but certainly television in the sense that TVO [TV Ontario], and channel 17 [PBS] have a lot of material that is very provocative and useful to use in class in one way or another.

Interviewer: Okay. Do you think your current media preferences and habits influence your version of Media Education in any way?

Brendan: Yes they probably do, uh, because my preferences tend to be, as I've said before, sort of analytical and so on, and the way I view film and books and newspapers tends to be with a fairly analytic, critical eye rather than from the production [angle]. And so I suspect that gets reflected in how I deal with it.

Interviewer: Could you reflect on how your biography might have a bearing on your decision to work in Media?

Brendan: I don't think there is any relationship. The only reason I'm working with Media at all, I think, is because it's mandated by the ministry.

Interviewer: What roles do the media play in the lives of the students you teach?

Brendan: I think it plays a very important role in the sense that, as we know, most of them are committed to television and video games and probably less so to newspapers. Although in the senior grades, and hopefully through our tutelage, more and more of them read newspapers and magazines. So, I think it plays a pretty important role in their lives.

Interviewer: Does this perception of the role it plays in their lives affect your curricular objectives?

Brendan: Again, I think our objectives are largely analytical, 'deconstructive' if that's the term you want to use, in that's also the approach that we use in literature. I mean both in literature and Media—I don't think there's a large difference because ultimately what they have to do is to understand how the media influences them. To me that's still the most important aspect of Media teaching, and that is an analytical process.

There is of course no linear, invariant relationship between media-biographic experience and a person's ultimate teaching orientation. There are, nevertheless, a number of themes that emerge from the extracts here and the interviews with other teachers of this generation. First is the idea that the 'critical stance' exhibited by many Media educators toward electronic media can be attributed in part to their personal experience. For many teachers over 40, television was introduced during midchildhood or adolescence. As in Alice's case, it entered their lives as a dramatic new technology, gradually acquiring the connotation of a family medium with shows everyone watched. It carried only a fraction of the channels and viewing hours available today, and was typically highly regulated by parents. Alice and Brendan's primary media relationship during childhood was to print and to books in particular. The rewards of this orientation included entry into the teaching profession. Their current media habits also reflect this bonding with print. As Alice states, "I'll choose the book because it's my preferred medium," whereas Brendan indicates "a lot of reading of newspapers, a lot of reading of books" as his preferred media choices.

During their youth, newspapers and radio were taken-for-granted sources of information, whereas watching a movie was a public event, an evening out. Brendan's weekly excursions with his colleagues to view artistically worthy "films" (students are more likely to speak of "movies") illustrates some of the aura still attached to this medium for this generation for whom going out to the "cinema" was "*very* important" (Alice). This might also account for the number of classic films, such as *Citizen Kane*, that feature in many Media courses during an era when students are more likely to view television movies-of-the-week.

Perhaps most important of all is how the bonding with print has affected the use and perception of other media. In Brendan's terms what's vital is that students understand how electronic "media influences them.... That's still the most important aspect of Media teaching." Print culture is associated with learning and critical analysis. Novels and films are useful to this analytical frame of mind to the extent that they are assimilated as socially significant fantasies and key sites for the cultivation of aesthetic taste. These values are evident in the hierarchical relations many teachers perceive between various media. It may be that many teachers' early experiences of particular media technologies work to establish taken-for-granted high/low culture associations with these forms. Thus older media, identified with high cultural capital and one's very subject formation, appear in a nostalgic, valorized light. In contrast, newer forms appear to be either intriguing (Alice), or alien and suspect (Brendan). Moreover, newer media are utilized and evaluated in terms of criteria appropriate to older media. For instance, asked about their current habits, Alice gestures to the high end of television, *Masterpiece Theatre* and CBC, while Brendan points to TVO (Ontario's educational service) and PBS (Public Broadcasting Service in the United States). All of these broadcasters produce a high percentage of 'classic' dramas, documentaries, and hour-long news programs, catering to an educated, urban, upper-middle class clientele.

Given this historical formation, then, the task of the Media teacher is fairly clear: to effect a conversion. As Brendan put it, "hopefully through our tutelage, more and more of them [will] read newspapers and magazines," while acquiring his own "analytic, critical eye" toward electronic media. Both of these teachers are aware of the media generation gap that exists between themselves and their students, most frequently experiencing it, in the words of one of their cohort, as the problem of "teaching against the grain." Still, there are significant differences that should not be glossed over among teachers of this generation. Alice is genuinely curious and exploratory in her approach, learning from her students, "many of [whom] know far more" about the new technologies than she does. Alice's interviewer remarked in his field notes that Alice left him with a sense of an "enthusiastic" Media teacher who, even if she regarded it her "duty" as an English teacher to oppose what she felt were the limitations of popular culture, had also recently become firmly committed to the possibilities of Media Education, even its "necessity." Perhaps her vital relationship with popular music as an adolescent grounds part of this stance. At any rate, she exhibits a fundamentally different orientation to the new mediascape than Brendan, who, like many teachers is resistant to Media Literacy, and only includes it in his teaching "because it was mandated by the Ministry."

The next pair of teachers, Colleen and Joel, are roughly at midcareer, both having taught for 18 years. Joel teaches in a large, ethnically diverse 'technical' high school that offers roughly equal numbers of 'general' and 'advanced' level courses. He described himself as a "casual" and "creative" teacher with university degrees in journalism and literary studies. He has taught Media Education for 5 years. Colleen works in an inner-city school with "a real mix of Spanish, Portuguese, Jamaican, Italian, [and] Polish" students. She claims to have taught media education in one form or another for 10 years. Representing a different generation than the first group of teachers, Colleen and Joel are similar to their students in growing up in televisual age, a period when electronic media generally played "a huge role" in one's social formation. Nevertheless, some of the same high/low, print/electronic media dichotomies and generational disparities are evident here.

Joel

Interviewer: What role did the media play in your own childhood and adolescence?

Joel: I think I was … your typical kid growing up in the 1960s and 1970s, so the media played a huge role. When I think back, you know we were, we watched a lot of TV and … movies.… We rushed out to buy the Beatle albums when they first came out, got the posters, the whole thing with Woodstock, the hippie thing— I mean, everything. The media fed it all back to us. It had a big impact I think, on shaping a lot of our values and attitudes, between the music we were listening to, the idea that the media telling us all the time that we were kind of like a generation in revolution.… History's shown that it hasn't been much of a revolution, but there was that aspect. And I was always, I still am, powerfully affected by film.… And I would even say that we were maybe more affected than the students now, in that there's a wider range of media. But you have to realize that in those days, you know … I was 6 or 7, the possibilities of TV were just starting. Like we were really hooked on TV. Like *Leave it to Beaver*, *Father Knows Best* or *Dick Van Dyke*, you kind of thought everybody lives in nice little houses in the suburbs, and the husbands and wives have twin beds … [laughter]. I forgot about that! … And you know, right down to where I can think of when I was 14 or 15, you think of what it would be like to get married you had this picture of a little table with placemats everywhere.… You'd run out and get your clothes on what was currently fashionable. The music of course had a major effect, major impact. So I think it was a time when we were really affected by the media.

Interviewer: More than now?

Joel: Well, I find in my general level students, they aren't as hugely consumers of the media as we were, because a lot of them have part time jobs so they don't, they're not watching TV as much. I actually don't know if it would be more or not, but I just know that there was such a fascination when we were kids because it was so new.... I think kids now growing up take TV for granted. I suppose it depends on what [your] definition of mass media is. If you want to go to things like videogames and all, then, maybe it does have more of an affect. But my observation is that kids I grew up with, we would get newspapers and we would read certain sections of the newspaper. These kids wouldn't bother, they just don't.... We probably read more.

Interviewer: What media do you tend to be least involved with and why?

Joel: Least involved with? Oh, television, yeah, 'cause I mean, it's basically so junkie, and I don't say that from a sort of snobbish posture. I just, I have a TV and lots of nights I feel like just relaxing and I look through or flip through to see what would I like to watch. I mean it's such crap, you know at least by my standards. But I'll watch baseball games and hockey games, but the sitcoms are so.... They're not clever like the old *Mash* series, or they're so slapstick and garbagy. I barely watch TV. I force myself to watch TV now, because the students talk about the commercials so I haven't seen any of them.... So I turn on the TV to see what the commercials are that they're talking about. Movies too. I don't have time to get out and watch any more the way I used to. I rent videos, not real frequently, but I do rent videos when I can.

Interviewer: Do you think your current preferences and habits influence your version of Media Education in any way?

Joel: Yeah, I think they do.... I'm not just sure the total effect it has.... Except when I ask the students about shows, for instance, they tell me about it and I don't know what they're talking about, so I have to go and check it out. But then again, when I talk about magazines and, you know, specialty markets, they don't know what I'm talking about.

Interviewer: Could you reflect on how your biography might have a bearing on your decision to work in this area?

Joel: One of the things I think that has affected it is when I took my journalism course.... It was taught by Wilson B. Key, who wrote the book *Subliminal Seduction and Media Sexploitation*, and he was a very dynamic lecturer.... I think because I got interested in that, that definitely had an effect and that's why I think I do a good job on the advertising section, particularly decoding. And I studied psychology, so a lot of the social psychology material that's out there around the media, I tend to pick up and read it and I bring that to them.

Interviewer: What roles do the media play in the lives of the students you teach?

Joel: Well, the major role is entertainment I think for most of the kids.... Some of them are not very high consumers of television because a lot of them have part time jobs. And I'll tell you it's very rare to find the general level that have much to do with magazines and newspapers. I mean, basically when we discussed the Tory ad [that] got withdrawn, their knowledge of politics is hazy at best. So there could be good issues for the classroom, but they just fall flat.... I dropped the magazine project, which I thought was a good project. They didn't seem to grasp what I wanted. Advertising always works—like, they get into talking about the way sex is used to sell, that gets them. And that's why I go into TV issues and movie issues, because that's basically where their expertise is. And you try to expose them a little bit to the newspaper, and, you know, how the media affects issues in the larger community. Say, you might talk about the Rodney King situation.... But, definitely I try to chose my curriculum based on what will interest them. Because if it doesn't interest them, it's really difficult.

Colleen

Interviewer: What role did the media play in your own childhood and adolescence?

Colleen: I grew up in a family of nine children. I was the third oldest.... It was quite an interesting thing to see how my mom and dad very quickly became quite aware of the fact that television and homework were two very diverse things. So, we had very strict rules about TV. I think any night that was a school night we were not allowed to watch TV after supper.... My grandmother also lived with us and it was interesting because she had her shows that she liked and it was extremely important that we as children made sure that she had her choices. And I think that's really something that I see missing nowadays, that there's so many TV's in a house and you know, everybody gets to have their way; there's no sharing. We had those moments, you know, the *Ed Sullivan Show*. If something was on that my dad or mom decided

Interviewer:

Colleen:

was Okay like *The Wizard of Oz*, it would be a Sunday event where you would sit down as a family.... But then that was it. It was something very regulated as opposed to just constantly being there .... With my students it's on all the time. The choices have just been you know, obliterated, and the control seems to really come from the machine as opposed to the people who own it. And we had the local newspaper, the radio, the local station was on quite often.... That was sort of a background sound. Films were a rare treat.

What roles do the media play in the lives of the students you teach?

Oh ... an incredibly crucial role, especially for my students who, in their situation in life right now, do not have very strong family units. I think that it becomes a role model for many students who are struggling. I believe at those very vulnerable years in teenage life a number of them make their life choices, you know, surrounding what they've seen on the media ... We talk about the issue quite often and it's incredible how many shows, for young people, really glorify the idea that as long as you're cool, you're the 'smart-Alec,' get the laughter and defy every authority going, you know, you'll get the laughs, get the support.... But don't ever be curious or ask a question or, you know, peruse a book or read more about something.... They are in those crucial years, and what ends up happening, their whole curiosity is sometimes cut. Or, what really gets me, is this whole focus on.... Finding a relationship, and especially with the girls.... Another big area—I've had many talks about this with the kids— sex. [Imitating a student] "Miss, you know, it just gets pushed upon us all the time.... " And so, you know, I see the effects.

These discursive overlaps and collisions in the teachers' remarks above are interesting. Joel, for instance, indicates he watched "a lot of television" when younger, is familiar with early sitcoms, and still actively follows many televised sporting events. Yet he experiences his historical difference from his students when they tell him he is out of touch with their viewing practices. On the other hand, he attempts and fails to interest them in magazines and newspapers, media that were more dominant when he was growing up. What is also salient are the tensions between the various discourses the two teachers previously mentioned draw on in their accounts of their past media experience, current preferences, and teaching practices. Joel alternates between a biographic discourse in which television is fondly recalled and a literary-critical one that positions him as a 'snobbish' media consumer. This literary-critical discourse is further buttressed by reference to another discourse from psychology and its premise of an unconscious, subliminal seduction. From this perspective, he neatly dismisses television as "junkie" and "crap ... by my standards." He thus retains the same suspicious eye, hierarchies of high and low media technologies, that characterized the first group of teachers. And having denounced television in such a totalizing way, he finds himself in the ironic position—for a Media teacher presumably interested in his field—of "forcing" himself to watch television (a sentiment not uncommon among this generation of teachers) in order to communicate with his students.

Colleen's remarks exhibit some of the same twists and turns. On the one hand she recalls how radio was a constant "background" in her childhood home. Moreover, television was frequently the site of shared family experience, and, in the case of her grandmother, an opportunity for intergenerational understanding. On the other hand television currently disseminates an array of antisocial values: pupils' premature sexual relationships, "racial tempers," antiauthoritarian postures, conflictual and violent behaviors—a virtual catalog of "youth problems" is laid on the doorstep of television. Students are represented as passive, indiscriminate viewers, directly parroting whatever they watch. Instead of providing positive "role models," television "pushes" dysfunctional worldviews and fosters a nihilism that stunts the social imagination of the next generation. Although both Joel and Colleen regard television as a negative force, they disagree about the nature and extent of its effects, or even how frequently their students actually watch it. Joel alleges that many of his students are "not very high consumers of television" because they maintain part-time jobs; Colleen's remarks imply that students base many of "their life choices" on what they see on television. Yet Joel is inconsistent on this theme, later indicating his curriculum deals with "TV issues.... Because that's.... Where their expertise is."

In general, teachers of this generation appeared to be caught between their mostly favorable past personal experiences of electronic media, and an acquired professional discourse that was hypercritical of media other than print, especially those forms most frequently discussed in Media classrooms: television, advertising, and videotape materials.[2] This critical stance is also reflected in the high frequency of advertising as a topic on the Media curricula we examined. It appeared to provide a rich field for deconstructive work that revealed popular media as manipulative. Considered from the angle of their classroom personae, therefore, teachers approached the media as a serious activity, one demanding rational discernment, a separation of the true from the false in media representations, and the sorting of media products into the authentic versus the debased. Left to their natural inclinations, students were seen as treating the media as mere "entertainment," thus risking

---

[2]The order here reflects teacher ranking on the provincial questionnaire of the most frequently examined media in the classroom. The most neglected media were: compact discs, photography, telephone, computer games, walkman, the internet, and multimedia.

"incorporation by the media." Teachers' own past media-biographic experience or present televisual pleasures, then, were rarely employed in relating to students' current uses of the media. Asked how their past or present media preferences might influence their teaching approach, several remarked that their "professionalism" and "objectivity" deflected any negative feelings they might hold about popular media. Most teachers were unable to directly draw on their past or present media experiences in their work in the media classroom. For example, the role television played in their own formation as a flawed, pervasive, and important cultural resource, a cultural forum in effect (Newcomb & Hirsch, 1994), remained largely unexamined in understanding students' current relationships with this medium.

Colleen's media critique is remarkable for its interweaving of a variety of adjacent discourses. It combines religious moralism (TV destroying family values, "corrupt[ing] young people's minds"), Parsonian sociology ("role models"), behavioral psychology (TV's unmediated "effects" on behavior), sociopolitical critique of "consumer culture," and, the baseline discourse of English teachers, print-centric notions of "critical autonomy" and aesthetic taste. That her critical perspective is a discursive patchwork in no way diminishes its power; most commentary is an intertextual mixture of this kind. Rather, focusing on her frequent shifts of discursive ground raises issues of the coherence of her model, what it enables or disables in her Media teaching, and the manner in which she invokes specific forms of student identity. When she directly imitates their voices, as she does at the end of the extract for example, she tends to constitute students as hapless victims of the media, thus justifying a pastoral role for herself as Media teacher.

Poster's (1995) work is suggestive in thinking about the dilemmas of this generation of Media teachers. Insisting on the links between particular technologies, historical change, and modes of identity, he viewed electronic communication systems as "new language formations" initiating profound and "extensive change[s] in the culture, in the way that identities are structured" (p. 24). What is at stake in the shift to electronic media is therefore not just a matter of increased efficiency in message transmission across a broader range of signs and information. Rather, they destabilize many of the intellectual traditions "profoundly rooted in print culture" (p. 57) such as the concept of the autonomous rational individual fostered by reading (p. 58), representational paradigms that stress decoding (p. 19), and binary distinctions between an enlightened, critical media user and a massified, media-controlled consumer (p. 49). Indeed, Poster asks us to note how most *a priori* rejections of electronic media as suitable vehicles of rational communication come from those raised within print-centric values (p. 5). This is certainly the position of that frequent keynote speaker at English teacher conferences, Neil Postman (1985). It is also the basic orientation of English, the 'sponsoring' subject for 'Media Literacy' in Ontario. Nonetheless, English teachers entering the profession after 1960 were also members of a culture that experienced an explosion of electronic media. They were part of "the broadcasting era" in which "a small number of producers" distributed information and images "to a large number of consumers" (Poster, 1995, p. 3). The ambiguities of this era (richness of information flow, lopsided ownership and control) help in part to explain the conflicted attitudes of Colleen and Joel who speak alternatively of "media effects" and their own media pleasures. Such teachers straddle both print and broadcasting eras even as their students engage with postmodern media forms like computer games, the Internet, multi-user displays, and interactive multimedia forms—all of which eventuate in new forms of subjectivity and sociality.

> Contemporary society contains modernist institutions and discourses which privilege certain configurations of the subject, those that support autonomous rationality.... But contemporary society also contains postmodernist institutions and discourses, such as electronically mediated communications, which support new configurations of the subject....There is a secular trend emanating from electronic communications that undermines the stability of the figure of the rational autonomous individual. Hence the outcry against these communications, the warning of their dangers by those adhering to modernist ... positions. (Poster, 1995, p. 76)

Poster's overall approach, then, focuses on the positioning of individuals in historically specific language/media patterns instead of assigning transhistorical values to media forms such as print, or privileging the critically autonomous subject of modernity. His attention to the discontinuities and overlaps between different technological contexts and the forms of subjectivity each supports can also be applied to teachers' media lives and teaching orientations.

The final pair of teachers are the closest in age to their students and are also new to teaching. Naum is in his third year of teaching within the Communications Technology area of a suburban High School. The program he works with is unusual in several ways because, as he notes, "we have the gravy train here ... as far as [communications] equipment requirements go," and he has become the 'pointman' for "integration with English." His particular strength as a teacher derives from his strong background in "radio and television arts." Derek has taught for 5 years, working in a large English department in a metropolitan academic school. He sees himself as providing "student-centered learning ... as a facilitator ... someone who is there to provide resources and forms of assistance." Like their students, these teachers had intense relationships with electronic media while young, and embody aspects of this experience in their teaching.

Naum

Interviewer: What role did the media play in your own childhood and adolescence?

Naum: Aside from watching a lot of television, I don't know. It's a powerful medium.... Very influential. Like it was a regular, youknow, viewing habit guiding you.... Very informational in a lot of areas.

Interviewer: Can you describe your viewing habits?

Naum: It unfortunately revolved a lot around television, you know the Saturday morning cartoons, a lot of sports and [my] parents were always into watching, you know, your *National Geographic* and all those types of nature things.... So there was good and bad with it. You know it can be, if you get hooked on it, a tough thing to get out of, but in that regard a lot of life revolved around it ....

Interviewer: What are your current media preferences and habits?

Naum: I read a lot more than I ever did. News magazines and so on. That's part of when you get into working in industry and like you kind of have to do it, so I absorb a lot more news magazines and not so much newspapers. I'm more magazine-oriented now than before—print, I should say.

Interviewer: How do you think your past and current media preferences influence your approach in Media Education?

Naum: Yeah, like video is so overwhelming you know, kids are just totally absorbed by the video portion without substance or any basis behind it. They watch a lot.... It's so passive, it's such a passive piece of entertainment I guess. I try to get them to do more writing. For the basic English skills, you know. You can't get by without it. It's an essential skill of life. Writing sentences.... This is the project, write. They're forced to write sentences, maybe under the guise of video [scripts]. It forces, you know, the kids that normally don't write well or anything to at least scratch something out on paper. It's kind of—God I hate to say—tricking them into doing it, but it, I suppose, forces them … [video] is the attraction, but I think they know up front, I tell them this is writing too, this is not just pictures and games and so on.

Interviewer: What role do the media play in the lives of the students you teach?

Naum: It's a major part of their life, whether you consider media to be the television and the print end or the computer end or whatever. I don't know, that just seems to be the world that we're growing up in now. The Information Age is what's dictating, I think what really drives them.

Derek

Interviewer: What role did the media play in your own childhood and adolescence?

Derek: It's enormous: both the role of radio and television and print media, all enormously influential.... The role of popular music generally. Television, early television. Um, and yeah, I think that gives me a very helpful perspective for the course, to see how those perspectives both coincide with and in some cases collide with the perspectives of people growing up today.

Interviewer: What are your current media preferences and habits?

Derek: My biggest interest outside of school, and inside of school, is music, so that's certainly the medium with which I'm most involved. But I try to be aware of developments in the media generally, whether it's television, films, or newspapers.

Interviewer: Which media do you tend to be least involved with?

Derek: That's a difficult question. I find that very difficult to answer. I mean, I'm involved in different media in different ways. I would suppose I would say magazines as a source of information. I'm more reliant on newspapers.

Interviewer: Do your current media preferences and habits influence your version of Media Education in any way?

Derek: I think inevitably they have to some way or another, even if it's just in terms of the activities that one constructs or the examples that one comes up with in class discussion.... It certainly helps to decide some of the issues that I think are worth examining, when we look at movies for example, television or newspapers.

Interviewer: Could you reflect on how your biography might have a bearing on your decision work in the area of Media Studies?

Derek: Well, I do have a background in various ways in media. As I say, I worked as a writer, journalist, teaching radio, playing music myself, so it's an area of enormous interest to me and I have huge interests in.... Film processing for example. So it's, as I say, something—I jumped at the chance to teach Media courses.

Interviewer: How do you think your past experience has affected your overall approach in this area?

Derek: I think I have a lot to bring in terms of just knowledge of media and media issues, to the course. And it excites me, so that's what I try and instill in students.

Interviewer: What roles do the media play in the lives of the students you teach? Also, does your perception of these roles affect your curricular objectives?

Derek: Yeah, very much so. My perception, what I make clear to the students at the beginning of the year, is that I think they know an enormous amount about the media generally, and it's in many ways the primary source of information, and my role is simply to give some shape to the understanding they have and to get them to look a little bit more critically at the media that are such a big part of their lives.

In many ways, these teachers represent an emerging trend in Media pedagogy, one different from the critical–interpretive tradition illustrated by the teachers cited so far. Both place strong emphasis on production work with their students, an orientation that arises from their grounding in another discursive framework than that of English. Naum's degree is from a technical college in the area of communication arts, whereas Derek has a background in cultural theory, journalism, audio recording, and film work. Yet, beyond the similarity of their technical knowledge about electronic media, there are major differences in outlook and in the way they draw on and interpret their past experiences of these technologies. Although Naum acknowledges television was "very informational" while growing up, he now mainly rejects his past televisual experience as "unfortunate," a case of being "hooked" and breaking a dependency. In a sense, his notion of Media teaching repeats his own history in miniature because, to a great extent, he attempts to wean students away from their "overwhelming" and "totally absorb[ing]" video pleasures by "tricking them" into his current preference for writing and print. Once again, high/low media polarities are active in his discourse, as well as the missionary project of saving those addicted to subrational media forms. In contrast, Derek's remark that his early music and televisual experience provides "a very helpful perspective for the course, to see how those perspectives both coincide with and in some cases collide with the perspectives of people growing up today" offers a rare example in our interviews of a teacher self-reflexively aware of the dialectical role his media-biographic experience plays in his teaching. He also astutely points out that he is "involved in different media in different ways," thus breaking with the media hierarchies evident in most other respondents' answers. His comments elsewhere also indicate a concerted effort to bypass the split between analysis and production that plagues many of the school programs in media we examined.

There is a final issue worth raising with respect to this younger generation of Media teachers. Although they are frequently the most enthusiastic advocates of 'Media Literacy' and generationally nearer to students' media experience— thus, like Derek, bringing "a lot ... in terms of knowledge of media and media issues"—they are also prone to what could be called the *disciplinary messiness* of Media Education. That is, Media pedagogy at its best is often a necessarily "messy," "relational" subject area because it explores the manner in which different technologies, social identities, and regions of culture interact. Just what counts as a technology or a significant media form is also often unclear. For example, the telephone, walkman, videogames, and school texts are rarely examined *as media* although they are pervasive in student experience. One younger teacher puts the issues in this way:

> What I find most challenging about teaching Media would be dealing with the prospect of having a course or a semester in front of you and coming to terms with what you can include and what you can't include. So I guess sometimes I find the whole thing difficult in that I have to be careful not to become overwhelmed or too immersed in a particular area.... Sometimes I find myself thinking, "Oh my God! Oh my God! I can't do any of this!" or "Where do I begin?" or "How do I organize it?" And, I mean, we do have the curriculum, but because you're talking about the media, obviously certain things will always be changing, you know, if you're pulling in current issues and that sort of thing. The critical framework stays the same ... to a certain extent. And some of the key concepts stay the same. So, I guess there's a comfort level with that. But every time I begin a course I sort of feel this overwhelming panic thinking how do I deliver this or what do I want the students to become involved in or engaged with. That's what I find the most difficult.... Media Education is really evolving and where Media teachers used to have a certain level of comfort, I really think that those areas don't exist any more. I mean it's difficult now just to teach about genre, just to teach about television, film, the music industry. That doesn't really work. The boundaries are all being blurred now.... So, I find that a real challenge, to know how to organize and present things for the students so that they can make sense of some of it, because I don't think things are as clear cut as they used to be.

There is, then, the problem of disciplinary clarity for many teachers who otherwise have usefully begun to question inherited subject boundaries. The idea that nearly anything is fair game for Media teachers has important consequences. First, like the teacher above, novice Media teachers often feel "overwhelmed" and "panicky" about what is focal to their work. If anything and everything is potential grist for 'Media Literacy', then teachers will inevitably prove themselves incompetent. It also leads to the almost frenzied sense some teachers have of needing to "watch and read everything their students watch and read" if they are to feel adequately prepared. Secondly, in the incisive commentary of one of the researchers, Arleen Schenke, this situation often produces:

> [a] kind of pluralism that avoids accountability for 'what' and 'why' you teach what you teach. Subjecting Media Education to 'anything' is to produce the circumstances of being 'nowhere'. There's no political project beyond the repetitious performance of deconstruction. There's no way of steering a path through the clutter of material. Elizabeth's classroom cupboards are full of 'pieces' of taped material that have no currency or context.... Beyond their existence as mere 'material.' On what grounds is she collecting what she's collecting? What does the discourse of Media teaching do to Media teachers? What is this scramble to collect 'everything' in order to be able to teach 'anything'?[3]

---

[3]I am indebted to Arleen Schenke for raising these issues in her field notes.

DECLARED AIMS OF MEDIA TEACHERS

Following is a sample of responses from the provincial survey to the linked questions. The primary focus is on the discursive patterns embedded in teachers' responses, but also on the implications of these patterns for classroom practice and student subjectivities.

(A)   *"How do you define the aims of Media Education?"*

(B)   *"What difference should Media Education make to students who take it?"*

(A1) To make students aware of the different media, their influences, power, the dangers, and the effects of each.

(B1) They should know how to deconstruct the messages delivered by the various media and be less vulnerable to manipulation. They should be critical thinkers about the media.

(A2) To have students develop a healthy skepticism and critical outlook on the various media, especially how information is manipulated and packaged; to empower them.

(B2) To be able to understand what the media are doing and be able to deconstruct [them].

(A3) To help students become more aware, more critical with respect to mass media.

(B3) They should question media more critically; be more aware of how media products are constructed.

(A4) To educate all students about the power of the media.

(B4) They should be aware of the influence media exerts on them. They should see how our culture and values are shaped by the media and respond accordingly.

(A5) To make the student more aware of the influences and choices in the media; to expose their bias and assumptions; to make intelligent choices regarding the impact of the media on oneself.

(B5) Their wariness of media and [their] impact should be remarkably heightened.

(A6) To offer intellectual self-defense for students, a critique of consumer society, and a challenge to stereotypes (race and gender).

(B6) These goals are largely reached according to student self-reporting.

(A7) Media are to be deconstructed as text.

(B7) To provide students with the ability to discriminate and judge the media and their messages; to protect themselves against manipulation; to enjoy the artistry of thoughtful media presentations.

The teachers' responses discussed here are loosely representative, providing a sense of the tone and framework within which many teachers appear to work. The language here is worth noting in some detail. Media are the active force in the relationship: "media are doing," they construct, act on, manipulate, seduce, influence identity, shape culture—exert power, in short; students, on the other hand, are done to, acted on, manipulated by, exposed or vulnerable to—do not exert power. The implicit assumptions are behavioristic: that adolescents are overwhelmingly passive in relation to media; second, that effects flow only in one direction, from media institutions outwards; third, media effects are "massive," overwhelmingly negative, and directly absorbed; fourth, that teachers counteract media influence by "empowering" students through turning them into "skeptical" "media consumers." This process involves learning to adopt the rational discourse modeled by teachers, one that can secure a discriminating taste, "critical autonomy" and "distance" in future media interactions. As one teacher remarked, "hopefully, they will think before flipping a switch on an electronic medium" once they have taken a Media Literacy course. In contrast to English, where the goal is to provoke a greater interest in books and reading, it seems the desired effect of 'Media Literacy' is less frequent media use, and a "resistant," "self-defensive" posture if one does succumb. The pastoral attitude overtly surfaces in the idea of students' confessional, self-monitoring of their media practices in B6, and in the state of "heightened" "wariness" to media sins in B5. That such views were widely held is implied by another respondent:

I have found overall:

1. a negative portrayal of the media [in media workshops and provided materials];
2. a constant implication that the media are involved in a conspiracy. Some of the workshops sound like Robert Ludlum novels;
3. a lack of knowledge about practical restrictions facing media [institutions]....

The concept of 'deconstruction' that figures prominently in several answers (B1, B2, B3, A7) directly echoes the primary 'key concept' in the Ontario *Media Literacy Resource Guide*: "all media are constructions" (Ministry of Education, 1989, p. 8). This widely endorsed axiom can obscure as much as it reveals. To the extent that analysis remains at the level of a structural parsing of contents, the performative aspects of media are underplayed. This approach neglects the fact that media texts are experienced as active social processes (e.g., watching television with others), and are constituted differently depending on the interpretive community in which they are activated. Constructivism in its textual mode thus has a tendency to discount the force of media practices, a move evident in A7 for example, in favor of textualized media products. Moreover, the notion that all media are constructed comfortably dovetails with conspiracy theory. Thus, references in teachers' comments to the constructed nature of media regularly occurred in conjunction with the discourse of manipulation.

> Jenny: The general one [aim] of course is that I simply want them to be able to be critical thinkers about the media. I mean critical in the sense they understand that media is a series of constructions and how that's put together.... And it's going to keep them from being duped in some way....
>
> Anna: Well, I would say that the aims of Media Education are to create in the minds of our students, questioners, critical thinkers, not just taking everything that they see for granted .... It's waking them up to understanding the connections and how media is constructed and just how much of a part of our daily lives it is and how it can affect us sometimes without noticing it.... I would like to see it as a relationship where they are able to meet the media on their terms and they are not controlled by it.

'Deconstruction,' in this context appears to simply involve exposing strategies of manipulation. The anatomizing of media texts somehow provides an antidote, results in a transition from an unconscious to a conscious state (being "duped" and "waking up"), a change from indiscriminate bodily pleasures and emotional responses to rationality ("critical thinkers"). A related premise is that if something is constructed, it is consciously designed, marked by a singular will and intention. What remains unexplored in this version of constructionism are the collective, impersonal dimensions of media production, as well as the dynamics of media appropriation.

The polarity in Anna's final sentence—either students control the media or are controlled by it—introduces a dichotomy at work in some of the other remarks cited: critical autonomy versus passive pleasure. In their 1973 research, Murdock and Phelps noted that becoming an English teacher seemed to require a "cut[ting] away or suppress[ing] large areas of personal experience" by supplanting their "involvement with popular culture" with a commitment to high culture and a 'critical' discourse on 'Mass Culture.' Instead, the authors recommended Media Education might usefully begin from another premise altogether: students' and teachers' own media lives and pleasures. Teachers in particular should attempt "to understand their own experience[s] of popular culture" if they expected to engage in "a constructive dialogue" with students about the media. The basic questions to ask in such an approach are "what is of value" in our media choices and preoccupations, and what is the basis of that value (Murdock & Phelps, 1973, pp. 148–149). For the most part, teachers appear to overlook their useful question: "not what are the mass media doing to adolescents, but what are adolescents doing with the media" (p. 141). Similar to the classrooms Murdock and Phelps investigated, the responses above illustrate an overemphasis on "deleting, criticizing, and inhibiting" media use, while at the same time teachers neglect the fact that most students already actively "make judgments and discriminations" about popular culture, "selecting ... and rejecting" what they encounter. In contrast, the Ontario *Media Literacy Resource Guide* suggests that it is principally the learning of "Media Literacy techniques" that "enables students to establish and maintain the kind of critical distance on their culture that makes possible critical autonomy: the ability to decode, encode, and evaluate the symbol systems that dominate their world" (Ministry of Education, 1989, p. 10). Indeed, code-cracking is the order of the day in most Media classrooms. This approach both confirms a long history of suspicion regarding the media within education (Lusted, 1985), and reinforces the view that the important meanings are the 'hidden' ones. This discourse dates back at least to F. R. Leavis' work and lives on in 'cultural heritage' approaches to teaching English.

RECOVERING LOST MEDIA LIVES

Discursive practices "are characterized by the delimitation of a field of objects, the definition of a legitimate perspective for the agent of knowledge, and the fixing of norms for the elaboration of concepts and theories" (Foucault, 1977, p. 199). This exploration of Ontario teachers' representations of Media pedagogy has attempted to highlight the manner in which their remarks constitute both the media as objects of classroom knowledge and roles for themselves and their students as "agents of knowledge." That is, the discourses teachers employ help to set the limits of what teachers may do, and the subjectivities students are invited to adopt, in the 'Media Literacy' classroom. A teacher's own historical experiences with the media are an important consideration in understanding the dominant paradigm in play in a given classroom. But the relationship that can be traced between a teacher's personal media experience and her/his subsequent version of pedagogy is never a simple or direct one. Rather, that teacher's past personal/social formation-in-media is constantly rearticulated by the mediating influences of acquired professional discourses, government policy initiatives, the technological imagination of the generation sitting in front of them, as well as their own current media preoccupations and pleasures. Generational media experience does appear, however, to determine which media are fondly remembered and treated as educationally significant. It thus needs to be accounted for in any calculation of the unstated assumptions and subjective investments that underpin or work to displace historically dominant models of Media Education. In this light, Hartley (1992) suggests we need "to think about where some of our critical assumptions have come from, and whether they are adequate for contemporary [cultural] production" (p. 137). Many of the questions he poses to himself as a television theorist—"[What] place [did] TV occupy in my own personal (social) formation? How does my own history fit in with that of TV? Where does my television consciousness come from and what did it feel like or connect with at the time?" (p. 138)—indicate the initial steps of a project that could equally well be undertaken by Media educators.

REFERENCES

Downing, D., Harkin, P., & Sosnoski, J. (1994). Configurations of lore: The changing relations of theory, research and pedagogy. In D. Downing (Ed.), *Changing classroom practices: Resources for literary and cultural studies* (pp. 3–34). Urbana: National Council of Teachers of English.

Durant, A. (1991, Winter). Noises off-screen: could a crisis of confidence be good for Media Studies? *Screen, 32*(4), 407–428.

Fairclough, N. (1992). *Discourse and social change*. Cambridge: Polity Press.

Foucault, M. (1977). *Language, counter-memory, practice*. Ithaca: Cornell University Press.

Hall, S. (1986). On postmodernism and articulation: An interview. *Journal of Communication Inquiry, 10*, 45–60.

Hartley, J. (1992). *Tele-ology*. London & New York: Routledge.

Lusted, D. (1985). A history of suspicion: Educational attitudes to television. In D. Lusted & P. Drummond (Eds.), *Television and schooling* (pp. 11–18). London: British Film Institute.

Masterman, L. (1985). *Teaching the media*. London: Comedia.

Ministry of Education and Training. (1995). *Broad-based Technological Education: Curriculum Guideline*. Toronto, Ontario: Queen's Printer.

Ministry of Education. (1986). *Visual arts: Curriculum guideline*. Toronto, Ontario: Queen's Printer.

Ministry of Education. (1987). *English curriculum guideline: Intermediate and senior divisions.* Toronto, Ontario: Queen's Printer.

Ministry of Education. (1989). Media literacy resource guide. Toronto, Ontario: Queen's Printer.

Murdock, G., & Phelps, G. (1973). *Mass media and the secondary school*. Basingstoke: Macmillan.

Newcomb, H., & Hirsch, P. (1994). Television as a cultural forum. In H. Newcomb (Ed.), *Television, the critical view* (5th ed., pp. 503–515). New York & Oxford: Oxford University Press.

Poster, M. (1995). *The second media age*. Cambridge, MA: Polity Press.

Postman, N. (1985). *Amusing ourselves to death*. New York: Penguin.

8

Conclusion:
Paradigms Revisited

Andrew Hart
University of Southampton

This concluding chapter summarizes and discusses the main findings of the project. A range of economic, cultural, social, and political variables are identified that encourage or repress the development of Media Education in different national contexts. Although we have found a rich variety of forms and practices within familiar basic paradigms, we have also found some surprising silences and some 'structured absences' in the teaching we observed. There was a recurrent lack of attention to: classroom interaction and dialogue about media; space for young people's own media experience and knowledge; opportunities for active involvement in the social production of texts; teaching in context through engagement with media processes and technologies; engagement with political issues; and learning about media institutions. School policies, support, and environment provide a local framework that mediates the power of larger sociocultural forces. We have found that the major factor in determining the teaching processes and strategies of English\Media teachers is autobiographical, and is therefore necessarily intimately related to their own developing experiences of media.

We also look back briefly at some of the specific issues raised by the different studies, and took forward to their implications for the development of effective Media Education on a global scale. Each chapter of the book presents a glimpse of the larger studies that they report on. None of the studies is representative of teaching approaches specific to any country, except in an indicative way. We have only just begun to retrieve teachers' sense of their aims and assumptions and the way they structure actual lessons. Even so, we can make some useful and productive comparisons, provided that they are tentative and provisional, pending further research.[1]

---

[1]I am grateful to Sue Court for her initial contribution to this chapter.

We have at least done something to remedy the "enormous dearth of descriptive work in classrooms" (Brumfit & Mitchell, 1989, p. 6). In addition, by analyzing what we have found, we have also uncovered a range of models and paradigms that English\Media teachers have drawn on with varying degrees of awareness and explicitness. We have shown how these models have been made operational according to the opportunities and limitations inherent in relatively uniform settings and with the same age-group of students (14- to 16-year-olds). We have shown, too, how strongly influential some paradigms have been (and remain) among teachers of English in most of the contexts we have studied. We hope that the recognition of these patterns will be more than simply reassuring to teachers of English\Media.[2] I hope this book enables them to reflect critically on their own practice and that of other teachers in order to evaluate and improve their own practice.

We recognize the limitations of the research here in terms of scale, depth, and scope. Future work on Media Education will need to expand beyond the limits of the English-speaking world and beyond the confines of English-teaching classrooms, especially in the Spanish-speaking world, where Media Education is recognized as of crucial importance for different reasons. It will also need to find ways of sampling more diverse classroom contexts. For example, in South Africa, it would be interesting to widen the sample to include more Indian teachers who have been involved in Media Education and, in the future, to look at developing work among native African communities. It will need to look at more cross-curricular work and at more specialized work in Media Studies. It will also need to find more sophisticated and methodologically rigorous ways of looking at teaching than observing single lessons, and provide a basis for generalization that selective case studies cannot claim to do. But no one should underestimate the difficulty or expense of doing so.

Toward a Framework for Comparative Analysis

This book began by raising some major questions about current practices in Media Education:

1. How are teachers living in the new multimedia world, both in their personal lives and in their classroom practice? How do they see this world in relation to their personal philosophies of teaching?
2. How are schools responding as institutions? To what extent do school policies recognize the importance of young people's extracurricular culture?
3. What influences are exerted by national and local curricular authorities? Do current formal curricula encourage engagement with new media technologies?

---

[2]This term is used throughout the chapter when Media Teaching within English is indicated.

It is clearly impossible to understand fully the vast complexity of concerns, motivations, aims, strategies, and methods that characterise the range of pedagogical approaches analyzed in this book. We can only try to trace some of the patterns and contours that may help us focus on the major issues in a very simplified form. The diagram in Fig. 8.1 is an attempt to represent some of the background factors that have affected, if not determined, the approaches of our teachers and the forms of teaching that they introduced into their classrooms. It may serve as a starting point and an analytical framework, however crude, for the more detailed comparative analysis that follows. As the discussion proceeds, it will become clear that some of these variables are necessary preconditions for systematic teaching about the media, whereas others are desirable but not vital to its growth. It is already clear that our research has shown that none of these variables in isolation can be considered sufficient to ensure effective Media teaching.

Teachers who read this book should be able to place themselves somewhere within the circle of variables, perhaps adding further factors of their own but, at least, understanding something of the complex pattern of autobiographical, cultural, curricular, and institutional constraints on their own teaching strategies and processes.

We focus first on how teachers are living in the new multimedia world, both in their personal lives and in their classroom practice, and how they see this world in relation to their personal philosophies of teaching. We then move on to address the issue of how schools are responding as institutions and to what extent school policies recognize the importance of young people's extracurricular culture. This necessarily entails analyzing some of the influences exerted by national and local curricular authorities and the extent to which current formal curricula encourage engagement with new media technologies.

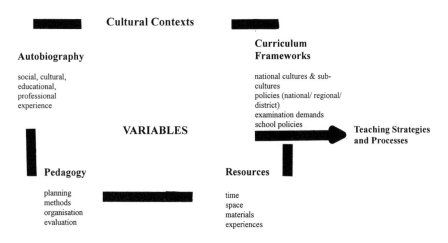

FIG. 8.1. Teaching strategy variables.

Teachers

The original research question was:

- **What are English teachers doing when they say they are doing Media Education at Key Stage (KS) 4 (ages 14–16) in secondary schools?**

In order to try to answer this question, we need to ask:

- Who teachers of English\Media are (their experiences, background, and training.
- How they see themselves in relation to schools and curricula.
- What they say (and think) about Media Education as a discipline.
- How they define their own approach to Media Education.
- What they actually do when they do Media Education.

Most of the English\Media teachers in the international project saw their work as closely related to their own values and their particular purposes in teaching. All agreed that their own teaching was informed by their views about media and society. Only one participant (Brendan in Ontario, see chap. 7, this volume) claims that he teaches Media merely because it is mandatory within the province. In South Africa, teachers who engage with Media Education seem to do so with a sense of its political importance and a conviction about its value. Court and Criticos (chap. 4, this volume) speak of the passion and enthusiasm of the teachers in the South African study, and teachers in the other studies often saw themselves as pioneers responding to the challenge of new terrain.

Teachers were often selected precisely because of their known involvement in Media teaching. In Australia and England, teachers were often selected for the research because of their links with local (often metropolitan) Media developments. Similarly, the South African study focussed on a relatively homogeneous grouping of nine White teachers and three Indian teachers, all of whom speak English as their first language. They are not representative of the English-speaking population, because less than 10% of the population as a whole are mother-tongue speakers of English, and the majority of English teachers speak English as a second language. The sample is drawn from one geographical area, one of the nine new provinces of South Africa, KwaZulu-Natal, which is again not representative of the ethnic and linguistic variety of the rest of South Africa. At the same time, as Court and Criticos point out in their overview of the history of South African education, the teachers studied are drawn from the previous White and Indian education authorities because it was in the Natal Education Department that Media Education first took root in the region, followed by the Indian education authority, the House of Delegates.

It is powerful evidence of the participants' commitment to Media teaching that they were willing to be observed by researchers and to spend a great deal of time in interviews discussing their motives and methods. Yet, as one of the teachers in the Ontario study explains, (Morgan, chap. 7, this volume), English\Media teachers often lack confidence. They are uncertain and uncomfortable about where they are going and how to get there:

> Media Education is really evolving and where Media teachers used to have a certain level of comfort, I really think that those areas don't exist any more. I mean it's difficult now just to teach about genre, just to teach about television, film, the music industry. That doesn't really work. The boundaries are all being blurred now.... So I find that a real challenge, to know how to organize and present things for the student so that they can make sense of some of it, because I don't think things are as clear cut as they used to be.

This lack of direction is not solely dependent on the intellectual breadth and diverse demands of Media teaching or even on the uncertainties of teaching in a postmodernist culture. It is something that is felt locally and personally. English\Media teachers often feel isolated and beleaguered by the indifference, suspicion or hostility that sometimes surrounds them. Hobbs (chap. 6, this volume) emphasizes how, with minimal state or district support in the United States, Media teachers often work alone and in spite of hostility toward their efforts. This sense of isolation and uncertainty may begin to explain some of the structured absences and silences in the range of work that we discovered.[3] As Collins (chap. 3, this volume) noted:

> The avoidance of Northern Ireland/Ireland perhaps is due, as one teacher pointed out, to the risk which many teachers associate with such topics. These matters are hot to handle and to address them may have repercussions in terms of parental response. It may also be the case that were teachers feeling more secure about Media Education generally, they would be less reluctant to embark on such work. But where an uncertainty as to its validity exists, and this is added to by the kind of response which attention to local media may elicit, the anticipated burden could be too much for most.

In such challenging circumstances, the support of colleagues and/or management is vital, as several of the studies have noted. In the South African study, 75% of the subjects regularly collaborated with colleagues in Media work. Hobbs notes a similar phenomenon in the Billerica initiative. In England, the strength and confidence of Jane's work, her willingness to listen and respond to her pupils' interventions and to structure Media work around their interests and emergent understandings, seems to be related to the fact that she works in a department that shares and creates its own resources and practices frequent team-teaching.

---

[3]This uncertainty was so great for some teachers in the U. S. study that they actually repeated for their observed lessons teaching that had involved the same pupils earlier in the year.

However, individual experience and training are clearly also important factors in determining the strategies and processes that Media teachers use in their work. Nearly all of the teachers in each study were experienced to the extent that they had been teaching for some time. All of the Western Australian teachers had been teaching for more than 5 years. More than 75% of the teachers in England had been teaching for more than 10 years (although two others were in their very first year of teaching). In South Africa, the average number of years of teaching experience was nearly 8, with an average of over 5 years for Media teaching. In Ontario, where three different 'generations' of teachers were deliberately selected, the four older teachers had between them taught for nearly 100 years![4]

It is very difficult to establish any consistent patterns in such small samples, but it seems to be the case that younger, less experienced, teachers offered a greater range of Media work and with more confidence than older, more experienced teachers, provided that they either had formal training in Media or Communications Studies or professional experience in the media (or, in some cases, both). The Ontario data go further than this in suggesting that there may be a three-way correlation among 'cultural heritage' approaches, print-orientation in classroom work, and older teachers. Conversely, it seems to be the case (Naum and Derek in Ontario, Jane in England) that the 'posttelevision generation', who have more experience of electronic media and more recent training, are also more comfortable with critical, 'representational' approaches. We need to explore this further in discussing the aims and forms of Media work that our studies have discovered.

Training

In Western Australia, as Quin explains (chap. 5, this volume) specialist Media teachers are required to teach English as their second teaching area. In England, there are no such requirements, but the majority of English\Media teachers (at least at KS4) come from a specialist English-teaching background and continue to teach English alongside Media. In fact, most teachers of English\Media in the English-speaking world have an initial qualification in English. As we have seen, this has advantages in terms of the critical approaches teachers of English bring to Media teaching, but it also poses some problems, in terms of the narrow 'textualism' of their focus and some of the aesthetic paraphernalia they may have inherited from the 'cultural heritage' tradition.

Where English\Media teachers have some formal training in Media teaching or some professional experience of media industries, it seems to make a difference, as in the case of Naum and Derek in Ontario, for example. In Northern Ireland, two of the teachers interviewed clearly benefited from the additional experience of working on the Northern Ireland Curriculum Council Working Party that consid-

---

[4]No data are available for the U.S. study.

ered the role of Media in relation to English (Helen). Although we collected data on teachers' gender in all of the studies and found an overrepresentation of women in England and Northern Ireland that is in line with gender differences within English teaching generally, this seemed not to be an important factor in determining general aims and classroom methods.

Predictably, nearly all of the teachers in each of the studies registered a desire for more and better training. Specifically, most of them pointed to the need for both a more systematic theoretical foundation within which they could work and for greater opportunities for practical or professional experience in the media industries. As Collins explains (chap. 3, this volume) none of the teachers interviewed in Northern Ireland was familiar with basic Media Education pedagogy texts, or had experienced specific training in Media Education:

> While a number of teachers have been willing to embrace Media Education, others have avoided the area because they have not had an opportunity to explore its nature fully. Some of those who have become involved in it have not had the kind of time or training to develop the area in ways they would wish ... It is certainly the case that most English teachers do lack a background in media theory. Most come to it accidentally, often through Drama. Thus their sense of their own inadequacy for the task may be well founded.

Similarly, although Initial and Continuing Education courses for teachers have been provided in a few places in England (notably London, Nottingham, and Southampton) since the 1970s, most English teachers have very little formal training in Media Education. Less than 25% of the teachers in the original study in England (including the two least experienced ones who were in their first year of teaching) had received any extended training in Media Education or Media Studies.

> Whatever growth there has been in schools and colleges of Media Education and Media Studies, there has not been a corresponding expansion of training and development opportunities for teachers. The result is that many work in isolation with little more than examination syllabuses to guide them. In-service support for Media Education has been severely reduced over the last 2 years as a result of funding changes and a National Curriculum focus on the core curriculum areas. Some teachers have simply inherited responsibility for Media courses from enthusiastic teachers who have moved on. Although some of these 'substitutes' often become enthusiasts themselves, they can too easily find themselves overwhelmed by the scope of the subject and by the unlimited material from which to choose ... Because few teachers have been formally trained in Media Education or Media Studies, there is inevitably a wide variation in theoretical understanding and classroom practice. Notions of Media Education may vary from showing a video recording of a Shakespeare play to the critical study of media institutions and audiences.[5]

---

[5]*Developing Media in English* (Hart & Hackman, 1995) is a series if structured practical exercises for trainers and teachers that uses the case studies reported in the original Southampton *Models of Media Education* project as a way of examining some of these different approaches to Media teaching within a Professional Development context. It provides criteria for lesson observation and evaluation that enables teachers to document and discuss their own colleagues' lessons.

By contrast, in South Africa, where the growth of Media Education has been more recent, all of the teachers interviewed had attended Professional Development courses for teachers and more than half of them had experienced formal training in Media Education. Not surprisingly, these were also the teachers who showed most awareness of basic Media pedagogy books and understanding of 'key concepts'. Nevertheless, as Court and Criticos emphasize, the teachers in their sample, chosen through links with Media Education work at the University of Natal, are untypical of South Africa as a whole, and there is a great need there for many more formal courses in Media Education for teachers.

In Western Australia, 25% of the interviewees had the experience of Professional Development courses and half were graduates in Communication or Cultural Studies in addition to their common background in Literature Studies. In Ontario, where a province-wide survey of English\Media teachers was undertaken as background to the case studies reported here, 87% of respondents had experienced no formal preparatory training in Media Education, and even those who had experienced some training often referred to an educational technology course rather than Media Education. In the United States, according to Hobbs, English\Media teachers are often self-taught, but there is currently some growth in the provision of Professional Development courses, particularly in metropolitan areas. The Billerica and Harvard Institute initiatives are clear examples of this growth.

Formal training for teachers in Media Education seems to be a necessary precondition for its effective development in classrooms throughout the world. However, training alone is not a sufficient guarantee of such development. As Robyn Quin points out (chap. 5, this volume):

> The presence or absence of a background in Media Studies/Communication Studies makes little or no difference as to whether teachers are confident in their ability to teach film and television. No teacher expressed doubts about their competencies in the area and nor did those without formal training express resentment at having to teach something they were not trained to do. Whether this confidence might be misplaced is another question.

Whereas more and better training at all levels is obviously desirable, we should be cautious in assuming that training alone will necessarily produce effective teaching. As Renee Hobbs notes in her study of Media teaching in Massachusetts (chap. 6, this volume), despite of their participation in intensive Professional Development through the Harvard and Billerica initiatives, several teachers were confused about their motives, educational goals, and classroom methods. They sometimes made references to 'key concepts' in a way that may have looked good on paper, but that were not made operational in the classroom. For example, Dave's work on newspapers and media violence is located ambivalently between a protectionist stance against pervasive media reportage of violence and formal analysis of generic presentational features. His approach embraces both individual and small group practical work and "soap-box" declamations about violence. He expects students to discover important concepts and principles about contemporary media through such work, but at the same time admits his complete ignorance of his students' actual newspaper reading habits and expresses dismay that they seem to be reading the wrong things. He seems to think that it is possible for teachers to 'know' about media without knowing their students' media habits, or even their students.[6] A similar contradiction between valuing students' opinions and responses on the one hand and privileging the teacher's own views on the other, is evident in the work of one of the Australian teachers on films.

There are often contradictions among the various discourses that a single teacher routinely draws on and between these discourses and actual classroom practice. We need to come back again to explore more specifically some of the confusions, tensions, and contradictions between liberal–progressive notions of 'empowerment' and 'critical autonomy' in the classroom and traditional whole-class didactic pedagogies. These are some of the parts of English\Media teaching that training does not reach.

Institutional and Curriculum Contexts

As explained in chapter 2 on the original research project in England, Media teachers have been supported in the development of their work in the classroom through curriculum guidance and lobbying by national bodies like the British Film Institute (BFI), and independent bodies like Film Education, and through formal training in University Education departments. They have also had the benefit of support within professional bodies like the National Association for the Teaching of English, the (now defunct) Society for Education in Film and Television, and the more recent Association for Media Education (AME). A series of statements and guidance on curriculum development and teaching methods has been supplemented by examination frameworks and occasional training from examination boards. Perhaps less well known is the degree to which local informal groupings of teachers, meeting regularly to share their problems and expertise, have been catalysts in the growth of effective Media work.[7] More debatable, but equally important, is the role that central government, through the Department for Education and Employment, Her Majesty's Inspectorate, the Schools Curriculum and Assessment Authority, and previously the National Curriculum Council (responsible for the Cox Report) have played in the formulation of National Curriculum policies, especially for English.

---

[6]This confusion of many teachers (despite formal training) is also evident from the way in which the observers in the U.S. study did not seem to know what they were looking for when observing colleagues in the classroom. Tis was the only one of the studies that used teacher-colleagues as observers rather than researchers but not the systematic observation schedule from the original study in England.

[7]The *Southampton Media Education Group*, for example, met regularly for 10 years until it was consolidated into the *Media Education Centre* at Southampton University in 1996 (Messenger Davies, 1991; Mottershead, 1995).

Many of the same forms of institutional support and curriculum demands have contributed to the growth of Media Education in Northern Ireland, as teachers in the study acknowledge. The Northern Ireland version of the Education Reform Act set out the curriculum framework, and the Northern Ireland Film Council along with the Northern Ireland Media Association have provided the kind of support that the BFI and AME have provided in England.

In Western Australia, the Screen Education Society, building initially on informal networks of teachers with an interest in film study, helped widen interest in the whole range of media and their relations with education. Sustained formal training, examination syllabuses, the School Commission's Innovation Program, and Higher Education programs all contributed to an environment favourable to the eventual introduction of mandatory Media Education across the whole continent in the late 1980s. In Ontario, 'Media Literacy' has been mandatory in the secondary curriculum for a decade, and the *Media Literacy Resource Guide* (1989) alongside the Association for Media Literacy has been a strongly influential form of support for Media teachers. In South Africa, Media Education is a crucial element in anti-Apartheid education, and around Durban the University of Natal has provided a focus of training and support for Media teachers, who are beginning to create informal networks to share their work. But, as Court and Criticos emphasize (chap. 4, this volume), with 80% of the population of South Africa never having experienced any form of Media Education, this is clearly not yet a national development as in England or Australia.

As with training, however, broad institutional support may be a necessary preconditions for the growth of effective Media Education but it is not sufficient in itself. Despite of the apparent consensus in Western Australia as to the importance of Media Education and the existence of established syllabuses, Quin notes that none of the teachers in her study made any reference to official syllabuses either to illustrate or justify their approaches to Media teaching (chap. 5, this volume). We also noted earlier how Brendan only taught Media because it was a requirement in Ontario.

As suggested in the Introduction to this book, there is no positive correlation between the spread of media and communication technologies and the growth of understanding about them. Indeed, the correlation may be an inverse one. Even where there is a genuine determination to update school curricula, the pace of technological change continues to outstrip educational responses. It still seems paradoxical, however, that the United States is, on the one hand, the major source of global media messages and a front-runner in technological innovation and, on the other, probably the most underdeveloped English-speaking country in the world regarding Media Education.

Tyner (1996), a prominent Media Education developer in the United States, also contrasts the way in which Media Education elsewhere has been mandated by central educational authorities with the piecemeal approach in the United States:

In the United States, where local control is the norm, Media Education has been practised idiosyncratically by dynamic teachers in K–12 education who include it across the curriculum in fragmented, often isolated efforts that are, by-and-large, marginalised and subject to budgetary caprice. (p. 9)

Kubey (1991) carried out research on the apparent obstacles to the growth of Media Education in the United States and agrees that the United States is "the only major English-speaking country in the world with virtually no formal Media Education in its schools." The reasons for this underdevelopment of Media Education are various. Unlike all of the countries we are comparing, the United States has as yet no formal provision for teacher education in Media. The United States is not only large but extremely diverse, with limited central control over educational policy (2.5 million teachers, 15,000 school districts, and 50 states, as Hobbs reminds us). As we have seen, Media teachers (like teachers of many other subjects) often work in isolation within their states, unable easily to form professional networks or to access those that do exist and lacking most of the institutional encouragement or support that has developed elsewhere. Any form of educational innovation is therefore difficult. At the same time, it is arguable that countries outside the United States have taken a greater interest in film and television as forms of communication, whether for aesthetic or protectionist reasons. Finally, it may be that one of the keys to the absence of developed forms of Media Education in the United States is the existence of a powerful tradition of 'prophetic' denunciation of the media. Such writers as Wilson Key, Jerry Mander, Neil Postman, and Marie Winn are well known within the United States (and beyond, as frequent mention by Ontario teachers show) but nowhere else have they managed virtually to monopolize the Media Education agenda and determine its most dominant discourse. As Hobbs clearly shows (chap. 6, this volume), the situation is beginning to change and the states of Massachusetts, New Mexico, and North Carolina, at least, have formally introduced some Media work, however it is almost as if the United States is determined to experience its own Leavisite tradition. Whatever the truth of this, it is clear that the major institutional frameworks in operation in the United States have not hitherto been supportive of Media Education and may, in fact, have functioned as negative constraints on its growth.

School Policies and Management of English\Media

Jane's and Kevin's experiences are similar to most of the other teachers in the original Southampton study and are fairly typical of where Media Education stands in relation to whole-school policies in England. At the departmental level, there is a clear expectation that English\Media work will occur as mandated by the National Curriculum for English, and there is often discussion and collaboration in the design of units of work that incorporate Media for students at KS4. So, despite of the fears and uncertainties of some teachers of English about how others (parents, head teachers, school governors) will see their Media work, it is incorporated into the routine work of English departments. It is rare, however, for Media to be written explicitly into whole-school policies. In Northern Ireland, as Collins points out (chap. 3, this volume), senior management often take an interest in Media when there is a large investment in equipment (although which causes which is a matter for debate):

> for Media Education to develop successfully, even within the English department, it needs the support of other staff. Several teachers pointed to the fact that the Vice-prin-cipal or Principal of the school was interested in Media Education, and related this to the school's investment in equipment. Beyond enhanced hardware acquisition, this support from management gave a confidence and credibility to the teachers' work. This management goodwill is probably important for any innovation in the school. Given that Media Education comes burdened with a popular sense of the media as entertainment source rather than valued subject of study, it is in particular need of acceptance throughout the school.

At the same time, the concern of many teachers of English in Northern Ireland to gain the support of senior managers for their English\Media work confirms the sense of nervousness and uncertainty about innovation that we referred to earlier.

It seems that only in South Africa among the places we investigated was there not only collaboration among teachers in their school but explicit whole-school policies for Media Education: Nearly half of the schools in the study either had Media policies or were currently revising them. Court and Criticos even suggest that such policies may have been the starting point for teaching about media for some of the teachers they interviewed (chap. 4, this volume).

Cross-Curricular Media Work

It is not necessary to have whole-school policies on Media Education for it to be present in areas of the curriculum other than English. Indeed, the U.S. study shows clearly that Media work is not confined there to the subject of English. Where Media Education should be located in school curricula has been a major debate in England and elsewhere, as explained in chapter 2 (see also Hart, 1992; Hart & Hackman, 1995). There is clearly some support for cross-curricular initiatives in England and in Australia. In Northern Ireland, the Education for Mutual Understanding and Cultural Heritage strands of the Cross-curricular Themes required by the National Curriculum seem to be used imaginatively for exploring social and political issues relevant to the communities by means of media texts, but there is little evidence in England of a desire to incorporate Media work into the Cross-curricular Themes. As Hobbs points out (chap. 6, this volume), there is debate in the United States between those who promote a cross-curricular approach based on literacy compe-tencies and those who favour a discipline-based approach to the mass media. Yet there is also the danger in the United States that cross-curricular approaches may evaporate into weak or instrumental forms of Media work or even into educational technology. In Canada, a broad-based Technology Education policy was introduced in 1995. However, all the individual studies suggest it is most likely that English Departments will remain the principal sites for Media Education, in South Africa, England, Australia, and Northern Ireland where Media Education has been introduced through the medium of the English curriculum. In South Africa, where there is no national policy on Media Education, it has been introduced into the curriculum through English and has been an optional extra, like Film Studies. The new core curricula are yet to be made public.

Irrespective of the educational politics of curriculum location, there are ample reasons for emphasizing the tremendous potential of Media teaching in diverse cultural settings especially, for example, in South Africa and the United States, where ethnic divisions are key factors. As Tyner (1996) argued:

> Sophisticated readings of familiar texts, coupled with experiences in media-making, are a powerful tool for teachers.... Image-making tools of expression, and video in particular, enable students to refine their own voices, to tell their own stories from an informed perspective and to promote cross-cultural understandings in formats that contribute to shared meaning. (p. 1)

Such a claim raises important issues about practical production and 'voice', that we need to come back to in our analysis of the classroom methods observed in our studies, but it is worth noting here as an additional dimension of cross-curricular work that is often forgotten in such contexts.

Aims and Approaches

We have discussed some of the personal perceptions of teachers that contribute to their motivation towards English\Media work, and I have touched on some of the larger discourses about culture, society, and the media that they draw on. These apparently individual notions can now be related to the general patterns that are already emerging and to the basic theoretical paradigms that were outlined earlier. The basic research question we began with was:

- **What Media Education aims are apparent?**

It is already clear to some readers that, although the precise terms may vary slightly, the three paradigms discussed by Masterman in the Foreword to this book are present in the stated aims and preferred approaches of most of the teachers in each of our separate studies.

The 'inoculatory' paradigm, which seeks to develop discrimination *against* certain kinds of media, corresponds closely to the 'cultural heritage'[8] approach

---

[8]'Culturl Heritage' is explicitly incorporated into the National Curriculum for English in Northern Ireland, where it means something quite different.

(England, Western Australia) referred to in the Cox Report (DES, 1989), to 'transmission' education (South Africa) and to 'protectionist' or 'defensive' strategies (Northern Ireland, Ontario, Massachusetts). The 'popular arts' paradigm, which seeks to encourage discrimination *between* media, corresponds to the 'personal growth' model (England, Western Australia) and to the 'Liberal–Humanist' approach (South Africa). The 'representational' paradigm, which seeks to address issues of ideology, power, and the politics of representation, corresponds to the 'cultural analysis' approach (England, Western Australia, South Africa) and to 'progressive', 'empowerment,' and 'oppositional' strategies (South Africa).

As has been seen here, these paradigms represent the three major phases since the development of Media Education in the 1940s, at least in England (see Fig. 8.2). Yet all three paradigms remain operational in every educational context that we have investigated. In Ontario, where we have richer biographical data than in the other studies, we can see how the three paradigms roughly correspond to three different 'generations' of teachers, and we can see something of the difference that the paradigms make to their classroom practices. Nevertheless, this is not just a matter of the age of teachers because there are continuing tensions and debates about their appropriateness in every location. There are, for example, clear schisms among educators in the United States between protectionist and empowerment paradigms. At the same time, there are arguably many features shared by 'protectionist' and 'representational' paradigms in terms of identifying texts, processes, and institutions for particular attention rather than others. Issues such as racism, sexism, and exploitation in various forms are central features of both paradigms.

	Title	Major Exponents	Cox Report equivalents (DES, 1989)
1	INOCULATORY\ PROTECTIONIST	Leavis and Thompson (1933)	Cultural heritage
2	DISCRIMINATORY\ POPULAR ARTS	Hall and Whannel (1964)	Personal growth
3	CRITICAL\ REPRESENTA1,ONAL\ SEMIOLOGICAL	Masterman (1985)	Cultural analysis

FIG. 8.2. Three Media Education paradigms.

The differences, however, are both ideological and pedagogical. Ideologically, the shift is from right-wing to left-wing politics and pedagogically from didacticism to dialogue.

The province-wide survey in Ontario revealed a quite narrow range of declared teacher aims that are nearly all confined to 'inoculatory' or 'discriminatory' paradigms, as shown in the responses tabulated by Morgan (chap. 7, this volume). Yet in the case studies a wider range of motivations was found. For example, Alice and Brendan, for whom television was a new phenomenon when they began teaching, show a clear sense of hierarchy in which the older, 'cool' media of print and film are superior to the newer, 'hot' electronic media, and they both have a mission to 'convert' their students away from their current preferences by "teaching against the grain" and focussing on the aesthetics and ethics of media texts. As Morgan comments (chap. 7, this volume):

> Older media, associated with high cultural capital, appear in a nostalgic, valorized light. In contrast, newer forms appear to be either intriguing (Alice), or alien and suspect (Brendan). Moreover, newer media are utilized and evaluated in terms of criteria appropriate to older media.

Joel and Colleen, representing the next 'generation' of teachers in the Ontario study, share some of the same cool–hot, high–low, and print–electronic dichotomies with Joel, in particular denouncing television. Yet Joel recognizes his own difference from his students and acknowledges their greater expertise by trying to keep in touch with 'their' media and by incorporating their interests into classroom work, often as a basis for discussion of social and political issues. Naum and Derek, the youngest 'generation' of teachers represented, with only 8 years of teaching experience between them, differ in that they do not have a hierarchical sense of media, although Naum is negative about television. Most important, however, is that they see media not simply as producing texts for consumption, but as forms of expression that are also available to young people. They do not share the same critical/analytical paradigm in their work as older teachers. They incorporate the kind of active production work in their approaches that envisaged in some of the Ontario curriculum documents of the last 10 years, but which few teachers have been able to adopt. As the province-wide survey showed, a willingness to focus on electronic media is still a rare phenomenon in Ontario, where the least-addressed media were: compact discs, photography, telephone, computer games, Walkman, Internet, and multimedia.

Media Education is not necessarily linked to sophisticated new technologies, but the majority of teachers in all of our studies seemed to be remarkably conservative in their choice of media for study. The print-centerdness that often characterizes the 'cultural heritage' approach was also evident in the South African study, where more than half the teachers expressed a preference for print media as classroom resources, although they also claimed to be happy teaching about electronic media where that was appropriate. The majority of this same group saw themselves as embracing a 'critical' paradigm, but did not always sound convincing in their understanding of what was meant by that. Similarly, print-centeredness was dominant in most of the classes we observed in England, and teachers (irrespective of their age) said they were happier handling traditional printed texts rather than electronic ones. In Northern Ireland, the 'inoculatory' paradigm seems still to dominate the study of advertising and of newspapers, with occasional references to Vance Packard. Only one classroom in the study focused on the medium of television and 'adult' newspapers were favored over comics and magazines.

In Western Australia, there is a range of motives for teaching Media but apparently a more general willingness to engage with a wide range of media forms (chap. 5, this volume). English\Media teachers in the Australian study estimated that they spent up to one third of their teaching time on nonprint media texts. Miss Smith embraces the 'cultural heritage' paradigm in treating films much the same as literature, whereas Mr. Jones focusses much more on a 'cultural analysis' approach, going beyond texts to examine institutional contexts and ideological formations in a wide range of print and electronic media. In England, some teachers were still treating media texts like literature, others using them instrumentally (like Kevin) as a springboard for discussion of social issues, whereas others (like Jane) tried to encourage young people to engage critically with their own forms of media (chap. 7, this volume).

However, none of these findings is intended to suggest more general patterns that may be endemic to particular cultures. In fact, all three paradigms may be traced in almost every Media teacher. It is also the case that a teacher may voice allegiance to one particular set of beliefs about the purposes of Media Education but actually contradict them in the classroom. So, before examining in more detail some of the classroom methods that teachers used, we can look briefly and more generally at the role that the three major paradigms seem to play in the approaches the teachers identified as characterizing their practice. We can look, in other words, at what they say they are doing before we look at what they are actually doing.

TEACHING: CLASSROOM METHODS

This section looks at what teachers actually do when they say they do Media Education, focussing on the original research question:

- **What forms of Media Education are apparent?**

The BFI newsletter referred to in Chapter 2 noted there is still "confusion over whether Media Education just means that the media are a convenient way of bolstering traditional English teaching, or that it entails specifically studying the media themselves" (BFI, 1993, p. 4).

In order to cut through the confusion, we used consistent observation categories. Chapter 1 outlined the categories used for observation of lessons (see especially Figs. 1.1 and 1.2). The main categories were lesson introduction, content items, method (structure/ organization/development), teacher-defined tasks, pupil activities, use of resources, and lesson conclusion. Each study demonstrates how these operated in practice and they are drawn on in the more general analysis that follows.

Some of the work we observed was on the periphery of Media Education as we have defined it and, in some cases, was not Media Education at all, but the use of media texts as a means of pursuing other goals. Although little of this kind of work has featured in the case studies selected for this book, the original international studies found ample evidence of instrumental uses of media both in the way some teachers described their own work and in their observed classroom strategies. Kevin's lesson on the television play *The Boy with the Transistor Radio* may stand as representative of this kind of work. For all its qualities in terms of pupil participation, dialogue, and relevance to their own social situations, the lesson did not even focus on the play as a text, let alone a particular kind of text for the particular medium of television. The question of why such a play was broadcast as part of programming for schools was not even asked. This is a singular use of a media text as a 'resource' but it is echoed in references to "use of media" in History, Drama, Afrikaans, and Geography in the South African study.

The related phenomenon of using film and television versions of literary texts in literature teaching is also common, as the BFI/NFER survey of English teachers showed (Dickson, 1994)[9] and, as the Northern Ireland study shows (chap. 3, this volume), this means that:

> The media ... act as conduits or vehicles for the delivery of enhanced understanding of literary texts, of more committed and thoughtful writing, of purposeful and enthusiastic listening. Less attention is paid to the ways in which the professional media operate. Such matters as ownership, or organisation, or media audiences, for example, are not highlighted.

However, our focus here is on the lessons that do fall into the category of English\Media Education as we have defined it. Although the work we have analyzed in each study covers a wide range of media, genres, and texts, there are some striking absences, especially in light of the recurrent themes expressed in teachers' accounts of their intentions. In most cases, the lessons we observed lacked:

- Interaction and dialogue (teacher–pupil or pupil–pupil) about media.
- Space for young people's own media experience and knowledge.
- Opportunities for active involvement in the social production of texts.

---

[9]See also the *Jane Eyre* example in the original Southampton study (Hart & Benson, 1993, pp. 38–42.)

- Teaching in context through engagement with media processes and technologies.
- Engagement with political issues.
- Learning about media institutions.

Interaction and Dialogue

Surprisingly, given the claims often made by Media educators of being innovative, none of the lessons observed in any of our studies was conducted in a way that departed radically from standard teaching methods. The 'lesson method', involving a brief introduction by the teacher, followed by informal small-group work (sometimes structured by worksheets), reporting back to the whole-class and occasional whole class discussion, was the norm. Most classes observed were dominated by teacher-talk, despite of widely held perceptions about the inappropriateness of teacher-dominated classrooms in the context of Media Education and sometimes in conflict with what teachers themselves said about the need for pupils to engage critically with their own cultural experience or express their own opinions. Despite teachers' occasional genuflections toward 'reader-response' theory, individual students rarely had the opportunity to develop their personal response in any depth or to listen to those of others. A surprising number of questions asked by teachers were 'closed' ones, intended to lead to apparently predetermined destinations. The results of personal research were rarely featured in classes, although there was occasionally some preparatory work designed to feed into lessons in a fairly closed way, as in Jane's (England), Joan's and Anita's (United States) classes. If it is important for young people to engage critically and productively with their own media cultures in order to develop 'critical autonomy', the lack of opportunity to do so in Media classrooms is problematic, as Tyner (1995) points out: "Although it is true that Media educators can be successful with a wide range of classroom methods, extreme teacher-centred approaches are in direct conflict with the goal of Media Education to encourage students to think independently" (p. 1).

Young People's Media Experience

It was suggested in the Introduction to this book that media teachers are engaging with three related cultural spheres:

1. The 'official' culture supported by the major public institutions: museums, libraries and, most importantly of all, the formal education system. Schools define what forms of knowledge and expression are to be considered valuable and how they are to be approached and used.
2. The culture produced by the major commercially organized communications, information, and leisure industries.

3. The vernacular cultures grounded in the life of particular neighbourhoods and/or social groupings (class, ethnic, and religious) that exist on the margins of official and commercial culture.

Most of the English\Media lessons we observed clearly engaged with (or even help to perpetuate) the first cultural sphere. Many of them also engaged with the second sphere, that of commercial communication, but usually as texts rather than as institutions. Rarely, however, did the vernacular sphere figure in the classroom. Exponents of a defensive 'cultural heritage' pedagogy have attempted and failed to resolve this problem either high-handedly by exclusion or paternalistically by 'discrimination'. Yet, on the other hand, to recognize and attempt to include such experiences in the classroom is inevitably to change them, because their value often lies precisely in the fact that they are part of a culture that is 'owned' by young people. 'Progressive' pedagogies, drawing theoretically on new approaches to studying audiences that emphasize their activeness and sophistication and recognize the existing knowledge and skills of students, have often done a disservice to them in an attempt to abolish the cultural and social authority of the teacher. The classroom emphasis is predominantly on spontaneity and informal group work, as compared to structured activity, planned learning experiences, and teacher direction. The danger of this position, as characterized by Ferguson (1996), is that it is:

> based around a pedagogy which does not only start with where the student is ... but tends to circle that position endlessly ... The new pedagogics which accompany too much of the new relationship to the media which teachers and researchers have constructed, are not demanding in the way that students are demanding of their own cultures. (pp. 62–67)

Given the unsatisfactoriness of both the 'discriminatory' and the 'progressive' positions, how can English\Media teachers address the dilemmas that arise from the necessarily unequal distribution in the classroom of social, political, and cultural experience between teachers and learners? Tyner (1995) neatly summed up the dilemma Media teachers face as like walking a tightrope:

> Teacher response to popular culture ranges from trashing it to embracing it. If teachers criticize popular communication forms, they run the risk of alienating and insulting the very culture that students value. If they embrace it, they risk looking like ridiculous fuddy-duddies who are trying too hard to appear up-to-date ... In the course of walking this tightrope, it isn't necessary for teachers to suppress personal distaste for popular culture artifacts, or to express glowing enthusiasm for every new pop culture trend. (p. 7)

The power of Media Education to be inclusive, to recognize and legitimate vernacular and commercial cultures in addition, rather than in opposition, to the 'official' cultures of schooling, represents an opportunity for intercultural education in situations of cultural diversity. Recognizing the ways in which commercial and vernacular texts are able to cross cultural boundaries effectively, but are then claimed and inflected in different ways by specific cultural and subcultural groups is fundamental to Media Education.

> Teachers and media producers see ample evidence that student use of texts goes far beyond the commercial intentions of the media industries … each generation carves out private modes of expression appropriate to prevailing social conditions and purposely keeps the expression coded and veiled to obscure understanding for adults. (Tyner, 1996, p. 5)

Study of this semantic traffic promises to take us beyond narrow forms of textualism.

Some of the teachers we observed made explicit references to the importance of young people's own cultural and media experience. In Australia, Miss Allen and a teacher who is not named both clearly expressed this view and attempted to incorporate it in their teaching:

> For a change they can prove they know something. When I am teaching print texts it is always the same. They know nothing and I know everything. At my school they are viewers, not readers and already know a lot about films and television. Media classes give them the chance to demonstrate their knowledge and so I exploit it heavily. The students really tap into it.

Similarly in Ontario, Alice reports:

> We had one presentation on CDs that I learned a great deal from. And this kid knows, as far as I could tell, everything about them, knows how they were developed, knows the technology, knows the future. You know, many of them know far more about certain aspects of that than I.

In England, Jane made space for pupils to bring in their own ideas and preferences about pop music. But all of these examples are exceptional: the norm is much closer to that described by Jude Collins (chap. 3, this volume), where teachers rarely acknowledge or draw on pupils' vernacular cultures as part of their English\Media lessons.

Textual Production in Social Contexts

Media production and teaching in social contexts are both strategies that can make the task of Media teachers easier. Specialist Media teachers frequently incorporate such approaches in their work. Yet one of the most surprising absences from Media teaching by the English/Media teachers whose work we have analyzed is the study of media texts in process or in action in actual social contexts. Twenty years ago, the first systematic study of education about the media in English schools strongly advocated the production by pupils of texts for particular contexts. Pupils' Media assignments, they suggested, "should be produced with a real audience or public in mind ... the school, or even better, the local neighbourhood" (Murdock & Phelps, 1973, p. 143).

Classrooms are, of course, highly artificial spaces and we should not expect to find actual media interactions occurring in them as in everyday social life. The real absence is the recognition of media as processes, events, and institutions that happen in the social world of young people beyond school. Morgan's research in Ontario led him to a similar conclusion about the conservatism of much current Media teaching: "The overall impression one gets from Media classrooms, conferences and educational theory is that the media have become 'texts-to-read', static props in a disciplinary theatre of interpretation" (Morgan, 1996, p. 29).

Although successive technological innovations like Super 8, portable video cameras and VCRs, and inexpensive electronic editing have provided an impetus in most countries for the systematic study of media, few teachers in our study routinely incorporated practical work in their teaching. None of the teachers in Australia did so except on rare occasions. One third of the teachers in the English study used practical group work in the lessons we observed, often involving presentations to the class, but this was always work of the planning or story-boarding kind, as was the case with Helen in Northern Ireland, who was apologetic about her inability to conclude her pupils' work in a finished product. Much of this absence can be explained by reference to lack of physical resources, access to appropriate facilities, or time constraints. However, as Hobbs points out (chap. 6, this volume), the arrival of *Channel 1* in Massachusetts, for example, has meant access to classroom hardware that would not otherwise have been available. The fact that technology is valued so highly in the United States also means that technology can be used as a 'gateway' for students' production to demonstrate how Media Education can enhance literacy, engage community interest, and promote "participatory citizenship." (Tyner, 1995, p. 2). There is a strong argument that media production can offer:

an opportunity for experiential, collaborative, problem-solving that enhances media analysis skills. Media-making also takes a refreshing approach to media representation ... it offers a space for students to define and redefine their own 'problems' with media and to explore their relationship with media. (Tyner, 1996, p. 12)

In particular, the opportunity offered by video production for young people to present their own experience can broaden their understanding of media forms and give them more confidence and competence in discussing representational codes, conventions, and discourses. The notion of 'voice', common in teaching about imaginative writing is central here. It means, of course, being able to articulate ideas in a public forum, being able to speak and write, as well as to listen and read. It means being heard and gaining access to public space for communication. It means having something of substance to say. It means developing a characteristic style that distinguishes the speaker in particular communicative contexts.

Yet there is nothing here that is not formally acknowledged by the English Cox Report as necessary for a fully developed English curriculum, nor by North American notions of 'Media Literacy'. Even a narrow literacy skills-based notion of Media Education recognizes the importance of utterance as well as reception. It is a critical aspect of citizenship education, even though its political consequences may not be fully acknowledged in either the 'adult needs' or 'personal growth' approaches to the teaching of English as described by Cox (DES, 1989, 2.21, 2.23). The problem is not acknowledging its importance but putting it into practice in classrooms.

Teaching in context encourages students to operate with confidence through guided practice in structured learning situations, so that they can "interpret their own experiences and make sense of their own learning" in a flexible way. Some of the work reported in the DEFT Project in England in Chapter 2 (Brown et. al., 1990) successfully follows this pattern of 'cognitive apprenticeship' (Tyner, 1996, p. 6). Given that fieldtrips form such an important aspect of the curriculum in such subjects as Geography, it is astonishing that, in a world saturated with media products and institutions, so few teachers interviewed or lessons observed made any reference to contact with actual media organizations or functions.

But video production is not the only means of learning in context or engaging with media technologies. Apart from one teacher in Australia using the Internet as a means of acquiring information, there is little reference by the teachers we interviewed to the newest forms of digital communication. The Media teacher of the future who recognizes the need to be in touch with the vernacular cultures of young people will need to incorporate information technology, in all its forms, in a curriculum that goes beyond embracing the traditional 'mass media' and that is not distracted by the inherent fascination of new technologies without reference to their ownership and sociopolitical functions. This will mean going beyond both the existing English\Media curriculum and the currently instrumental role of digital technologies in education as expressive tools. It will mean including critical examination of software developments and information exchange and even employment patterns on a global scale. As Ferguson (1996) argued, the new Media educator will need to "develop a viable and ongoing engagement with the evolution of new technologies as industries, and with the ways in which multimedia approaches are being utilized for educational and other purposes" (p. 68).

Political Issues

Both the Northern Ireland and South African studies show teachers at work in a highly conflictual and frequently violent political context. In Northern Ireland, many teachers seem cautious on politically sensitive areas, even to the extent of not using local newspapers for study. In South Africa, on the other hand, possibly because the 'revolution' is over, Media Education was perceived as having a real potential to dismantle the legacy of Apartheid. Elsewhere, political issues and even more general issues of power in society seemed to be systematically avoided. Partly, this is the result of the dominant forms of textualism that we have noted, but it is also related to the kinds of text chosen and the particular emphases of teachers on the personal. For example, in England, Kevin did not choose to relate the individual concerns with un/employment in Willie Russell's play to wider political issues. Perhaps English teachers do not feel able to explore the more general issues of power that media texts so often raise. They certainly focus only rarely on the institutional contexts of media production and, in one case reported by Court and Criticos (chap. 4, this volume), consciously exclude such concerns.

Media Institutions

Institutions like schools or broadcasting organizations are recognizable by the changing forms and norms that they establish over time. They demand certain kinds of discourses, values, professional allegiances, and practices that are often made visible in the way that they speak about themselves publicly through job advertisements, information packs, and annual reports. Study of media institutions is especially significant because it is an area in which young people are most inexperienced and in most need of learning from adults who may have such experience. It involves asking questions like "What is this text for?" rather than "What is it like?", "How was it made and how does it work?" rather than simply "What does it mean?", and "What are its values?" rather than "What is its value?" (Branston, 1984, 1987). It means looking for the unexpected and for uncertainties in the ways in which media organizations operate, rather than seeing them as monolithic structures that may be encompassed in thinking about the media as singular rather than plural. Unfortunately, it seems to be an area in which most English\Media teachers are also most inexperienced (Naum and Derek in Ontario are obvious exceptions). The habit of ignoring or avoiding production, financial, and institutional contexts in the study of advertising noted by Jude Collins in Northern Ireland (chap. 3, this volume) is surprisingly widespread.

> What was notable by its absence throughout all the lessons observed was attention to the way advertising relates to a wider social/political system in a consumer society. Equally, there was little attention to the relationship between program-making and advertisements, or how advertisements relate to program-funding. For the most part, work on advertisements tended to ignore context, focussing largely on what was in front of the pupils, considering examples of stereotyping, emotive language, and a general concern to deceive.

It may be that the influence of the BFI's 'Signpost Questions' on English teachers in England and Northern Ireland bears some responsibility here. Although the questions provide key concepts that are clear and flexible, the framework does not explicitly include study of institutions. It therefore risks downgrading the importance of power relationships in the production, distribution, and consumption of media texts. The separation of 'Agency' and 'Production' into distinct categories is in danger of de-socializing and de-politicizing media processes. This is hardly surprising, because the 'Signpost Questions' are very much a compromise produced from a long process of consultation and discussion with teachers. They are an attempt to provide a consensual framework with which most teachers would be comfortable. But their blandness is a potential weakness. So too with the BFI's widely quoted definition of Media Education, as reproduced in the Cox Report:

> Media Education … seeks to increase children's critical understanding of the media … [It] aims to develop systematically children's critical and creative powers through analysis and production of media artefacts … Media Education aims to create more active and critical media users who will demand, and could contribute to, a greater range and diversity of media products. (DES 1989, 9. 6)

As Ferguson (1996) complained:

> It is a definition which astutely avoids any contact with the political. There is no mention in it of a term like 'society', nor of the exercise of power in and through the media … We are thus left with an approach to pedagogy and Media Education which is sadly emasculated. (p. 66)

The original study In England suggests, in referring to the habit of "institutional acquiescence," that Media teaching in English may only see institutional procedures and professional practices as something to be imitated and emulated, rather than critically examined. Only 1 of the 11 lessons observed in the English study was concerned with exploring the industrial context of the texts analyzed (i.e., Promoting a Pop Group). Morgan detected an avoidance of the "collective, impersonal dimensions of media production, as well as the dynamics of media appropriation" (chap. 7, this volume) among teachers in Ontario. In Australia, Quin (chap. 5, this volume) shows how, in the featured *Gallipoli* lesson, the teacher avoided institutional questions related to ownership, promotion, and distribution. She concludes that: "Wider issues about cross-media ownership, marketing, and power relations are not included in the syllabus and considered by most teachers to be inappropriate to Media Education in the English classroom."

McMahon (1996) also claimed that Media Education in Australia characteristically avoids the "political economy questions about media: questions of ownership and control, questions of policy, and questions of access equity" (p. 166). This is a crucial failure in light of the increasing privatization of Media Education resources, as media organizations set about colonizing the curriculum with 'free', glossy materials for classroom use, and teachers deprived of adequate resources and training eagerly drink from the poisoned chalice of sponsorship. Instead of allowing new marketing strategies to define and narrow the Media Education agenda, teachers with an understanding of institutions might be expected, as Len Masterman reminds in his Foreword, to actively incorporate the study of marketing into the Media curriculum. Otherwise the sphere of 'commercial' culture we referred to above is likely to dominate not only the 'official' but also the 'vernacular' culture.

Our research confirms rather disturbingly the conclusion reached by Ferguson (1996) about current English\Media teaching in England: "For both teachers and those concerned with the preparation of teachers, there seems to be little mileage in a pedagogy which is concerned with identifying in specific ways the operations of power and subordination in societies"(p. 64).

THE DEVELOPMENT OF MEDIA EDUCATION

This international research shows that both the general cultural contexts of media power and access on the one hand and, on the other, the perceptions of educators, administrators, and social commentators of the media's importance in shaping values and social competencies are crucial to decisions about curriculum direction. The discourses that emerge from tensions around 'mediatization' provide many of the philosophical and educational justifications used by English\Media teachers for including Media Education in their work and determine the particular accents and emphases of their classroom pedagogies. Their confidence and competence in the classroom are also partially determined by their experience of and access to training and to local support networks, curriculum materials, and critical\theoretical literature. School policies, the support of colleagues, appropriate facilities, and necessary resources offer a framework within which larger sociocultural forces operate locally. But the major factor in determining the teaching processes and strategies of English\Media teachers seems to be autobiographical and necessarily, therefore, intimately related to their own developing experiences of media. This is most obviously the case in relation to interactive teaching strategies, teaching in context, and incorporation of practical production work in the classroom.

We have found that teachers who operate within a 'popular arts' or 'representational' paradigm are more likely to be comfortable with these interactive, contextual and practical approaches than those working within an 'inoculatory' one. Indeed, there is an ironic symmetry between the belief of some teachers in the manipulative power of media and their vain hope that didactic, teacher-centered pedagogies can make any difference to what young people think and feel about the media. On the other hand, teachers who see the media as significant and powerful ideological forces that systematically represent the world and specific values to particular social and cultural groups with their own semantic power as interpretive communities, often adopt more pupil-centered approaches and find a place for pupils' extracurricular media experience and knowledge. As has been suggested, Media Education examines both the way we make sense of the world and the way others make sense of the world for us (Prinsloo & Criticos, 1992, p. 20). But our research shows a dominant concern among English teachers with the first part of this definition at the expense of the second. English teachers are consistently more concerned with individual perception, language forms, and responses than with social interactions, institutions, technology, and production.

What precisely determines the basic operational paradigms of English\Media teachers remains open to debate, but it seems that the crucial factors are autobiographical. Training and formal policies may make an impact on teachers' motivations, but only indirectly: they may be necessary factors but they are not sufficient. Ultimately, the commitment of teachers when properly resourced physically, culturally, and intellectually, seems to be the major factor in involvement in Media Education. Its long-term development on a scale commensurate with the globalization of media processes and institutions depends on such individual experience and commitment.

We have already pointed many of the elements that are likely to be important in the Media Education of the future. As Masterman (1991) said:

> ... successful Media Education involves an empowerment of learners essential to the creation and sustaining of an active democracy and of a public which is not easily manipulable but whose opinion counts on media issues because it is critically informed and capable of making its own independent judgments. (p. 4)

Summarizing a more detailed description of Media Education in Europe in the 1990s, he focussed on three essential elements that relate closely to human rights (Masterman, 1996, p. 75). These elements may act as the criteria by which the Media Education of the future will be judged: a Commitment to Democratic Values, a Negotiated Curriculum, and a Fostering of Critical Autonomy.

All three elements are present in emergent forms in much of the work we have examined in our research. Although a great deal of the classroom work analyzed here has been based on a fairly narrow range of possibilities and is basically conservative, there is a recognition by most of the teachers of the need to move forward and develop new curricula and teaching strategies that are more appropriate to the needs of 21st-Century citizens. Such a project was envisaged by the recent Declaration of the World Council for Media Education at La Coruna (World Council for Media Education, 1996:

> All media are human inventions. They provide information and pleasure, but they also construct and transmit images of the world, re–presenting it to us in particular ways. The development and application of new information and communication technologies now offer us opportunities for informal educational processes which work in parallel with the existing formal structures of schooling. But they may also work in tension or in conflict with conventional education.

It is therefore vital that we become literate and competent users of the media, so that we may understand and benefit from them. This involves education about the variety of content, forms and methods of the media. Educated citizens of the 21st Century should be able to use media in a critical and confident way.

Achieving this goal on a global basis requires the development of Media Education strategies which will be appropriate and effective in different cultural contexts. The increasing globalization of information and communication media makes it important that Media Education should encourage individual autonomy and strengthen democratic procedures throughout the world.

The *World Council for Media Education* therefore seeks to foster international efforts for the development of strategies and procedures for the exchange of information, the advancement of research and the production of learning resources which will provide a solid foundation in Media Education for all citizens of the world.

We hope that this book encourages others—teachers, administrators, and policymakers—to join us in this global challenge.

REFERENCES

Branston, G. (1984). TV as institution: Strategies for teaching. *Screen, 25*(2), 85–94.

Branston, G. (1987). *Teaching media institutions*. London: British Film Institute.

British Film Institute. (1993, Autumn). *Media Education News Update* (MENU; Vol. 4). London: Author.

Brown, J. (1990). *Developing English for TVEI*. Leeds: Leeds University

Brumfit, C. J., & Mitchell, R. F. (1989). The language classroom as a focus for research. In C. J. Brumfit & R. F. Mitchell (Eds.), *Research in the language classroom* (pp. 3–15). Basingstoke: Macmillan.

Department of Education and Science. (1989). (The Cox Report) *English for ages 5–16*. London: HMSO.

Dickson, P. (1994). *A survey of Media Education in schools and colleges*. London: BFI

Ferguson, R. (1996). 2000. *Continuum, 9*(2), 58–72.

Hart, A. (1992). Mis-reading English: Media, English and the secondary curriculum. *The English and Media Magazine, 26,* 43–46.

Hart, A., & Benson, A. (1993). *Media in the classroom*. Southhampton: Southampton Media Education Group .

Hart, A., & Hackman, S. (1995). *Developing media in English*. London: Hodder.

Kubey R. (1991). *Obstacles to the development of media literacy in the United States* (Report to the Trustees of the Annenberg School for Communication). Philadelphia, PA: Annenberg School for Communication.

Masterman, L., (1991). An overview of Media Education in Europe. *Media Development, 27*(1).

Masterman, L. (1996). Media Education and human rights. *Continuum, 9*(2), 73–77.

McMahon, B. (1996). Resharpening the edge: The educational riddle: *Continuum 9*(2) 161–171.

Messenger Davies, M. (1991). *Co-operation between media educators, media professionals and parents*. London: British Film Institute for United Nations Educational Scientific and Cultural Organizations.

Morgan, R. (1996). Pantextualism, everyday life and media education. *Continuum, 9*(2), 14–34.

Mottershead, C. (1995). *Regional support for media education*. London: British Film Institute.

Murdock, G., & Phelps, G. (1973). *Mass media and the secondary school*. Basingstoke: Macmillan.

Prinsloo, J., & Criticos, C. (Eds.). (1991). *Media matters in South Africa.* Durban: University of Natal, Media Resource Centre.

Tyner, K. (1995). *Shooting back: Video and authentic education.* Paper presented at the fourth *Pedagoxia da Imaxe* congress, La Coruna, Spain.

Tyner, K. (1996). *Representing diversity: Media analysis in practice.* Paper presented at the fifth *Pedagoxia da Imaxe* congress, La Coruna, Spain.

Contributors

Dr. Jude Collins is a Senior Lecturer in the School of Education at the University of Ulster. Over a 10-year period he taught high school English in Ireland (North and South) and in Canada. For the past 18 years he has taught at the University of Ulster, where he presently works in the PGCE (English with Drama and Media Studies) and the PGD/MEd programs. In 1993, the University of Ulster selected him for its Distinguished Teaching Award. He has written and presented radio reports, dramas, and documentaries for the CBC, BBC Radio Ulster, BBC Radio Newcastle, BBC Radio 4, and BBC Radio 5.

Sue Court is a Lecturer in the Department of Education at the University of Natal in Durban, South Africa, where she teaches English courses for the Master's and Bachelor of Education programs as well as for the Postgraduate Diploma in Initial Teacher Education. She began her career as a secondary school teacher of English in the United Kingdom and Rhodesia. In 1979, she took up an appointment in the English Department at the University of Durban–Westville where she worked for 8 years before moving to the Department of Education at the University of Natal in 1987. She has published in the fields of English language and Media Education. Her particular research interests include Media Education and the methodology of English teaching as both first and second language.

Costas Criticos is a Senior Lecturer in Education at the University of Natal in Durban, South Africa. He is also Director of the Media Resource Center, which is based in the Department of Education. He has published in the field of educational media and progressive education. His research interests include Media Education, experiential learning, and school architecture. Costas has been involved in educational media and Media Education for more than 20 years. Unlike most of his colleagues in Media Education he has a science and engineering background, and has come to Media Education from an involvement in production rather than textual studies. A graduate of both the University of Natal and Syracuse University, Costas has received a number of awards in support of his work. These include a British Council Fellowship Fulbright Scholarship. He is currently a representative of South Africa on the *World Council for Media Education*.

Dr. Andrew Hart is a Senior Lecturer in Education at the Research and Graduate School of Educational Studies, University of Southampton, where he teaches Media Studies on the MA(Ed) programs and supervises MPhil/PhD research. He also teaches in the postgraduate Initial Training course in English, Drama, and Media Studies. He has published widely on Media Education and has worked closely with teachers as Director of the Southampton Media Education Group (winner of the British Film Institute's Paddy Whannel Award for innovation in Media Education), as Director of the Southern Media Education Research Network, and of the recently established Media Education Center. He currently represents the United Kingdom on the *World Council for Media Education*. Recent publications include *Teaching Television, Making 'The Real World'* (CUP, 1988) and *Understanding the Media* (Routledge, 1991). He also wrote, with Gordon Cooper, the BBC Radio 4 series *Understanding the Media* on which the book was based. His most recent book was with Sue Hackman: *Developing Media in English (Hodder, 1995)*.

Dr. Renee Hobbs is Associate Professor of Communication at Babson College. She directed the Harvard Institute on Media Education at Harvard Education School, the first national-level teacher education program in Media literacy in the United States. She created KNOW TV, a curriculum for critically analyzing the documentary, which won the 1995 Golden Cable Ace Award. She has worked with teachers in many school districts to include media analysis and media production activities in the context of existing curricula.

After working for many years as a Secondary School English and Media teacher, **Dr. Robert Morgan** taught in North America's oldest Cultural Studies Department at Trent University. He is presently an Associate Professor in the Department of Curriculum, Teaching and Learning at the Ontario Institute for Studies in Education at the University of Toronto, Canada. His current research interests are in the areas of the theory and practice of English in secondary schooling, the role of television in adolescent lives, and the implications of Cultural Studies theory for curriculum. Recent articles were published in *Discourse* and *Continuum* (1996).

Robyn Quin is as Associate Professor of Media Studies at Edith Cowan University in Perth, Western Australia. She was a teacher and later an educational consultant in Media Education before moving to University teaching. She has published media textbooks for students and teachers, in collaboration with Barrie McMahon. Their publications include *Exploring Images* (1984), *Real Images* (1986, 1995), *Australian Images* (1990), *Meet the Media I* (1990), *Stories and Stereotypes* (1987), *Teaching Viewing and Visual Texts* (1995). She was one of the originators of the *World Council for Media Education*, on which she currently represents Western Australia.

REFERENCES

Hart, A. P. (1988). *Teaching television*. Cambridge: Cambridge University Press.
Hart, A. P. (1988). *Making "The Reel World."* Cambridge: Cambridge University Press.
Hart, A. P. (1991). *Understanding the media*. London: Routledge.

Hart, A. P. (1991). *Understanding the media.* London & Southampton: BBC & Southampton Media
   Education Group.

Quin, R. (1984). *Exploring images.* Perth: Bookland.

Quin, R. (1986). *Real images.* Melbourne: MacMillan.

Quin, R. (1987). *Stories and stereotypes.* Melbourne: MacMillan.

Quin, R. (1990). *Australian images.* Sydney: Science Press and the Australian Film Commission.

Quin, R. (1990). *Meet the media.* Toronto: Globe.

Quin, R. (1995). *Real images* (2nd ed.). Melbourne: MacMillan.

Quin, R. (1995). *Teaching viewing and visual texts: Using the national profiles in English.* Victorial:
   Curriculum Corp.

Author Index

The letter *f* following a page number indicates a figure; *n* denotes a footnote

Subject Index

The letter *f* following a page number indicates a figure; *n* denotes a footnote; *t* indicates tabular material.